Praise for *Me, Chi, and Bruce Lee*

"His book's good cheer and infectious enthusiasm for the subject should make readers willing to accept that too."
—*Globe & Mail*

"Preston had me following him every step of the way as he traveled the globe on his quest for understanding of martial arts."
—*Chronicle Herald (Halifax)*

"One seriously funny book. Part travelogue, part journey of discovery, part aeiiiiiiiiya! chop suey adventure: What's not to like?"
—Will Ferguson, author of *Happiness* and
Beauty Tips from Moosejaw

"One broken rib later, Preston ditches kung fu in favor of a less rough-and-tumble art where he walks around in circles. Which is ironic, as this fun and insightful book thoroughly kicks ass."
—*Metro (UK)*

"An entertaining and self-deprecating journey around martial arts."
—*The Guardian*

"It's engaging stuff.... He won't win any fights with his fists but he could talk an opponent into submission."
—*The First Post*

"At its heart, this is a road book, with Preston serving as a martial arts naif looking for wisdom and enough moxie to defend himself in an emergency. As with any good road book, the magic is in the trip, not the destination."
—*Quill & Quire*

Also by Brian Preston

Pot Planet:
Adventures in Global Marijuana Culture

ME, CHI, AND BRUCE LEE

★

ADVENTURES IN MARTIAL ARTS FROM THE SHAOLIN TEMPLE TO THE ULTIMATE FIGHTING CHAMPIONSHIP

BRIAN PRESTON

BERKELEY, CALIFORNIA

Published by Blue Snake Books

Blue Snake Books' publications are distributed by
North Atlantic Books
P.O. Box 12327
Berkeley, California 94712

Originally published by Penguin Group (Canada) 2007
Cover design by Kerrin Hands
Printed in the United States of America

Me, Chi, and Bruce Lee: Adventures in Martial Arts from the Shaolin Temple to the Ultimate Fighting Championship is sponsored by the Society for the Study of Native Arts and Sciences, a nonprofit educational corporation whose goals are to develop an educational and cross-cultural perspective linking various scientific, social, and artistic fields; to nurture a holistic view of arts, sciences, humanities, and healing; and to publish and distribute literature on the relationship of mind, body, and nature.

North Atlantic Books' publications are available through most bookstores. For further information, call 800-733-3000 or visit our Web sites at www.northatlanticbooks.com and www.bluesnakebooks.com.

Library of Congress Cataloging-in-Publication Data
Preston, Brian, 1957–
  Me, chi, and Bruce Lee : adventures from the Shaolin temple to the ultimate fighting championship / Brian Preston.
    p. cm.
  ISBN 978-1-58394-268-0
  1. Martial arts. 2. Preston, Brian, 1957–. I. Title.

  GV1101.P74 2009
  796.8--dc22
                          2008040997

        1 2 3 4 5 6 7 8 9 UNITED 14 13 12 11 10 09

For Gigi,
born helpless and invincible

Part 1

A GOOD EXCUSE

1

☆

Fear and Disequilibrium to the Age 47

Any growing boy can find a socially acceptable way to knock the crap out of his peers, if he likes that kind of thing. In other parts of the world it might be boxing or Karate, Tae Kwon Do, or Judo. In Canada it's ice hockey that separates the men from the boys.

Hockey for me started early. In the winter of my fourth year my dad made a backyard skating rink. To compact and level the snow, Dad like a draft horse pulled a three-foot-wide snow shovel back and forth across the yard; behind him my older brother Bill squatted down on the scoop of the shovel to give it weight, holding onto the shaft with both hands like a witch riding a broom. When I was older, Bill would do the pulling, me the riding. After flattening the snow, it was just a matter of repeatedly applying a fine mist of water over the hardpack until it was thick enough to support the weight of boys in sharp-bladed skates.

I learned to skate that first winter by pushing around an old tube-framed summer lawn chair. From the start a kid understands that skating is something special. It's frictionless. You can twist and turn and glide, or build up speed then effortlessly coast. It gets you oh so close to how birds must feel when they fly.

☆

By age six I was playing organized hockey, and for the next half dozen years the game was a celebration of movement, balance, and artistry. It was all about skating, stickhandling, passing, and play-making. It was beautiful. Then, at age twelve, around the time arena dressing rooms started to stink like jockstrap fungus and other extravagant hormonal discharge, the graceful game completely changed. Full body contact and fighting was suddenly acceptable, encouraged even. Fathers who used to watch our games through the glass windows of the heated room at the end of the rink started to come out into the unheated arena and take a sterner interest, shouting in deep booming Dad voices. "Hit 'im! Go get 'im! Knock him on his ass!" Suddenly kids whom God had graced with an early growth spurt, kids a foot taller than yours truly, kids with faint moustaches and chipped front teeth, wanted to drop their hockey gloves and punch my lights out.

There was no complicated art to it, no sweet science. If you were right-handed, you grabbed the neck of your opponent's jersey in your left hand. If he didn't fall, if he seemed sturdy, you could use him for balance, to support yourself at the same time that you tried to hit him—you were, after all, wearing ice skates, teetering atop thin blades of steel. Skates are like a bicycle, much more easily balanced during motion than while standing still. They really are the most idiotic things to wear for two people who want to fight each other; it's like putting boxers in high heels.

But you do your best: you start throwing right-hand round-house punches, hoping to land more to his face than he does to yours.

Simple slugging. Years later as a journalist I asked Gino Odjick, then of the National Hockey League's Vancouver Canucks, one of the best fighters in the best hockey league in the world, how he acquired his technique: "Did I have to *learn* to fight?" he asked rhetorically. "No, I just said to myself, I'll keep punching till I go down. And that's what I've always done. And it ended up working all right. As long as you're punching you're not getting beat. It's when you stop—and the other guy keeps punching—that you're in trouble."

At twelve my peers and I were suddenly granted license to pummel each other bare-fisted, just like our idols in the NHL. Conn Smythe, founder of the Toronto Maple Leafs, is credited with one of the cornerstone clichés of the game, one that's been handed down through the generations: "If you can't beat 'em in the alley, you can't beat 'em on the ice." At twelve our impromptu scraps never lasted long; very quickly someone would get pulled or punched off balance and the fiery duo would fall together to the cooling ice. The linesmen would kneel down to pry apart a tangle of intertwined limbs, and then the referee would banish two boys to the penalty box for five whole minutes, after which they were allowed to return to the game, and do it all over again if they felt like it.

☆

I never felt like it in the first place. One time in my twelfth winter I was skating around during a game, minding my own business, following my bliss as it were, when I heard my name called from the stands. It was my brother Bill screaming at me to Get In There and Get The Puck! I felt obliged to make an effort, so I skated over to the corner of the rink, where a couple of players were bumping shoulders with that black disc at their feet. Ignoring them, I tried to poke the puck free, when out of nowhere a huge kid slammed me into the boards and I started to fall. Arcing backwards, I swung my stick up for balance, and it inadvertently hit my adversary in the face.

By the time I got back to my feet the puck was long gone, but this big goon had dropped his stick and his gloves, the thick padded gloves hockey players wear, and was holding his fists in the classic "just like the pros" pre-fight ritualistic stance, rocking back and forth on his skates. In his eyes there shone a joyous madness, a crazy rage completely out of proportion to the wrong done, and it scared me shitless. I wanted to say, "It was an accident!" but no words came. I turned on my skates and made a bee-line for the safety of the team bench, trying to pretend I wasn't in a full-on skate-for-your-lives panic. In the ice-cold echo chamber of the arena I heard him call me a gutless pussy. Or maybe it was pansy. I made it to the bench, but found no comfort there, no words of kindness, no forgiving pat on the shoulder pads from my coach or teammates. For a few minutes I couldn't look anyone in the eye. When I finally did lift my head and look at someone, it was my brother Bill in the stands. He shook his head slightly, a bemused smile on his face, as if to say, "That's all right kid. You're a sad specimen, but I still love you."

At the end of the season, I quit hockey.

☆

The next summer my parents loaded me, two siblings, and a Weimaraner into a 1965 Chrysler and drove three thousand miles west. My dad checked out houses and job prospects in various towns on the way, but nothing suited until we ran out of west, hit the coast, and took the ferry to Vancouver Island, where it rains monotonously all winter, so much rain that rooftops turn to mossy green carpets and hallucinogenic mushrooms sprout on suburban lawns. In other words, backyard ice rinks are an impossibility, hockey loosens its stranglehold as a male proving ground, and adolescent boys have to find other ways to terrorize each other.

For a time at Mount Newton Junior Secondary School I was terrorized by a kid named Ben Platz. It started in drama class when we were doing a read-through of Orson Welles' infamous radio play, *The War of the Worlds*. Ben Platz had the role of a news announcer. Called upon to read aloud a line that began, "Speaking at a dinner in Los Angeles," such and such an expert said such and such, Ben unexpectedly mispronounced a key word: "Speaking at a *diner* in Los Angeles," he said, and it struck me as so hilarious I laughed out loud, not because I was making fun of Ben Platz's ignorance of the difference between *dinner* and *diner*, but because in my mind's eye I had instantly pictured some greasy spoon of a lunch counter, and some UFO expert rising from his swivel stool to deliver his address to the startled waitress and short-order cook, and that image made me laugh.

There was no explaining that to Ben Platz, of course. I had publicly mocked and embarrassed him and I would be made to pay. He was a tough kid.

Years later I ran into him in a bar in our home town and he claimed he'd become a member of a motorcycle gang called the Crypt Kickers. He told me tales of how they ran cocaine and amphetamines up the West Coast, and how he could go into any strip club from California to Canada and, if he laid his club's "colors" on the table, the stripper had to fuck him. Again we almost had a misunderstanding over pronunciation, because at first I thought he said Crib Kickers and that didn't sound very tough to me. This time, though, I kept my mouth shut and didn't laugh. I'd learned my lesson in grade ten.

In the days after Ben Platz let it be known he was going to lay a beating on my adolescent ass, I spent minimal time outdoors. It was straight home after school, pedaling furiously on a brakeless bicycle my brother had cobbled together out of junk parts he'd found, imagining Ben Platz lurking behind every parked car or roadside shrub.

I think he enjoyed *not* catching me. He could torture me that way, mutter threats at me in the halls and classrooms, watch me flinch and wince at his promises of pain. He lacked elegance of language but the sincerity of his anger made up for that. "I'm gonna *kill* you, Preston. I'm gonna fucking *hurt* you, man."

One day, in a little-used corridor in the basement, quite by accident, we had our High Noon. I came around a corner and we were face to face, just the two of us, each surprised as the other. He reacted instinctively with force—his arm shot out to my neck, and he took hold and pinned me up against a row of lockers. For mercy's sake I manufactured tears as a child does: half cunning fakery, half terrified, sincere repentance. I think it was the last time I ever cried fake tears; I was really, really far too old for that. Fifteen. Immediately afterward I was ashamed of myself, but at the critical moment abject submission was the strategy that came naturally, spontaneously. Possibly it saved me a beating. One solid punch to the forehead that made me see stars, and Ben Platz walked away, satisfied we were even.

☆

When I was twenty-one years old I worked on a railroad gang a hundred miles east of the Rocky Mountains, in Edson, Alberta. Gangs like ours, building new switches and repairing track, lived in railroad cars parked on sidings. When we settled in alongside the quaint little station in a two-bar frontier town like Edson (there was the bar, and the Indian bar), the nightly incursion of a crew of twenty horny young outsiders threw the whole town's mating patterns into chaos.

A bunch of us were in the bar, and I was dancing with a native girl, cute faced, plump but not fat. A girlfriend of hers came onto the dance floor, took hold of my arm, spun me around, and shouted above the music, "Dance with me instead." The plump girl was taken, she yelled in my ear, and the boyfriend was the jealous kind. This girl was scrawny, and plain enough that when she said she had her own trailer all to herself and we could go there later, I still preferred to take my chances with plump and cute.

So I turned away and went back to dancing with girl number one, when, sure enough, her boyfriend appeared out of nowhere. He was a hot-tempered asshole, you could just tell. He yanked her by the elbow, marched her off the dance floor, and steered her against her resistance to a table in a less crowded corner of the bar, where I watched them argue. She hung her head mutely, he was in a rage. Then he slapped her.

I felt I had no choice but to go over and do the right thing. When I got to their table, he stood up and faced me. I told him not to hit her, and then we just stood there, almost chest to chest. He took a step back and struck a boxer's pose; he was shorter but much better built than me, well-muscled, and held his fists clenched, one under his chin and the other between his nipples. They looked spring-loaded and cocked to me. I felt like if I even dared bring my fists up to a similar classic pose, he'd take that as a sign I wanted to fight and then he'd beat the crap out of me. So I kept my hands at my sides, leaving myself open from belly to face—wide open.

I don't remember what we said to each other. But I remember the tautness of the moment, my body clenched to attention, my eyes on his face, my attention focused on his fists.

He backed down, and sat down, probably because my railroad buddies had all stood up from their nearby table. He had no back-up, I had half a dozen. The buds bought me beer to honor the willow-thin college boy who had not flinched when faced with the loaded fists of a local wife-beater. They saw it as bravery, but you can't flinch when you're petrified.

The plump native girl left with her boyfriend and I got drunk, and then she came back without him, looking for me. The guys all encouraged me to go for it, but I was spooked. It just seemed far too likely that the worst-case scenario would play out: I'd go home with her, get naked, and suddenly the boyfriend would be there smashing down the door to get at me, only this time I wouldn't have back-up watching conveniently from any nearby table.

☆

One more, at age thirty, old enough to know better.

Belize is an easily overlooked little mangrove swamp of a country on the Caribbean coast of Central America, where the citizens are mostly black and sound like Jamaicans. On my second day in Belize City, I was trying to get a boat out to the quais— pronounced *keys,* reef islands where the snorkelling was reputed to be supreme. By the harbor I met a guy who seemed a bit low-life and dicey but he said he had a boat and could take me there. I said sure and stopped for some fried eggs and beans at a street food stall on the way, where this old Hispanic lady tugged me by the T-shirt when he wasn't looking, and made a gesture of throat slitting, then pointed at him, then did it again a few times to make sure I caught her drift. I was very grateful for her kindness, tipped her well, and ditched the guy. Then I found another guy who said he had a boat, a younger, clean-cut kid who seemed more on the up and up and not at all like a petty criminal, which was the vibe I'd picked up off the first guy even before the nice lady warned me. So this guy starts taking me to his boat, and I start to get a bad feeling about him, too, a feeling like something was wrong with this picture—like, hey, aren't the docks over the other way, shouldn't we be going that direction—but I didn't act on it, instead I just plodded along like a dopey trusting cow herded to an abattoir. Once we were well away from the main streets, four young sleazy-Belizey dudes cornered me and then put on an absurd pretense of being under-cover cops. One of them stuffed a little baggie in my front pocket, pulled it right back out, and accused me of possession of mari-juana, then the rest demanded my wallet and passport "for identi-fication." Two of them grabbed me by the forearms and held me. I struggled a bit, enough that my cheap rubber flip-flop sandals slid off my sweaty un-acclimatized non-tropical feet. Then I felt even more silly, like I couldn't even run away because you can't run away on pavement in bare feet. So two guys held me in place like court-room bailiffs, and I just stood there slackly, utterly nonplussed as to *counters*. I had no clue how to defend myself. For a second I pictured me as James Bond or Bruce Lee kicking and chopping at them all in just the right places, but that was fantasy. In reality I was stymied for ideas. Lucky for me, these guys were gentle: they threw no gratuitous punches. There were no cheap shots; two held my arms, while another displayed a little knife blade at a respectable distance, and yet another searched my wallet for money. In the end they left me the wallet, my passport, and even my travellers' checks. They strolled away, casually satisfied with a hundred and fifty bucks in cash to split five ways.

I slipped my flip-flops back on my bare feet while a gaggle of shantytown six-year-olds gathered round to gawk as the sad white man pulled himself together and shuffled off the stage of their little dead-end street. I was actually feeling giddy: unbruised, my hair barely mussed, I still had my passport and most of my money. It could have been so much worse. The mothers of the gawking kids sat in tin hut doorways in their poverty, looking right through me as if I were a cloud, and I did feel like a wispy non-presence, floating out of their morning and away from there, back to the first world forever.

2

☆

A Proposition

We were drinking Czech beer at a rickety picnic table outside a pub near Great Ormond Street, in weather warm enough to drink outside if you kept your coat on and your legs crossed. The British publisher said, "You should do your next book about Kung Fu."

I could feel myself making a pained face. Sometimes the body decides before the mind, and the body had long ago decided: Kung Fu was definitely not me. Physical, disciplined, violent, and potentially dangerous, it seemed the opposite of me. I'm more like cerebral, haphazard, pacifistic, unfailingly harmless.

"I like to write things that make a difference, that right a wrong, expose an injustice, accomplish some good," I said. As excuses go, this was heavily self-flattering, and also a stretch: I've written plenty of trash to pay the rent. Short-term, you can hold your nose and do it.

I think of myself as a journeyman scribe, no Martin Amis but I make the most of limited skills. To make a living in the early twenty-first century, a journeyman scribe can't pick and choose assignments. To make a living, you take orders from magazine editors, who in turn need to please advertisers. Which means you end up writing advertorial bullshit. And months later, when you're almost over the fact you wrote it, back it comes, delivered to your door in a glossy magazine to remind you all over again that you're just a cog in the Age of Consumption, selling crap to people who don't need it. The orangutans of Borneo are in full retreat, watching their formerly lush and munificent rainforest strip-logged for disposable chopsticks and patio furniture, and you're writing articles for airline magazines about where to eat in Las Vegas. Sell-out! One of a million Neros clattering on keyboards while the planet burns.

☆

Books are better. In a book you can say anything you like, like what I just said. No magazine editor will pay you money for what I just said. At best, some lefty rag that survives on grants will give you a free subscription. So, better to write books, but writing a book is a long haul; it's essentially a cohabitation, you and the book have to move in together. Really, it's like a marriage: you'd better be sincerely fucking enthused about it before you sign on.

"Martial Arts are hot right now. Look at *Crouching Tiger, Hidden Dragon*. Look at *Kill Bill*. Film is our most dominant medium, and Kung Fu is tremendously influential," said the publisher. "Everyone knows about it on a fantasy level. But books are about reality. Non-fiction is your métier. You spend a year getting a black belt, tell us what you learn from it. Everyone would love a black belt, but few do it. If you write the book, they'll live it through you."

☆

At this point I could have told him about hockey, or Ben Platz, or Belize, but another story came to mind. I'll keep it short. A few years ago I was in the heart of Glasgow, a very rough and tumble town, on assignment to write about the night life there for an American magazine. I was alone, around about midnight, heading to a nightclub, and took a shortcut down an alley. Two drunken boys came out of the shadows. One of them had a short-bladed knife and was muttering about how he wanted to cut me. Apparently, for certain Glasgow boys it's a rite of passage: they need to slit someone's nostril with a knife or razor, then they feel like they're a man. Now, these were two very drunk, spindly-limbed boys, fourteen or fifteen, sixteen at the oldest. One of them slumped against a chain link fence, the other, barely able to stand, waved his little blade in my direction, and kept snivelling, "I'll cut you."

What did I do? I turned around and ran.

That revived them. Dogs and sharks smell fear, and likewise adolescent boys. I ran, they chased, I sprinted, they gained, panting and slobbering, "I'll cut you!" The muted rubberized *thomp thomp thomp* of their Nikes on the pavement followed me all the long way around the block, to the entrance of the very nightclub I'd been looking for, where I sought refuge in the long shadows of the bouncers guarding the door. The boys stopped short and turned away, like jackals from a campfire. Once I'd caught my breath and explained to the bouncers what had happened, one of them snorted, "Ye just bark at them to Fook Right Off."

"When I told people about it afterward, every man in Scotland gave me that same advice," I told the publisher. "It's just something you know how to do if you're Scottish: shout 'Fook off' with credible menace so fourteen-year-olds intent on mayhem slink away to scope out wimpier prey. Like me."

☆

So the subject was dropped. We parted and I went off to have dinner with my friend Chris, a marijuana activist I'd met researching my first book. We hadn't seen each other in four years but the merry mood of reunion, further heightened by fine hashish rolled up with dodgy British tobacco, started to sour when we got into an argument over the Iraq War. Chris, iconoclastically alone among his lefty pothead friends, supported Tony Blair's sending the troops to bring down Saddam. He supported using the British military to remove any dictator anywhere who uses violence and terror against his own people. "Appeasement does not work," he said. "The only way to stand up to violence is with violence. Sad but true."

I'm a pacifist. I'm also an appeaser. On the whole I find arguing tiresome and fruitless, maybe because I so seldom win. To avoid it with Chris I changed the subject: I told him about the Kung Fu book idea. His enthusiasm surprised me. "Fantastic," he exclaimed. "You must do it! We're getting to that age, as men, where our faith in ourselves starts to falter, because the body begins to betray us, right? Men start chasing younger women, just to reclaim some feeling of youth and vitality and virility, right?"

"I'm happily married," I reminded him. "Then again, my wife is ten years younger. Your point is?"

"Studying a martial art would be a great way for you to make peace with the physical aspect of your nature, which you've likely neglected your whole adult life. Most men have. Even the athletic types, the jocks, just play out the athleticism of their youth like a poker hand, then they throw in the cards. By forty they fold."

He'd struck a nerve. I had to admit it, I'd folded long ago, practically in childhood, under the assumption I'd been dealt a bad hand to begin with. I was always the scrawny kid who couldn't even manage twenty push-ups to earn the merit badge. You've heard all my fight stories. Yep, that's all of them. You know I'm timid as a trout, darting for the bottom when a pebble plops into the pond. I'd done nothing in the three and a half decades since I quit hockey to change the self-image I had when I was twelve. "You're right," I said to Chris. "If someone's willing to pay me money to transform myself from a wary, timid, middle-aged pantywaist into a Kung Fu killer, who am I to turn up my nose at this amazing opportunity? I should count myself blessed, and just go for it!"

Back in the publisher's office the next day, I told him I'd had a change of heart, an epiphany of sorts, and was now eager to write a book about the phenomenon of Martial Arts, where it came from, where it's going, and what it all means, and also eager to find out first-hand what happens when a wimpy forty-something wuss, with the heartfelt zealousness and sincere vigor of the newly converted, takes up the study of Kung Fu.

3

★

Sifu Bob

I n 540 AD, at a Buddhist monastery called Shaolin, in Henan province, China, a monk from India named Bodhidharma was overseeing the translation of sacred texts from the original Sanskrit into Mandarin. The Chinese monks were about what you'd expect from a bunch of pencil-neck manuscript transcribers who passed their work days hunched over their writing tables, slowly going myopic. On days off they would sit frozen in meditative poses of intense stillness, which wasn't exactly a recipe for physical robustness either. Once in a while these sad specimens would venture timidly from the temple to the outer world, only to encounter bandits and other nasty antisocial types who would beat the snot out of them and steal whatever a monk had worth stealing.

Taking matters in hand, Bodhidharma began to teach these overly cerebral scribblers how to exercise their bodies properly, and how to defend themselves, based on patterns of movement from Indian yoga. The central principle of his self-defense classes: one should only respond with the amount of force necessary to defeat or subdue one's attacker. If he blocks your path, go around. If he shoves you, step back. If he punches you, block it. If he punches again, punch back. If he insists on trying to kill you, well, in that case, all bets are off. This self-defense philosophy is derived from Chan Buddhism, better known as Zen, the name given it when it later spread to Japan. It was born at the famous Shaolin Temple.

☆

Fifteen hundred years later, another pencil-neck scribe, namely me, is feeling a strong kinship to those Shaolin pioneers. We pretty much lead the same cloistered existence of eye-strain and disregard for office isometrics, only instead of a monastery I hide out in my suburban split level, and instead of a calligraphy brush I've got a laptop. The biggest difference between us: martial arts training came to the monks unbidden, the gift of a saint. I'll go forth and seek my Kung Fu in a marketplace saturated with choices.

My hometown has a quarter-million people; it's by far the biggest city on an island two-thirds the size of Ireland. Do you know Vancouver Island? It hangs down the west coast of North America like a giant dribble of snot from Alaska's massive nose. The island I call home was covered by half a mile of ice until eight thousand years ago; then the glaciers melted, and before you knew it huge cedars, firs, and hemlocks sprang up and covered the place in a lush green pelt. Then Europeans arrived and looked upon the trees as weeds to be cleared to make farmland, or lumber to be cleared to make a quick buck. Most of the original old growth has been chopped down now, and what's growing back is a patchy beard of farmed trees and scrub bush.

Even here, in my quiet backwater of the world, a half-dozen schools list themselves under Martial Arts in the local yellow pages, and I see plenty more clubs around town. Goes to show how ubiquitous martial arts have become. Schools blossom from Beijing to Buenos Aires. Tens of thousands claim to possess the knowledge, and they offer it up for sale to the millions who crave the knowledge.

One of the listed schools was The Kung Fu Academy, and when I phoned it up I liked the recorded message. It ended with a hokey aphorism, or affirmation, delivered in an almost ironic, take-it-or-leave-it tone of voice: "Be True to Yourself and You Will Succeed." The Academy is in Colwood, a working-class suburb of Victoria. People in Colwood drive huge pickup trucks with bumper stickers that say things like, "Are You An Environmentalist Or Do You Work For A Living?" or "Hug a Logger: You'll Never Go Back To Trees." I phoned up and made an appointment to meet with Bob, the owner, and on the grey autumn day I first drove out to the Kung Fu Academy, I almost missed it on account of being distracted by a big sign board out front that read, BUBBLY IN TIME FOR THE HOLIDAYS. It's tucked away in a tiny strip mall next to Brew Byou, a place where they help you make vast quantities of affordable beer and wine.

☆

Bob ushered me into his office and sat at his desk with his back to a wall of photos of his students. The proud possessors of black belts had been awarded their own individual photos, striking kicking poses with full leg extensions and well-groomed hair. Their photos formed an outer defense wall around an inner sanctum of group photos shot from high above, of forty students in neat rows on a deep green lawn, all of them in what I would soon recognize to be a left-leaning horse stance.

They looked so disciplined and bonded in purpose in their matching uniforms that it conjured up mental echoes of the evil Han's island in *Enter the Dragon,* the absurdly cartoonish yet absolutely all-time seminal martial arts movie starring Bruce Lee.

You see, I was already heavily into my research of Kung Fu primary sources, and you start with Bruce Lee. Four of the five (a mere five!) feature films Bruce Lee ever starred in are available at the public library here in Victoria, and by then I'd seen them all. They're all laughably silly, except for the moments when Bruce Lee is demonstrating his bodily perfection of movement.

Apparently Lee's astounding and extraordinary gracefulness was an innate trait: as a nineteen-year-old ballroom dancer he was Hong Kong Cha-Cha champion. The fluid confidence—the charisma he brings to the screen—is closer in its effect to film dancers like Fred Astaire or Gene Kelly than to martial artists. When Bruce Lee is fighting, you cannot look away.

☆

Bob has the healthy good looks of a pool lifeguard, or a bartender in the kind of bar where women want to sleep with the bartender. Big white teeth, eyes that hold your gaze, and black hair falling in boyish bangs. He comes across a little bit too shy to be a real leader-of-men type. There's a slight air of his mind being elsewhere, like he'd rather be surfing.

In setting up the meeting I'd presented myself as both a prospective student and a journalist writing a book. First thing I wanted was Bob's life story. "I'm forty-one years old," he told me. "My dad was a Golden Gloves boxer in the Navy, so there was parental pressure to box. I started at sixteen, and fought for four years.

"But boxing took me on the wrong path. At that age, kids have a lot of adrenaline. I'm not an aggressive guy, but at that age confrontations were never a turn-down. If someone were to say something to me, I would never back down, I'd be right back at them: 'What did you say? Bring it on. Let's fight.' Kind of a challenge lifestyle."

Bob credits his early boxing training for developing hand speed and footwork. "I don't think I would be as fast as I am today without it. My dad being a boxer, I had good training. I was unde-feated for those four years." Outside the ring he was getting into scrapes where his boxing proved inadequate: multiple fighters, or gang-style beatings. "I emerged out of boxing into martial arts in part because it was more versatile; you could use your whole body, as opposed to just using your hands. Boxing is a sport art, like Judo. Boxing is striking but no throwing or grappling; Judo is throwing and grappling, but no striking. Both are good as sport arts, but not complete systems. The other negativity about boxing is, even as a kid doing it, you're aware of rumors of head injuries, and you see aging fighters who have not aged well. So it's not a long-lasting art you can pursue and practice for the rest of your life."

When he took up Kung Fu, Bob was attracted to the under-lying Buddhist philosophy of pacifism that ran through it. He dropped the challenge lifestyle. Raised a Catholic, he has moved on from the Church. "You can hear Catholics and, for example, Jehovah's Witnesses arguing with each other, who's right or wrong. When you start to believe that your religion is the only religion, that steers me away. Buddhism is a little bit different. To this day I've never heard Buddhists talking down to anyone else."

There you have Bob. A decent, thoughtful guy, who has taken a youthful love of fighting and turned it into a path to peace.

☆

Time to talk about me. Glasgow. Bob listened to my story about how when Scottish punks threatened to kick my ass and cut my nostril, I skittered away like a wuss.

"You did the right thing," he said.

"I did?"

"You achieved the best possible result: no one got hurt."

We talked for about an hour: I told him I'd just finished reading *Bruce Lee: Fighting Spirit,* a biography by Bruce Thomas, better known as the bass player in the Attractions, Elvis Costello's old band.

"And what did you think of Bruce Lee?"

Thomas' book is like a father's criticism: unsparing in the details, yet underneath it all, generous, admiring, loving even. Bruce Lee is portrayed as a flawed human being. Notwithstanding that he talked a good line about Kung Fu being a spiritual calling, Lee never really outgrew the street fighter ethos of his rough and ragged teenage years in Hong Kong. Violently ambitious about his movie career, a mercurial, temperamental artist imprisoned by impulse, he died in the bed of a woman not his wife at a mere thirty-two years of age.

"I was totally impressed with his physical training," I told Bob. "You can see it in his movies, his physical conditioning is second to none." In fact, in *Way of the Dragon,* when he fights Chuck Norris in the Coliseum in Rome, Norris looks flabby and slow, but Lee is like a walking (and kicking!) embodiment of one of those medical school maps of human musculature. You can see the individual fibers pulsing through his taut skin. "But as a teacher, as a husband, as a man, Bruce Lee was deeply flawed."

"Exactly," said Sifu Bob. "He's not an example we aspire to follow around here. He was a hothead. He had awesome talent, no doubt, and a desire to study a hundred systems, hone the best techniques into his own style, to synthesize and then to teach—it's really too bad he died so young. He might have evolved so much further. But dying young was characteristic of his attitude to life. We teach a different style. Our role models are men who live to be a hundred."

"Doesn't that go against the whole warrior ethos? I've been reading up on the Martial Arts, and somewhere it said that for the Samurai of Japan, their greatest disgrace was to die of old age or disease, and not in battle."

"Samurai are extinct," he said.

☆

I'd already looked at Bob's Academy's website, so I knew that he calls the system he teaches Shaolin Kempo Kung Fu. The website states, "Shaolin Temple represents a first organized attempt to blend fighting techniques with moral and spiritual principles in an effort to understand violence and to deal with it in a way that best promotes the virtues of compassion and peace recommended by Chan Buddhism. The difficulties and significance of this spiritual and moral challenge have remained fascinating until the present day, and at Kung Fu Academy we see ourselves as continuing to address this challenge."

I liked that. It made the Academy sound like the thinking person's Kung Fu School. I also liked this phrase on Bob's website: *The only person you compete against is the person you were yesterday.*

Hopefully I can beat that sucker.

4

☆

Chi

There are more than five hundred styles or systems of Kung Fu in China. In an exhaustive list compiled by John Corcoran, you'll note styles with poetic names like Phoenix Eye Fist, White Tiger, or Six Harmonies, and other styles that just sound weird: Drunken Monkey, Plum Flower Praying Mantis, or my personal favorite, Eight Drunken Fairies. Kung Fu is used here in the West as an umbrella term for all Chinese martial arts, but it's really a misnomer. Kung Fu means "accomplishment through hard work," or to use an English idiom, "practice makes perfect." In that sense, self-improvement in any art, from archery to piano, requires Kung Fu. A better term for Chinese martial arts is *wushu*—*wu* meaning fighting, *shu* meaning arts.

Ed Parker, back in the 1950s and '60s, was one of the main players responsible for bringing Asian martial arts to mainstream America. He called the art he taught Okinawan Kempo Karate, and it's that art, sometimes called Chinese Karate, that forms the base of what Bob teaches at the Kung Fu Academy. In one of his many books, Ed Parker addressed beginners like me: "The Martial Arts are a real and tangible subject. Although they have taken on mystical connotations over the years, they are by no means mystical. When the unknown becomes known, the mysticism disappears."

Do you know what Chi is? It's sometimes spelled Ch'i, and it's Qi in Pinyin, the Chinese government's official system for translating Mandarin into the Roman alphabet, but I'm going to stick with a spelling that for English eyes looks as it's pronounced. Chi is the Asian concept of the life force, the energy that created the universe, permeates the universe, and continues to play out in every breath, every fart, every muscle movement, every moment from birth to death, by every creature that ever lived.

Generally I like quantifiable proof of a thing's existence before I buy into it. I can't imagine ever getting to a point where I could accept God or Allah as being any more real than Zeus or Krishna. Man invented God, not the other way around—any rational thinker accepts that. But on some level I'm a sucker for the promise of the kind of magical experience that's understood when people speak of mysticism. It's not a God I'm after, it's a phenomenon, a feeling. If I'm going to set myself to learning martial arts, then I really do want to experience Chi.

☆

Bob and I discussed Chi at our very first meeting. "Chi can be developed and harnessed by martial arts training," he told me. "It's not something to be understood mentally, really. On that level it's like God, it's just too big to worry about. Ever had acupuncture?"

"No."

"That's a more direct manner of restoring balance to the flow of Chi in the body. Our martial arts training is also a way to regulate Chi. It really starts with breathing. With training, you'll feel your body in a new equilibrium."

One of the first things Bob taught me was how to breathe from the dantien, the motherlode of Chi in the body. "The dantien draws the air to the bottom of the lungs, so it allows you to breathe at full capacity. If you're drawing it from your chest muscles, you're only breathing at half capacity," he said. He had me face a mirrored wall, and directed me to place a finger on my collarbone, and another on my dantien, a point two finger-widths below the belly button. "As you breathe, the belly or lower diaphragm should be moving in and out, and your collarbone should never move," he said. It took some practice, the type of soft practice where you relax and don't try to force it, before I got the hang of it. Once I had it, I noticed that in situations where previously I would have been easily winded, sucking short jagged breaths to recover, I now suffered less lung burn, and my breathing stayed deep and even. It's a simple improvement anyone could make, and once you know about it you wonder why everyone isn't let in on the secret. They should make it mandatory for schoolchildren: Today, kids, we learn how to breathe properly.

☆

"How long would it take to get a black belt?" I asked Bob that first day, as he showed me around the club.

"Depends how much effort you put in. But minimum five years."

Five years!

It almost made me wish I was a celebrity. Ed Parker took serious heat from Karate purists in the sixties for granting a black belt to a clearly undeserving Elvis Presley. Not the young, agile, pelvis-palpitating Elvis. We're talking paunchy, drugged-out Elvis, mixing a few lame-ass Karate kicks into the strutting stage routines of his latter and last days.

I noticed a class schedule taped to the wall that said free-style sparring was open to blue belts and higher. "Think I could get a blue belt within a year?"

"Possibly," Bob said. "You'd have to work at it. Train almost daily."

On the wall of the training room the line of belts ran from novice white up the scale through yellow, orange, purple, green, blue, and brown, then a two-tone brown–black belt called pre-black, then black. But it didn't end there. Beyond black there were another four wider belts made of silk. Bob called them sashes. The top end, the highest of the high, was a white sash, symbolically indicating that when you achieve that level, you go back to white, the color of a novice. "You never stop learning."

"But who could teach you? You run the school."

"True, this is my school, but that doesn't mean I'm not still a student. I train under two masters here in town."

"Oh. Do *they* have schools?"

"No, neither of them has a formal school, they just take on a student or two to pass along their knowledge, keep it alive: one's a Filipino who specializes in the physical, fighting arts; the other's a doctor of Chinese medicine who teaches me the Shaolin philosophy, more of what's called the *internal* arts. And he has a master too: my master's master is close to a hundred years old. His knowledge comes to me secondhand, but I trust my master to pass it on as he sees fit, when he determines I'm ready and deserving of the higher levels of that knowledge."

5

☆

My Master's Master

I wanted to take the measure of my master's master, and so it came to pass that I found myself in a small, slightly shabby house in a blue-collar neighborhood of town, in an upstairs room where the walls slanted in from the roofline, and the low winter sun streamed across the carpet, illuminating a chess board set with well-worn wooden pieces. My master's master has a Buddhist name, Shi Yao Hai, and also an English name, Don. He gave me the option of calling him by either name; I chose Don because I just can't bring myself to call a white person a strange non-white-person type name that he didn't come by naturally. It seems so *affected*.

The name you are born with should be respected. A series of events beyond your control brought you into existence—in other words it's a fluke you were born. When you were given a name at birth it was also beyond your control, so your original name should be kept as a reminder of the fluke of your existence. Unless it's something like Assman.

☆

Don certainly was not what you'd expect a great martial artist to look like. Whereas Sifu Bob is tall, well-muscled, and graceful, Don is short and on the roly-poly side. He was wearing gold slippers, a red T-shirt, and orange beads on a little wristband tied with a yellow thread that tufted out like a bird feather past the knot. He fiddled with that tuft for much of our talk.

Don's sect practices Parayana Buddhism, which means "beyond vehicles." The Parayana order recognizes as their premier saint Pao Jaco, a large Indian man who brought Buddhism to China a hundred years before Bodhidharma. "He's the one they depict as the fat Buddha," says Don. "Buddha himself could never have been fat. After six years of fasting, he wouldn't have had any fat cells left." The Parayana sect believes a true Buddha figure comes along every five hundred to fifteen hundred years to refresh the world's memory about the need to be enlightened. "They bring a new dispensation, you could say. In the outer sense they reveal a new religion." He counts Zoroaster, Krishna, Moses, Jesus, and Muhammad, but says there are others we don't know, who were enlightened but never found a following to pass on their message.

I told Don I was planning to visit the Shaolin Temple in China as part of my martial arts research, and he said, "You're going to have trouble finding the real thing—when the Chinese took over in '49 they did the same thing they are now in trouble for in Tibet: they broke up the monasteries, tortured the monks, forced monks and nuns to fornicate, all that.

"The ones who saw it coming had escaped, and most of them have not been back to China. They would be put in prison to this day. A little over a decade ago, China started opening monasteries again, and decreed that Buddhism was acceptable again, from the position that you have to be Communist first and a Buddhist second. So the Shaolin monasteries that do exist now in China have two features: most monks joining are resolute Communists, and the masters teaching, especially those who teach martial arts, are not real masters, not by our standards, anyway. Now, to speak on their behalf, they're undeniably great when it comes to conditioning. But their style is the hard style. It's very physical. It's gymnastics."

☆

Don is forty-nine and has been studying Buddhism and martial arts for thirty-seven years. When he was twelve he was sitting on a park bench, "opening and closing a book on Buddhism, thinking about the contents," when an older Chinese gentleman approached and invited him to classes he taught in meditation and Buddhist psychology.

"Today I'm the highest ranking monk in our order in North America at this time," Don says.

"What about your first master, whom you met in the park as a boy?"

"He was born and trained in China, and got out when the Communists came to power. He lived here for a long time, but he's in Jakarta now, in Indonesia, coming up to his one hundred fifth birthday this August, and still wandering around like a youngster."

I told Don that what attracted me most in Kung Fu was the Buddhist principles behind it, that one should never strike first, but always and only use the art in self-defense. I asked if there is any situation in which a Kung Fu fighter would be justified in initiating violence. "Most schools of martial arts reinforce an egotistic position: you have the right to defend yourself," he responded. "This creates an aggressive–responsive person. The nature of the response is aggressive, and that is not the Buddhist way. From our perspective, if you know violence is coming, you leave. Because the only reason you would stay would be to protect your ego."

He got up and stood beside a tall-backed chair, facing it like an imaginary opponent. "If I'm not into the attitude that I have to defend myself, then the strike will come to within twelve to fourteen inches of me before I respond. Now if I'm standing my ground, I'm going to be hit. If I'm not standing my ground, then I'll step back, and he can't touch me, his arm or leg becomes my target, and I can reach a nerve area, and disable him from continuing to fight. You're better off not standing up for your rights, in a psychological sense."

"Are there not times when you need to stand up for your rights?"

"No. No such thing."

"Really?"

"There are times when you might choose to protect someone's life, or body, or your own. But there is a principle superior to that: develop a mind that does not need to be protected, that does not view life from that perspective. So if you are in a fight, your mind is such that you don't need to protect yourself. Your emotional energy is such that you don't need to protect yourself.

"It fits so well with Buddha's teaching," Don continued. "Buddha himself taught that if you acted from the framework of justice, and did only what was necessary, without revenge or anger, you were following his way. He was speaking to military people and judges when he said this.

"When we work with the martial arts and start to teach people the depths of it, as they learn, it changes in turn how they learn. Right now your training with Bob at his school is reflexes, movement, and balance, but the depth of your technique is very superficial. After two or three years, you'll start to understand what it is you are doing, and why. Most martial arts don't teach an understanding of what it is they are doing—the world's top competitors in the full contact martial arts rely purely on physical prowess and technical knowledge, that's their ceiling."

Physical prowess and technical knowledge sound like an unbeatable combination to me. What more is there?

"Those professional fights are all *external* arts, concerned with the physical, and what you can do with your body. There are also internal arts. Internal recognizes the physical, but also that there are other assets you can draw on. A person who studies an internal system would never negate an external physical asset, but they know also they will not always be young and as physically impressive as they might be in their prime, so they have to incorporate understandings that are strategic, that are physics-based, that are movement dynamics-based. The nature of balance, what creates it, and what disrupts it, force, what creates it, what disrupts it, and how you utilize the assets of another person against him. That's an internal arts understanding."

By then the winter sun had dropped low in the sky, slanting light through the window, making Don's ears glow translucent orangey pink. He asked me to stand and stood facing me with his arm outstretched, palm resting on my shoulder. He invited me to put my hands on his elbow and pull down with all my strength. "All your strength," he repeated. I gave it my best and made some progress, causing him to bend a little. "I'm trying to resist you using my biceps," he explained. "Now we try another way."

This time he just extended his arm as though reaching past me for a cup in a cupboard, not trying to resist me at all. Now his arm was solid as a rock, and couldn't be bent, no matter how hard I pulled down on it. "That's just physics, that's not Chi, anyone can do that," he said. "People who have learned the soft arts have learned hundreds of those, if not thousands. If you look at all the pieces, there are probably hundreds of thousands."

6

☆

Brazilian Jiu Jitsu Conquers the World

After Don had introduced to me the concept of soft, internal arts, and proclaimed them superior to the purely hard, external styles employed by even the greatest of today's professional fighters, I thought I'd better track down a top pro martial artist and see for myself exactly what those guys are up to. Browsing the internet I came across the legendary Brazilian Royce Gracie's website, which was trumpeting his recent victory in a bout on New Year's Eve in a stadium in Japan. In front of fifty thousand spectators and a TV audience of twenty million, he had forced the four hundred ninety-pound Japanese sumo star Akebono to submit in just two minutes and thirteen seconds.

A sidebar on the site listed all of Royce's upcoming martial arts seminars, in places like Orlando, Houston, London, and Glasgow. Right in the middle, sandwiched between Orlando and London, one seminar didn't seem to fit. It was scheduled for February fourth and fifth in Vanderhoof, British Columbia. In other words, in my neck of the woods.

Vanderhoof is a lumber town of four thousand that sits smack dab in the middle of the vast scruffy pine forests of my home province. The contact for the Gracie seminar was Scott Stewart, at the Northern Institute of Brazilian Jiu Jitsu, so I phoned, and Scott's wife did her best to help me while simultaneously trying to soothe an inconsolable baby. She didn't know much, except she'd been told by Scott to tell anyone who called that Royce Gracie was the Wayne Gretzky of martial arts, which would make him the Michael Jordan of martial arts to Americans, or the Zinedine Zidane of martial arts to the rest of the world. A legendary superstar.

She took my number so that Scott could phone me back. When he did I found out he works as a bouncer on weekends in the bar at the Northern Lights Inn. It's the premier dance club in Vanderhoof because it's the only dance club in Vanderhoof. Scott works a regular day job as a contractor doing kitchen renovations and such-like, and as a sideline he runs the Northern Institute of Brazilian Jiu Jitsu, which meets Monday and Wednesday evenings in a room at the local high school.

Scott is a huge fan of Royce Gracie and sounded downright rapturous that he had managed to convince a genuine martial arts legend to come to Vanderhoof, a town best known for good fishing and moose hunting in the surrounding woods, in other words for things you don't even do in a town. "I'm talking to his agent, but sometimes I don't really believe he's his agent," Scott told me. "I still don't believe he'll actually make it. Like he'll cancel at the last minute. Or his plane won't be able to land in the fog." The nearest town with an airport is Prince George, sixty miles away; apparently in the winter, fog often rolls in and fucks up the flight schedules. It can last days.

☆

As I talked to Scott I thought, wouldn't it be great if I flew up there
to Prince George and timed my arrival to match Royce Gracie's,
arrived with the superstar himself, on the same flight, and Scott
could pick us both up in his truck and drive us to Vanderhoof on
a lonely road called the Yellowhead Highway that runs from Prince
George five hundred miles to the sea at Prince Rupert? Wouldn't it
be fantastic, rocketing through the icy night, bifurcating an endless
army of snow-laden pine trees in the dark, with the town emerging
at last like a beacon of warmth and humanity against the brutal
cold, and then hanging out with Royce all weekend because there
would be nothing else for him to do up there, we'd be marooned
together at the Northern Lights Inn, and in the end Scott would
drive us back to Prince George, and Royce and I would part like
friends for life after catching a plane out of that frozen hellhole?

☆

And that's pretty much how it worked out, or at least some of it.
We didn't part as friends for life exactly, and lots of strange shit
happened. And some of it really, really hurt. I had a premonition
about that.

My premonition manifested itself in me asking Scott on the
telephone, "If I came up there and took the seminar with Royce
Gracie, and I'm like a near-total novice, I mean, I'm enrolled in the
Kung Fu Academy and I've learned the first Kempo, or Form,
Kempo One, in which I make like a crane or dragon, or a tiger, and
I sort of, like I twirl, and I slink around in a stylized manner, and
punch the air at some imaginary foes, but really I've never sparred
yet, or grappled, not since high school wrestling, I mean I remember when I was like thirteen, and stood four foot something and
weighed eighty-nine pounds—I didn't get my growth spurt until
sixteen—and the coach approached me and asked me to join the

school wrestling team because they needed someone in the under-ninety-pound category, but at that time I had nary a wisp of pubic hair so I shrank from any sport where I'd be expected to strip down afterward and shower, especially shower with macho manly wrestling-type guys from the older grades with birdsnests of curls above their drooping hoses, I was terrified of that shameful hairless communal shower scenario, so I didn't wrestle, so I don't know grappling, but would it still be all right if I took the seminar, or is everyone a serious Jiu Jitsu practitioner who'll make mincemeat out of me?"

Of course I didn't exactly phrase it like that, but when I spat out the essential kernel of the question, Scott said, "No problem, don't worry about it, there'll be tons of beginners. Half my school is beginners, and they'll all be there."

"Okay, good. Do people wear jocks?"

"Some do, some don't, it's personal choice. I don't. And I don't like the ones that do. When they do an arm bar, it scrapes my elbow all to shit."

An arm bar is a Jiu Jitsu or Judo move where if it's done to you, you're lying on your back and so is your opponent and he's got your wrist locked up with his hands against his chest and his bum is under your shoulder with his thighs on either side of your upper arm and one leg across your neck and the other across your torso, and he starts arching his back until his crotch is against your elbow. He can arch until your elbow breaks, or you tap the mat to make him stop. It's all about leverage.

☆

Now if you're like me, or at least me a few short months ago, before I started on my martial arts quest, you're wondering, who the hell is Royce Gracie and what's this Brazilian Jiu Jitsu all about? Listen up.

The largest Japanese community anywhere in the world outside of Japan is in Brazil, the result of a massive wave of immigration in the early twentieth century. One of the leaders of that immigration, Mitsuyou Maeda, was a Japanese champion of Jiu Jitsu, a martial art that's the rougher, nastier ancestor of the sport of Judo. Like Judo, Jiu Jitsu emphasizes throws, take-downs, and submission holds over striking.

In establishing a Japanese colony in Brazil, Maeda was helped by a Brazilian of Scottish descent, Gastao Gracie. In gratitude, Maeda offered to teach Jiu Jitsu to Gracie's son, Carlos. Carlos trained under Maeda for six years, until Maeda returned to Japan.

Like much of Japanese culture, Jiu Jitsu in Japan was highly formal, ritualized, and tradition-bound. Brazilian culture is pretty much the polar opposite: intuitive, impulsive, anarchic, passionate. Left to his own devices, Carlos began to pass his training on to his four younger brothers. The Gracies let their imaginations loose. No limits. *Vale tudo*. Anything goes.

In 1925 Carlos opened an Academy in Rio de Janeiro, publicizing it with a provocative newspaper ad: "If you want a broken arm or rib, contact Carlos Gracie." Thus was born the famous Gracie Challenge, in which Carlos, and later his younger brother Helio, and eventually any one of their multitude of sons or nephews, would take on anybody, anytime, in a no-holds-barred fight.

Carlos was a big, aggressive fighter, and his Jiu Jitsu style played to his strengths. His younger brother Helio, on the other hand, was a frail kid who suffered from dizzy spells. He spent his youth in the Gracie school watching his other brothers spar and teach. Then came "the fateful day that changed the course of jiu-jitsu forever," as Gracie biographer Kid Peligro puts it. The son of a high ranking politician came in for his lesson from Carlos, who was delayed for some reason. The student asked Helio to "play" until Carlos arrived.

The smaller, weaker Helio proved a tough opponent, an excellent teacher of technique over strength, and the student insisted from then on that Helio teach him.

Given his slight frame and lack of power, Helio set himself to developing fighting moves that relied on leverage, not brute strength. He was a brilliant innovator, and soon Carlos had stopped fighting, turning the challenges over to his brother. The young phenom proved unbeatable against a legion of local Brazilian boxers and brawlers who took up the challenge against him. He had no trouble defeating the street styles of much larger men. His best weapon: grappling, or forcing the battle to the ground, where he could maneuver his opponent into a joint lock, or choke hold. The choke was not strangulation as it's commonly thought of (cutting air to the lungs), but rather constriction of the carotid artery, cutting off blood to the brain, causing loss of consciousness. The Brazilian Jiu Jitsu as developed by the Gracies was a tried and tested fighting style, constantly evolving and battle-tested. The tough Brazilian bouts very quickly revealed to Helio which techniques worked in "real life" and which were better abandoned or reworked.

☆

Helio Gracie had seven sons, and gave them all names that begin with the letter R. According to a system akin to numerology developed by Helio himself, R is a particularly powerful letter, especially at the start of a name. All of these sons followed in their father's footsteps and became martial artists. They seem to have had no choice in the matter. Jiu Jitsu was the family business. Check out Kid Peligro's book *The Gracie Way*, which serves up a fusillade of family photos, and you'll find a hilarious example of how young they start 'em: Helio's eldest son Rorion, maybe three years old, stands on a chair in front of his birthday cake, a sugar-coated replica of the padded floor mats of a training gym, complete with two little dolls getting set to rumble, each dressed in a *gi,* the traditional Jiu Jitsu heavy cotton long-sleeved buttonless shirt tied with a cloth belt.

By the 1980s, Rorion had grown into a man and moved to California, where he set up a modest Martial Arts Academy in his garage and began to proselytize the Gracie style in America. Eventually he was joined by one of his younger brothers, Royce. "I was seventeen when I came to the States," Royce remembers. "Rorion's club had an open challenge. A student will come up and say, 'I got a friend of mine who's got a black belt in Karate, nobody can take him down.' 'Okay, bring him over. He comes over, you do your thing, I'll do my thing, let's go.' We never lost."

So the Gracie Challenge had been transplanted from Brazil to America, albeit at first in a less public, more word-of-mouth form. It wasn't until 1993 that Gracie-style Jiu Jitsu made its mark on martial arts on a wider stage. Rorion and a couple of Pay-Per-View promoters arranged "The Ultimate Fighting Championship," a Brazilian-style no-holds-barred competition that would bring together the best fighters from various martial arts styles, and let them compete. Put up or shut up time for kickboxers versus Karate Kids versus Kung Fu Fighters versus Tae Kwon Do boys versus good old fashioned Marquess of Queensberry pugilists, dropping the gloves to go at it bare-knuckle.

Rorion chose his brother Royce to defend the Gracie family's honor, and do battle under the banner of Brazilian Jiu Jitsu. At one hundred seventy-five pounds, Royce Gracie was outweighed in each bout by fifty pounds or more. His first bout was against a boxer, Art Jimmerson. Once he'd slipped inside the punches for a clinch, Royce took him to the ground and quickly forced him to submit. Next up was Ken Shamrock, a skilled shoot-fighter, a style big in Japan that is sort of a cross between Jiu Jitsu, kickboxing, and Western-style wrestling. Again Royce was able to get his opponent down on the mat, this time winning with a choke hold using his *gi*. In the last fight of the night Royce faced a six-foot-five-inch kickboxing giant by the name of Gerard Gordeau. Once again it went to the ground and Gordeau was choked out.

Royce Gracie's victory in the first Ultimate Fighting Championship proved that the fancy kicks and showy combinations so popular in Chop Socky Kung Fu movies are useless against a patient fighter who knows how to wrestle you to the floor. They also made Royce and the rest of the Gracies the undisputed world leaders in a new form of fighting: Mixed Martial Arts.

7

☆

Royce and Me

"There's a light dusting of snow on the tarmac. Watch your step, it could be slippy," says the flight attendant over the PA as our plane rolls up to the terminal in Prince George. As we deplane (formerly known as disembark) from the little twin-prop aircraft, she's waiting to mouth a mandatory smiley-faced perky "Buh-bye!" to each and every passenger, and the guy ahead of me asks her, "*Slippy*? Whatever happened to *slippery*?" Exactly what I was thinking. The English language is elastic, that's what's great about it, so why is it so irritating when people adulterate perfectly good words? It's like not respecting your elders.

☆

Scott is supposed to meet me right about now, at eight P.M., then we're going to go for a beer in town, then come back and get Royce Gracie, who's landing at ten. I'm peering into every face that looks like it could belong to a bouncer/Jiu Jitsu instructor from Vanderhoof, but the pickings are slim. Most of the guys look like they work in the parts departments of car dealerships. They all quickly rendezvous with their intendeds and head for home.

The airport gets eerily empty. The restaurant and gift shop are closed. The only diversion is the brochure rack of local attractions. Believe it or not, there's one that says, "Introducing Assman's Funeral Chapel." The brochure opens into a triptych of photos of the facilities, all of them eerily empty. Devoid of life, you could say. Printed across the bottom: If This Booklet Has Come To You At An Inappropriate Time, Please Accept Our Apologies. I hate southern sophisticates mocking northern backwaters, therefore I hate myself right now. On a more intriguing note, the brochure touting "Lingerie Secrets" says Prince George's most complete lingerie store carries bra sizes from A to I. I'm familiar with E's, and even triple E's, those porno-popular twin dirigibles, and I think I've heard of F's. But never G's or H's. And then there's I's? The north country must be home to some truly monumental ladies.

It's minus six outside but when he finally shows up Scott's dressed in jeans, a short-sleeved black T-shirt, and a cowboy hat. The only thing missing is the pickup truck. He does have one, but it wouldn't sit three comfortably so he's brought the wife's car, a Chevy sedan he's customized with an eerie blue light under the dash that stays on all the time and faintly illuminates our feet.

Less than two hours to go till Royce appears, and Scott can hardly contain his anticipation. He's a bit of an overgrown kid, a self-described "rough and tough farm boy," and this is the eve of one of the greatest days of his life: the day he hosts his hero, Royce.

In that last phrase there's alliteration, in case you're not aware: being Brazilian, Royce pronounces his name in the Portuguese manner. The R is like H. Royce becomes *Hoyce*.

When my flight came in there had been more than a little of the dreaded fog lurking about. It could easily thicken in two hours and shut down the airport. So we head into town with our excitement slightly tempered. Royce may not make it.

The sky is faintly orange, the tree line is black. It's pine forest out the window, looking exactly like the unbroken phalanx of snowy-shouldered soldiers I'd imagined. When we get near town, bright man-made lights make the snow shine impossibly white. We pass a car dealership where the vehicles covered in six inches of snow look like sugar-coated bonbons. Meanwhile we make conversation and I get the scoop on Scott: he's thirty-one, his dad was in the Navy, later turned to farming and lumber mill work, and in his spare time taught his boys to fight. Growing up, Scott was in about fifty scraps, bar brawls, and the like, before he became a bouncer. At that point he thought some technical training might be good.

"I studied Tae Kwon Do from a guy in Vanderhoof, then he went and got some training under Carson Gracie Jr., came back, and started mixing the two. Then he left town and there was no school for a while, until I took over. Now I don't remember any of the forms or Kata from Tae Kwon Do at all. It's strictly Gracie-style Jiu Jitsu. I get it off the internet. I go to bjj.org and they have all the techniques, broken down, picture by picture by picture, with a written explanation. So I spend twenty minutes and try to go through the movements of it, and try to remember it, and then take it down to the club and show 'em how to do it. I usually remember about two out of four—I get down and find out, okay, hmmm, this doesn't work…."

"You should print up the web pages, so you've got the pictures."

"Yeah, I know. I gotta buy a printer."

"Have you ever had to use any Brazilian Jiu Jitsu as a bouncer?"

"Not really. Generally the best approach to bouncing is minimal force. But I've been in a few situations where I've been shitting myself. I made the mistake once of kicking out a biker. Not a Hell's Angel but a group affiliated with them around here.

"The next night two enforcers came in. One blindsided me, and the other weighed three hundred pounds of pure muscle. That's probably the most scared I've ever been."

"How did he blindside you?"

"I was sitting on a stool by the door, and he just came up on the blind side and punched me right in the face." He points to his cheek just below the eye socket. "I didn't go down though. I came off the stool onto my feet, and steadied myself, then I just grabbed his hand and shook it, and said, 'All right bud, have a good night!' The big guy started laughing, and the other guy didn't know what to do. The big guy ended up giving me a hug later. Turns out in jail he'd been cellmates with one of my brothers."

Speaking of bikers, he points out the prime biker bar in Prince George, as our sedan grumbles along the snowy streets, our tires making that squeaky, scrunching sound of dry snow getting crushed. If you've never heard it, imagine driving over a three-inch layer of sponge toffee. "We're not going in there," he says, gesturing to the bar. "If you bump against a biker in there by accident, they'll put you on the floor and stomp you good. Then the bouncers'll drag your limp corpse outside and scold you—'You know better than to cross that guy!'"

☆

Eventually we settle our asses into the padded chairs of another bar. This one's pretty tame. Drinking and small talk, shouted over Guns N' Roses. Scott tells me a long story of a great fight he and a buddy had in Vancouver recently, rescuing an old Chinese man from being humiliated by a gang of teenagers, fifteen, sixteen years old, in a Subway sandwich shop. The last straw was when the punks knocked the elderly gent's glasses off. Scott and his buddy took on eight kids and whipped their asses.

"You had righteousness on your side," I say.

"My dad taught me, never fight unless you're right. Never be the first one to swing, but always be the first one to hit."

An ad comes up on the TV screen for UFC 51, the latest episode of the Ultimate Fighting Championship. Victor Balfour is fighting Tito Ortiz in the main event. "We're all going to watch it tomorrow night in the bar after the seminar," Scott says. "Royce is keen—he told his agent to make sure we had a place to watch."

I tell him I'm not a fan of the Ultimate Fighting Championships. It's devolved over the last dozen years into spectacle that comes perilously close to the antics of the World Wrestling gang's smash 'em, bash 'em cartoons for the defectively naïve. I'm against the very concept of martial artists fighting for cash and glory. True martial artists are above that. It goes against the whole Buddhist ethos. As I blather on in this vein the fire of my righteousness is stoked by my third beer in an hour. I'm a cheap drunk.

"Buddhist monks will still challenge each other," Scott insists. "I believe if a martial artist takes on another martial artist, that's great. If a martial artist challenges anyone else, that's horse shit. Once anyone starts training in my club, if I hear they're out challenging guys, that's it, they're gone, they're out of the club."

☆

It's getting near ten, time to go get Hoyce, I mean Royce. But try to think of it in your mind as Hoyce. Back in the car, Scott takes the last swig from a plastic bottle of Coke and drops the empty onto the passenger side floor. "That's one thing you never see in a car, an actual spot for a trash can," he mutters. "Just an idea."

We drive in silence.

"It's funny how nerves play on your mind," he says. "Is this really happening?"

It really is. I wander off to phone my wife, and by the time I get back I've missed the actual moment when Royce enters the terminal from the slippy tarmac. He and Scott are standing by the single luggage belt waiting for two big duffel bags containing T-shirts and hats and other Gracie logo-laden sales stuff, and Scott's jabbering away in full-on starstruck giddiness, hooting, "I can't believe you're here!"

Next to big goofy Scott, who stands about six foot three and weighs two hundred ten pounds, Royce looks unimposing. Six foot one, one hundred eighty-five pounds. But he has great presence, in the sense of being *present:* he looks pretty damn sharp and composed for someone who just spent twenty hours getting from Orlando, Florida, to Vanderhoof, British Columbia.

First impressions will hold true all weekend: a taciturn, classy Brazilian gentleman. A sense of humor tempered by the weight of expectations and responsibilities. The most celebrated Gracie, he's the family's top travelling salesman, the premier peddler of his uncle Carlos' and his dad Helio's original recipe. He spends half the year on the road these days, leading seminars like the one scheduled for tomorrow, and he's accustomed to all kinds of odd towns and eccentric hosts. He just goes about his business.

☆

We pile into the sedan and head off into the cold dark night. Scott and Royce are up front, faces slightly illuminated by that blue under-dashboard glow. I'm in the back trying to scribble notes in pitch black.

"You got grizzly bears up here?" Royce asks.

"Yeah, huge ones, fourteen hundred pounds. But they're hibernating right now. They sleep all winter."

"They're dangerous, right?"

"The biggest part is not to be afraid of it," Scott answers.

"Yeah, right," Royce says. "I'll be patient enough playing dead when the bear is trying to eat me, so he leaves me alone. Just lie down, play dead, he'll go away, is that true?"

"Grizzly bears yes, black bears no. Black bears, they eat dead things all the time."

"But black bears are not that aggressive," I say, just to remind them there's someone in the back seat.

"So if a grizzly bear attacks you?"

"Lie down," Scott says.

"Hell no, I'll take my chances on the foot chase."

"Black bear, you turn around and fight 'em," Scott says.

"Try to look as big as you can," I add.

"Yep. What you do is if you got trees around you, you grab a tree and shake the whole tree, like a little tree, small enough to shake but big enough to look big, so then to the bear, you look big."

Scott starts babbling about other matters, apologizing in advance for his club. The Northern Institute of Brazilian Jiu Jitsu only has about twelve regulars. "Eighteen is a large class," he says. "The biggest problem being in a small town is there's no one to teach me. I gotta learn it all from the internet."

"It's up to you to *create*," says Royce. "Create the guys that can give you a hard time."

"I tell my students, my goal is to teach them to be good enough to beat me."

"That's the right goal."

"I didn't start training until I was twenty-two, and that was because of the Ultimate Fighting Championship," Scott says. "I love it."

Royce doesn't say anything. He's left the UFC to fight now with K–1, a rival Mixed Martial Arts promotions outfit based in Japan.

"Which would you rather fight in, The Octagon or a boxing ring?" Scott demands eagerly.

"Makes no difference," says Royce.

"How old are your kids?"

"Seven, six, and two."

"Seven, six, and two. Awesome!"

That seems to mark an exhaustion of potential conversation-starting gambits on the part of Scott. It's my turn. From the back seat I tell Royce how I'm a novice, I've never done any Jiu Jitsu or Judo-type throws, but I'm going to give it a shot—

"I've got beginners, and guys who are really good," Scott interjects.

"That's okay, I can juggle," says Royce.

The ghostly pines slide by outside.

"I'm missing a funeral tomorrow," Scott says. "My wife's best friend. Twenty-three, and she died of cancer of the brain. She sang the song my wife walked up the aisle to, at our wedding."

For a long time after that, the only sound is the heater blasting.

From the back seat, I address the back left side of Royce's head. "Royce, is this as far north as you've ever been?"

"I've been in Sweden. Is that farther?"

We can't be sure.

"The North Pole is a fifteen-hour drive from here," says Scott.

"Really?" says Royce.

"No, not really."

I try to get journalistic. "Royce, growing up, did you have a real genuine interest in learning martial arts, or, being a Gracie and all, was it just expected of you?"

He turns slightly so that I see him in profile. "My father always said, you can have any profession, but you have to know how to fight," he says. Then he looks out the window at the black nothing, or maybe he can see a faint, blue-lit outline of himself reflected back off the glass. "It's a heavy burden, the name Gracie."

Though snowbanks line the road, the asphalt itself is clean and dry, and we in our gasoline-powered cocoon watch the miles roll by, until an outpost of human activity appears, a flood-lit fuel stop for logging trucks. Then a few businesses, most notably Extreme Toyz, selling snowmobiles and jet-skis. Finally we can see a thicket of lights in the distance ahead.

"Civilization at last," I say.

"Good," Royce says. "For a while I thought it was going to get like *Deliverance*."

"I don't know how Ned Beatty ever got talked into that role," Scott says with great feeling. "I could *never* take that role."

☆

Every guy drinking in the pub at the Northern Lights Inn stands in exactly the same pose: one hand holds a beer bottle, and the other, like a half-sheathed knife, is tucked to the second knuckle in their jeans front pocket. The only exception to this rule is Royce Gracie, who sets his orange juice on a countertop and stands comfortably with his hands at his sides, in his customary pose of relaxed alertness.

There's nothing snobby about small-town Canadian bars. They can't afford pretense and exclusivity, they need to cater to every taste in town. To drive home that point, the DJ plays these three songs in a row: a rocker by AC/DC, followed by some country tune with a chorus of "Save a horse, ride a cowboy," then Outkast asserting over a funkified bass-line that Roses Really Smell Like Poo Poo Poo. On the dance floor there's a clutch of middle-aged native ladies in oversized hockey sweaters, and a gaggle of teenaged girls, northern beauties in jeans and tight tops, adeptly, adaptably, finding the right way to move to any and all of the wildly variant songs. To my way of thinking, small-town Canadian girls are the most tolerant and grounded women on the planet.

I say as much to Scott, and he says, "When I was fourteen I asked my ninety-five-year-old grandpa, what's yer biggest regret, and you know what he said to me?"

I shake my head and take another swig of my Kokanee. That's the beer around here.

"He said, 'I don't care if you've got a girlfriend, or you're married, or what you are. If you get a chance to run a girl, you do it! Never turn down any woman who wants you!'"

Scott, who is married and resides in a small town, obviously can't afford to live by this creed, but he's encouraging me to, because men like to live vicariously when they can't live freely. If he wants to live a little through me, unfortunately I can't oblige. I'm happily married, which sets a man up for exquisite torment when he's alone and hundreds of miles from home, watching cute women shake their sweet things in a sweaty midnight crowd. Temptation is dangling there before my eyes like Eve's apple, but let's get serious, given my age and looks, it's not on offer for me. I'd have to get super-proactive to stand a chance. Royce, on the other hand, just by dint of being here, has some ripe and tasty-looking girls coming around to be introduced. Apparently he is also a happily married man, and shows zero interest, not even bothering to flirt, and soon excuses himself to go to bed. It's been a long day, and tomorrow he has to work.

☆

Royce Gracie is an extremely gracious individual. In the bar Scott must have introduced him to half of Vanderhoof, a raft of inarticulate young men in awe of him, some of them dragging along their dads to shake the hand of the Martial Arts star, dads who mostly had no clue who Royce Gracie is or what he's done to make their sons insist they meet him, but Royce was patient with everyone.

He was gracious even to a gang of four stoners who momentarily congregated just outside his room, just next to my room, at the end of the hall on the main floor, as far as you can get from the bar without going outside. It was by default the most discreet and convenient place to toke when it's sixteen below outside.

Although he declined the offer of a toke, just as he had declined the offer of alcohol in the bar, Royce chatted with them for a few minutes before excusing himself after a long day. He was so nice, in fact, that one of them wandered back half an hour later with more of his best buddies in tow, to meet the famous Royce Gracie, and in his enthusiasm and intoxication banged his fist on Royce's motel room door.

Royce dragged himself out of bed and answered the door, still amazingly civil to these stupid fucking yahoos. I could hear it all through my door, because the Northern Lights Inn is the kind of place where the mere sound of shoes on the carpet in the halls carries through the walls, let alone the coughs, farts, whistles, or great sucking tokes of drunken bipeds staggering around. Without even getting out of my bed I had the pleasure of listening to some skinny white kid dressed like a rapper (I'd met him earlier in the bar, noting particularly the silly oversized iceberg-white baseball hat plopped sideways on his nearly-as-white scalp), telling Royce, "These are my buds, 'n' I just wanted 'em to meet you 'cause it's like a huge honor to meet you Royce," and worst of all to my ears the idiot pronounced it with an R, not *Hoyce* as it should be but *Rrrroyce*.

I could picture Royce shaking everyone's hand, because I could hear him saying it's good to meet them too, how ya doin', then very softly, but firmly, he mentions he just spent more than twenty hours getting from Orlando, Florida, to Vanderhoof, British Columbia, and it's well after one o'clock in the morning, and he's got to get up and lead an all-day seminar early tomorrow. "Okay, now you've met me, let me sleep," he says, then he shuts the door and goes back to bed. When the bar closes at two thirty A.M. the parking lot right outside our ground floor windows comes alive with drunks, women cackling, men blustering, diesel engines of oversized pickup trucks roaring to life, and that squeaky, penetrating, all-permeating scrunch of tires on dry cold snow. When I ask him about it in the morning Royce looks puzzled, and says he slept right through.

☆

The seminar is booked for the local high school, in a mat-covered wrestling and gymnastics room up on the second floor, overlooking the gymnasium. Down in the gym there's a basketball tournament this weekend, with the Vanderhoof Vikings (boys) and Viqueens (girls) battling other small-town schools from lonely northern outposts like Fraser Lake and Fort St. John. Competing with the crowd noise, Royce calls for the seminar students to gather around him, sets his laptop on the floor, and has us watch his most recent fight on it. First up is a "tale of the tape" graphic, showing six-foot-eight, four-hundred-ninety-pound Akebono towering over six-foot-one, one-hundred-eighty-five-pound Royce Gracie. "Uhm, which one is you?" pipes up a comic among the twenty-four men and one woman who have paid a hundred and seventy-five bucks for this day of Brazilian Jiu Jitsu. The joke gets a big laugh—the energy at this point is high, nervous, and giggly, with no one certain what to expect.

We crowd around the tiny screen and watch the fight start. "I knew I couldn't stand and trade punches with him, so my strategy was to bring him to the floor and catch him in a shoulder lock," Royce says. "When he came in the ring, I knew I was inside his head. I told my corner I could beat him in five minutes." Onscreen, quickly Akebono has flopped down on top of him, and the fight announcers are bawling apoplectically in Japanese, a good language for sportscasting, full of terse, blunt, explosive syllables in short sentences that sound like they end in half a dozen exclamation marks. Royce—underneath all that blubber—has his arms free to repeatedly punch Akebono in the head, while the bigger man seems like he's trying to get up.

"He's not putting his weight on you," Scott comments.

"He's trying to create space to punch me," Royce explains. "And that allows me to slip out."

Sure enough, when the big man lifts his torso up on one arm and attempts to punch with the other, Royce is able to slip sideways, so that he's lying almost perpendicular to the Sumo, slips his legs around one of his shoulders, and has him in a basic arm lock. At risk of a broken elbow, the big man taps the mat in submission, and the fight is over, at two minutes and thirteen seconds.

"Was he strong?" someone asks.

"He's just heavy," Royce says. "Kimo is stronger. When I fought him I could feel the blood rushing through his veins." The Japanese martial artist Kimo and Royce fought a legendary bout in 2000. It ended when Royce suffered a broken foot.

We watch the fight a second time, then Royce has us spread around the floor to do some stretches. Guessing at club affiliations by people's T-shirts, I can see the Judo club in Prince George has close to ten members here, then there are a few from a Shodokan Karate club in Fraser Lake, and a Tae Kwon Do club from Houston, a small town four hours' drive west. A mixed bag of martial artists. After stretches Royce orders us to pair up, completely randomly, just take a look around and find a partner.

My eyes meet those of Gord, a Vanderhoof kid of twenty-five. How to describe Gord? Well, at the end of this experience, on the drive back to the airport in Prince George, Royce will ask Scott, "Who was that kid from your club, with the goatee?"

"Gord."

"Tough kid."

"Oh yeah," Scott will answer. "He works in the sawmill in town, throwing lumber around all day. Sometimes he straps weights to his wrists while he works—he started out with one pound, then two, then five, now he straps eight pounds on each wrist." Gord has fought in four semi-pro No Holds Barred or Extreme Fighting matches, in Prince George and Vancouver.

So Gord, who is extremely solidly muscled, tense, and serious, is to be my partner, and there is no time to explain to him that I'm a novice, and he should go easy on me, because Royce has selected a guinea pig and is demonstrating what must be done, namely he wants us to take turns with each other, rehearsing and absorbing this exercise: you throw a punch at your opponent's face, and then fall and slide forward to one knee, the other knee slipping between his legs, then you wrap your arms around his waist, drive your shoulder into his belly, pick him up onto your shoulder, turn his legs from vertical to horizontal, and lay him on his back on the floor, coming down with your torso across his, chest to chest crossways, pinning him.

Fine. I feel I'm doing quite well at this, although Gord finds the punch I throw toward his head (the opening move in the series) to be a rather feeble, tentative affair, and says so: "You gotta work on your hand speed, buddy." I make a mental note of that.

Then it's Gord's turn to try it out on me, and I can see what he means: his fist lashes out to within a few inches of my face, and I know if he actually struck me my nose would be splayed open like a gutted trout. Then he's driving his shoulder into my belly and picking me up and slamming me down on my back, and I'm really wishing I had a better idea how to fall properly. It all seems to happen in slow motion, that sense of weightlessness as I wait for my back to connect with a huge thud to the padded (thank God) floor. Even with padding there are a couple of times when I feel the wind almost knocked out of me, feel myself vibrate with after-shocks.

So we keep repeating this maneuver on each other, which is merely the first maneuver of a day full of them, and on Gord's tenth attempt or so, he lifts me up by the gut and throws me down on the floor and comes down on top of me, and this time he's a little overenthusiastic maybe, and by accident he drives his skull into my chest, and a horrible popping sound issues from my rib cage, a sharp snap barely muffled by the fleshy blanket of my skin.

"Sorry dude," says Gord. "You okay?"

"Oh yeah, I'm fine," I croak. "No problem."

☆

But within half an hour there is definitely a problem. I can barely move without excruciating agony, and although I'm trying to be a gamer, it's obvious I'm not up to the standards of what is expected. Royce, wandering from pair to pair, pulls the third wheel off the only threesome (we're odd-numbered at twenty-five participants) and brings him to join Gord and me. We're doing some more grappling stuff, which I wish I could describe explicitly to you in terms of the details of the moves, but I was basically by then in "protect ribs at all costs" mode, and not highly cognizant of much, except that Gord had grown increasingly irritated, impatient with my lack of moxie. "You need to work on your flexibility, *pal*," I remember him saying. There's a way of saying the word *pal* so it sounds battered in sarcasm and deep fried in condescension, until it doesn't mean pal at all, but anti-pal; it means, "You are not my pal, because you are not in my league." That's the way he said it. The stinging "pal."

Gamely I tried to keep up with the big boys, the younger, more flexible, stronger guys who could instantly, effortlessly reproduce the grappling moves Royce demonstrated only once or twice. But have you ever cracked or broken your ribs? It hurts like hell, in almost every position a body can be put into. Standing erect was okay, although it still hurt to breathe deeply. Bending over was agony. Lying on my front or side was nearly unbearable. I found I was no longer paying attention to what we were supposed to be doing—it involved you, after a fall, getting your heels up and tucked into the opponent's hips to prevent him pinning you, then wriggling to the side and wrapping one leg around his head and tucking a heel into his collarbone for leverage—all very tricky technical stuff and quite out of my league even if I hadn't been in excruciating agony. Every time I moved I felt agonizing pain, like a broken shard of rib bone was busy carving its initials into my liver.

☆

I had busted some ribs. I had a perfectly good excuse to bail. I began to search for, to wait for, to live for, that one special moment. The appropriate moment to bail.

How many ribs I cracked or broke, and how severely, I'll never know. I saw my doctor three days after my injury. He ran a finger over my ribcage for all of five seconds, wrote me a codeine prescription and told me ribs heal themselves, there's no point X-raying them because an X-ray won't change the remedy. A week later, my sister who's a nurse told me about a friend of hers who fell off a ladder and died because the rib she broke punctured her liver. My break was also on the liver side, and the pain seemed to come from the front ribs, and the back ribs, and the floating rib, breaks aplenty, breaks all over the place—even before she told me about her fatal friend I'd felt sure I'd bruised my liver. I spent most of the five painful weeks it took my ribs to heal in a state of exaggerated hypochondriacal fretfulness, convinced my liver was fucked and soon to fail.

I must say that even through the intense pain that came immediately after the injury, during that brief half-hour or so while I gamely tried to grapple on, other sensations made themselves known. Some of them were even pleasing. There's intimacy in grappling, rolling around on the floor in a wrestling clutch with an opponent who's doing it as sport, not out of malevolent intent. Memory comes strongly through smell they say, and having my nose squished up against Gord's neck or chest or the back of his knee transported me back to childhood wrestling matches with my brother, who's two years younger than I am. There was a kind of non-sexual physical comfort in it that I'd forgotten existed. Male intimacy, based on camaraderie and trust.

☆

Finally Royce called for a break, by simply shouting "Get some water." He was displeased with one aspect of our performance so far: we were being far too rough on each other, and he wanted us to tone down the violence. "Loosen up eve'body, you've already proven to me you're tough," he said. "I mean, look where you live!"

That got a laugh, and sucked some of the tension out of the room. Everyone had been over-pumped, way too eager to show a famous Gracie how strong and fearless they were. Now everyone relaxed a little. But it came too late for my ribs.

I sidled over to Royce and told him that I had to quit, the pain was too much. There was real "loss of face" in this for me, and Royce did nothing to lessen the sense of shame. No words of sympathy, no comfort. He gave me the fiercest, most severe look of disapproval, a look like if we weren't standing on these mats, if we were outside on the street, he would turn and spit on the ground.

Now to tell Scott I was quitting. Like a giddy puppy, he was wrestling right through the water break, taking on his brother Kevin, an even bigger, older version of himself. Kevin had driven all the way from the town of Kamloops to be here, leaving yesterday afternoon after work, six P.M., and driving steady through long wintry roads until four this morning. The two of them were rolling around on the floor, four hundred fifty pounds of men acting like boys acting like bear cubs wrassling.

"You two look pretty evenly matched," I said. In this type of situation you can't just walk up and say "I quit." Gotta ease into it.

"He's got more power, but he's lost technique through lack of practice," Scott said.

"'Course, he knows I punch him and he's down," said Kevin. "One thing I still have over him is the six-inch knuckle punch."

Scott spots two teenaged boys loitering in the doorway.

"Go get your *gi* and your pants," he yells at the taller of them. "You can still sign up for eighty-five bucks."

"No money," the kid says. "I'll give you five bucks."

"I'll give you a buck for a minute," says his buddy.

"Maybe he can take my place," I say. I explain about my ribs and how I'm going to pack it in.

They're having none of it.

"C'mon man, tough it out!" says Scott.

"Suck it up!" says his brother.

Before I can resist Scott drags me down on the floor with two-hundred-twenty-five-pound Kevin, calling upon me to prove that at least I've learned something. He wants me to perform that series of moves where you start with your heels dug into the opponent's hips as he comes down on top of you, and you're supposed to swivel out to the side and wrap a foot across his neck and lock it with a heel, meanwhile manipulating him into an arm bar and putting pressure on the arm until he thinks his elbow might snap, making him tap out. It was a totally macho moment, the kind I've pretty much got through forty-seven years without ever having to tackle. I was being called upon to prove I wasn't a quitter, that I was game. Okay, I'm game. I'll show you I'm game.

I tried my best to slither out from under heavy Kevin's torso, which was snugly clothed in a black T-shirt that said, Work Harder: Millions of People on Welfare Depend on You. I did manage it, but there was no way I could have gotten my leg over him like I was supposed to if he had offered resistance. Basically he let me break free. Even then, with my ribs busted, fuck did it ever hurt! But I did suck it up, I did tough it out, and felt a little better for it, like I'd paid pocket change in dues to the great god Machismo.

And then I quit.

☆

At the end of the break Royce divided the class into guys who had more than a year's experience with Judo or Jiu Jitsu, and those who had less. The lesser beings were told to sit along the edge of the room while he paired off the remaining hardcore grapplers according to experience. I sat my ass on the floor and leaned my back against the wall and talked to some guy who worked in the Forestry Office in Burns Lake, eighty miles away. "I was expecting there'd be more *attitude*," he said, meaning more macho strutting and posturing. Guys were keeping that in check because, well, you don't swagger in front of Royce Gracie. You'll just look like a jerk.

Royce Gracie is the real deal and he wasn't swaggering, he kept it very low-key and cool, just taking his turn sparring with some of the better fighters from the Judo club, maintaining a consistent expression of calm concentration, never seeming to strain or wrench his muscles as he searched for leverage and position. It was like watching a spider play with a fly. Slowly, methodically wrapping him up. "For getting near forty he's tremendously fucking agile," said the guy from Burns Lake. Supple would be another word.

☆

At lunch I went to 7–Eleven to buy extra-strength Tylenol, then found a little bakery café that had chicken noodle soup. I felt slightly better walking back in the cold. When I came back to the school someone was asking Royce, "What do we have to do to get you to move up here?"

"Turn the heat up."

Then everyone chimed in at once: "This is *nothing*!" "Last year it was minus forty for five weeks straight!"—that kind of thing.

A television crew showed up from Prince George looking for Royce Gracie, and had to be straightened out that it's pronounced *Hoyce*. Royce stood at attention in the blinding glare of the built-in camera light, and went to work answering what must be all the old familiar questions.

So you were the first Ultimate Fighting Champion. Tell me about that.

"The first one was eight men. Three fights in one night. The second, sixteen men. Four fights in one night. Back then there were no gloves, no time limit. Just fight until someone gives. The first, second, and fourth championships, I won."

How does that make you feel?

Royce hesitates at this one. Maybe he's remembering how he felt, a decade younger, when sudden success and fame pulsed through his veins, when at first it might have felt bigger than his heart and mind could contain. Maybe he's thinking about how he feels now, making a good but not great living, conducting seminars like today's in far-flung towns big and small, feeling his body age and his fighting skills gradually diminish.

"In a perfect world I probably never would have been a fighter," he says. "I never had a fight in the street. I'm not aggressive. I'm just good at what I do."

☆

For the afternoon session I snag one of the two chairs on the edge of the mat near the entranceway. Yeah, the chairs are for the invalids, me with the busted ribs, and a woman named Claire, seven months pregnant. She asks if I train in Brazilian Jiu Jitsu in Victoria. Ah, no. Never done it before.

"Really? I was watching you, you looked like you knew what you were doing."

It makes my day. Only it hurts to smile.

Her ten-year-old son Connor is the youngest participant today; he's paired with a twelve-year-old. Everyone else is a grown-up. Claire is here because Connor is a diabetic and needs to have his insulin level checked regularly, something he's prone to forget in the excitement of this kind of event. She watches him struggle against the bigger boy and says, "As far as martial arts go, this Brazilian Jiu Jitsu is really the best for kids. Karate and Kung Fu is all striking, but I've noticed when kids fight, they always end up with their arms around each other's necks, in headlocks, trying to twist each other to the ground. This sport deals with exactly those kinds of real fight situations."

On the mats in front of us it's grappling central, with a dozen bouts in progress. Now it may be, as Claire has just pointed out, that Jiu Jitsu is more realistic than the fancy flying kicks of Kung Fu, but that doesn't make it more attractive to look at. A sport like kickboxing may be unrealistic (in a street situation, would you allow someone to stand back and repeatedly kick you? No— instinctively you would rush 'em and try to get 'em in a headlock, just like you did when you were seven), but kickboxing is fun to watch. It's action-packed when two good kickboxers tee off on each other in the controlled setting of a boxing ring. Grappling, however, does not look good. It's like wrestling, not the slick, silly high-arcing trajectory overhead throws and body slams of professional wrestling, no, I'm talking here about competitive wrestling that no one in the world gives a shit about until the Olympics every four years, and even then in watchability it ranks somewhere below weight lifting and above archery. Pure grappling is unphotogenic, and we live in a visual age. A grappling star has yet to become a movie star, partly because in the full flowering of his martial art, even in the moment of victory, the grappler is likely to have half his face mashed into the mat, and the other half tucked out of sight under his opponent's armpit. It doesn't have to look pretty to work. In fact, sometimes it looks almost comically rude, like two guys playing full-contact Twister.

☆

Inevitably Claire asks why I'm not still out there. The guys are all, "Suck it up, wimp!" but when I mention the ribs she goes all motherly. There's no hospital in town, but they have a clinic, and I should go right this instant and get checked out, especially if it hurts to breathe. Should I? I almost think I should, but what if something really spectacular happens, like some hot-headed local decides he can take Royce Gracie down, and takes a serious run at him, and Royce suddenly sheds his gentlemanly cool and starts beating severely on the guy, and I miss it 'cause I'm in a three-hour line-up for painkillers halfway across this frozen burg? I'd never forgive myself.

No, I'm here for the rest of the day and evening and all day tomorrow, so alcohol and Tylenol will have to do. Alcohol and Tylenol. Be a good name for a country song. But as a painkilling combo, it's not that effective: I'll be so sore by bedtime, fumbling with the medicine bottle at my little motel sink, that getting the childproof cap off will become unbearable agony.

☆

By the end of day one, Royce is losing his voice in the cold dry northern air. As the session winds down with a question and answer you can hardly hear him. Someone asks how he thinks Mixed Martial Arts is evolving, how it's changed since he first fought and won.

"At first it was style versus style, now it's athlete versus athlete, because everyone cross-trains," he says. "And now with time limits built into the fights, not always the best wins, sometimes it's just the most aggressive."

What advice can you give to fighters going into a fight?

"You win a fight in training camp. Discipline to get up and go train, no matter what. Get up. Do it. Just being tough is not enough."

Then it's photo time. The boys from the Prince George Judo club want a group shot with Royce. Mushed in close together, grinning like a winning rugby team, they wait for the local professional photographer to fiddle with a setting, and the frozen smiles start to thaw. One of them says to another, "Do you wanna take your hand off my ass?"

"I think it's Royce's," is the deadpan response.

Then the wife of one of the Judo guys wants a photo of herself kissing Royce. "This cannot go on the internet," Royce says. "My wife will kill me."

☆

Later, in the bar, a couple walks behind my stool.

"We're stuck," says the woman.

"I thought only dogs got stuck," says the man.

Repartee like that would normally make me wanna turn in my chair to get a look at them. Too painful. Did I tell you about my ribs?

A lot of the Judo boys have stuck around to drink beer and watch the Ultimate Fighting Championship on Pay-Per-View in the bar. They're clustered in the low chairs and little round tables below the big TV screen. Macho stoics to a man, it's hilarious to watch them drag themselves to their feet and ever so slowly, stiffly, make their way toward the can when they need to take a leak. From the way they move you can tell they've severely stretched or strained every major muscle in their bodies. They're bruised and battered for sure, but admitting it is not an option. "Suck it up! Tough it out!" The Jiu Jitsu mantra.

Royce is sitting farther back at a more elevated table with Scott, who's asking him, "What's the youngest you ever saw a kid in a *gi*?"

"My son, two days old."

"Damn! My daughter's just got her first at four months."

"So I beat you," Royce says, smiling.

"Yeah, but did you ever see a *pink* belt?"

A bit later in one of the UFC bouts a journeyman fighter named Pete Sell beats some guy named Baroni with a choke hold, and the announcer proclaims, "Royce Gracie 101!!" Everyone in the place turns to look at Royce but he hasn't heard it. He's not even watching. He's left his chair and gone to the bar to get himself another cola.

☆

The next morning I drag myself to Royce's seminar, this one designed specifically for police, bodyguards, and other security types. It's a different crowd, a different vibe. Much more no-nonsense and professional. One of the cops, one of four who've driven down together from Terrace, a town eight hours' drive up the Yellowhead, tells me, "A policeman cannot ever afford to lose a fight, so anything goes." At the same time, he says, it's hard for cops to train, especially in small towns, because they don't want to join the local martial arts club, lose a fight in practice, and then have some dipshit bragging in the pub how he humiliated Officer So and So on the mat last night.

Royce begins by demonstrating a somewhat complicated but elegant technique for turning a suspect over onto his belly and getting the handcuffs on him behind his back, starting from a situation where he's pulled you down on top of him and you're face to face on the ground. The technique is all leverage and little strength. The cops are impressed. Scott, meanwhile, is looking uptight about something.

"I'm stressed out," he tells me. "I got an email saying Royce has to fly out of Prince George at four o'clock today, so that means class has to end at two, at the latest. His wife wants him home."

Apparently Mrs. Royce Gracie is sick of her husband always being on the road, tired of playing the lone police officer and disciplinarian to three rambunctious young sons chewing up the furniture at home. She can't believe their dad is on the same continent, in the same time zone, yet so far out in the middle of fucking nowhere that he'll finish a seminar at four P.M. Sunday and not be home in Los Angeles until late Monday night. Taking matters into her own hands, she has phoned his agent and gotten hold of the flight schedule, phoned the airlines and rearranged and rebooked it, and phoned the agent back to tell him to tell Royce to get his ass home Sunday night.

So Royce is spending a lot of time on his cell phone with his agent, while the cops practice. He gets off the phone and pauses for a minute to watch some locals in the gym below, grown men playing indoor soccer. I make a joke: "As a Brazilian, this must be painful to your eyes." The play on display is clumsy, awkward, all-around god-awful. Hoser soccer.

"The wife changed the flight on me," he says.

Scott comes over and Royce tells him, "What we can do is go straight through with no lunch break to two o'clock, and give everyone a free T-shirt."

"How do you think the guys will take that?" I wonder.

"I don't know," Scott says. "There's only fourteen guys, but there's bound to be one that'll be sour about it. But the worst is, Royce was all excited because we were going to take him out for moose meat dinner at the in-laws' tonight."

When the change of schedule is announced, the cops take it in stride. For those with long lonely drives home, it's good news, an earlier start. Scott calls the photographer from yesterday and tells him to hustle his ass over early to take the souvenir photos. When he arrives and hears why the day is being cut short, he says, "Behind every strong man—there's gotta be an expression there somewhere."

Scott nails it: "You can be the toughest man in the world, and still be ruled by a skirt."

☆

The clock's a-tickin'—T-shirt and photo signing always gobble up more time than budgeted. We'll be sprinting for the gate at the Prince George airport, but first there's the long drive in Scott's wife's sedan. The sunlight off the snow is squinty bright. Royce in the front passenger seat as always looks the cool customer in shades perfect for a Brazilian beach. I'm in the back seat wolfing down a Subway sandwich and scattering shredded lettuce all over like Christmas tinsel. My knees are up by my ribs, and when Scott hits one of the numerous potholes in the road, the pain is excruciating. As a fighter, I ain't much, but as a writer, I'm tough. I keep peppering him with questions, and Royce, ever the gracious gentleman, answers them all. But he's also the strong silent type, the anti-raconteur, and gives mostly short, terse answers.

Sometimes his responses sound a bit too well-practiced: "Like my father said, 'Everything what I am is Jiu Jitsu. I made from the techniques and dignity of the sport, a flag, and I'll take care of my family with sweat, affection, and blood.'" Or, "It's good to be scared. It makes you duck the punch. The guys not scared of getting hit, those are the guys that get knocked out."

What about the future of the Gracies as fighters, now that everyone studies their methods and emulates their style?

"We'll be involved in martial arts for generations. As long as my sons are around. For the next fifty years we're still gonna be around."

And what if your sons aren't interested in being fighters?

"They'll follow in my footsteps only if they want to, it's not an obligation, they are not under contract. But I have a very big family. My father had nine kids, my uncle had twenty-one, together they have over a hundred grandchildren, together they have over fifty great-grandchildren and still growing. Every day there's a new one being born. With this kind of family, we will have

Gracie Jiu Jitsu for the next hundred years. We're not going to quit just because everybody else has learned Jiu Jitsu."

There's a lonely gas station and general store at the halfway point of the drive. As we cruise past it Scott checks his gas gauge and realizes we need to double back and fill up. Precious minutes wasted. It's really going to be tight getting Royce to L.A. tonight.

As Scott feeds the gas tank a customer comes out onto the porch of the general store, hurries down three wooden stairs, slips on an icy patch at the bottom, and totally wipes out. Ass over tit, as the Pogues song goes. Scott, ever the jester, yells "Safe!" like a baseball umpire. The guy truly crash-landed hard; he gets up shaken, bruised, and not amused, but he sucks it up and limps to his car with one snow-smeared ice-smacked kneecap mark on his pant leg.

Royce emerges a minute later from the store with a coffee and a postcard of a moose.

"Caribou is bigger than a moose?" he asks.

"Smaller, but bigger antlers," Scott answers.

8

★

Kung Fu Revenge

Almost everyone I've met who practices martial arts got hooked on it as an impressionable teenager. They saw a Bruce Lee movie, or a Jet Li movie, or some guy on TV splitting bricks with the blade of his bare palm, or Royce Gracie kicking ass in the UFC. The adolescent mind easily surrenders to fantasy, and the majority of fantasies fall neatly into three categories: success, sex, and revenge. In life we tend to outgrow our teenage fantasies of success—at twenty you realize you'll never drive Formula One or score on a penalty at the World Cup, at thirty you admit you'll never be a rock star and open for U2, at forty you accept you'll never be president or prime minister. That leaves sex and revenge as lifelong fodder for fantasy. Sex needn't concern us here. This is about revenge.

When I got back from Vanderhoof I started psyching myself to write a newspaper article I'd sold about the trip, a feature for the metropolitan daily closest to where I live. I took a few days to mull over the material. This phase of mental editing is also called procrastination. Before I got any further than that, an editor at the paper called. She sounded very, very sorry. She was killing the story.

It seems the paper was no longer willing to pay for features longer than fifteen column inches, about seven hundred words. I'd been contracted to write twenty-five hundred, therefore my services were no longer required. Insert your favorite obscenities here. I got off the phone royally pissed.

Shortly afterward, I was asked to give a public reading for World Press Freedom Day, and a reporter from that selfsame paper called me up for an interview. Because I wrote a book about smoking pot all over the world, an act perceived by many mainstream media types as a career-killer, she thinks I must be fearless when it comes to speaking my mind. She's young and trying to be "edgy" so she asks me, "What can you think to say that would be so 'out there' this paper might not even dare print it?" So I go into a rant about how humble generalist scribes like me will soon be as extinct as the Japanese Samurai, directly because of the policies of her goddamn paper's owners, who hand out awards for promoting "literacy," but for whom literacy equates to teaching cretins just enough so they can read the ads, but don't you dare overload their anemic little attention spans beyond seven hundred words. It feels good to get that off my chest.

A few days later I get an email from the reporter: she's depressed. Her tape recorder didn't work, she has no transcript of our interview. Could we please do the whole thing over again? So we do, only this time the first interview's "edgy" question goes AWOL. I ask what happened, and she says, "I ran it by my editor, and he says it's a no-go."

In that moment I felt utterly powerless, a peon shat upon by the potentates of print. There was no way to alter my powerlessness, nothing I could do but fantasize about what I'd *love* to do. Anger clenched my mind into a fist of fury, screaming *REVENGE!* in my head like Bruce Lee in his first feature film, *The Big Boss*. Have you seen it? He's sitting on the banks of the river, staring into a water-fall, when suddenly, superimposed on the tumbling, gurgling white water, he sees the faces of his dead comrades. They've all been murdered by The Big Boss's henchmen. *"I don't care what becomes of me. REVENGE! I'll get revenge!"* So says a seething Bruce Lee, in voiceover.

Revenge! Is there a homo sapien alive who has never felt dark, delicious fantasies of *getting even* bubble up through the murk of the 23.5 trillion synapses that make up the private universe of consciousness?

The mind can't be edited, and mine succumbed to a savory moment of pure, unadulterated Kung Fu revenge: on the day I truly master the deadly art, I'll stride confidently into the corporate headquarters of the media empire that screwed me over, bust down the door of the greedhead who runs the show, and proceed to break his nose with my toes. Peck his eyes out with my fingers! "You love literacy? How about learning some *Braille,* motherfucker?!!!" Heeyap! *Guuudap! Wump,* Weeeeee-sknapnip!!! End with the sweet muffled *thadump* of body hitting broadloom. Roll credits.

9

☆

More Revenge Fantasies

I'm keeping a diary of my progress at the Kung Fu Academy. Most recently, it noted that today I learned how to fall on my face. Rule one for falling forward: make a window. Touch your thumbs and forefingers together in front of your face to make a little triangular window to look through. Hold that pose. Now fall to your knees, then forward. You won't hurt your wrists or elbows this way; you'll absorb the shock equally from elbow along forearm to palms, all of which should slap the mat simultaneously.

I was practicing this technique when Lacy, a plump twenty-something gal in the back corner of the club, observing the kicking technique of another student, urged her to pretend to "Kick the water bucket, like in *Kill Bill 2*." Everything stopped for a moment because Sifu Bob couldn't remember a kicked water bucket in *Kill Bill 2*. Apparently Lacy has watched *Kill Bill* more than once.

There and then I made a note to watch *Kill Bill,* but only got around to it after I went to China and stocked up on pirated DVDs. A buck apiece, I mean who can resist? I bought them at a state-owned store, proving that the Chinese government's assurances they're cracking down on video piracy are a complete joke. I got *Unleashed,* also known as *Danny the Dog,* a recent and, for my money, instant classic martial arts movie produced and written by Luc Besson, starring Jet Li, with a soundtrack by Massive Attack, and with Bob Hoskins as the mouth-frothing bad guy; I got a seven-disc deluxe boxed set of Bruce Lee; I got *House of Flying Daggers,* Kurosawa's *Seven Samurai,* and some Indian movie I still haven't gotten around to watching that's supposed to be Bollywood's attempt at martial arts; I got a three-disc box of Shaolin movies, including *Shaolin Temple,* the film that turned the teenaged Jet Li into a star. And I also got *Kill Bill 1* and *2,* Quentin Tarantino's homage to (or is it parody of?) martial arts movies. So eventually I watched *Kill Bill 1,* and then *2,* and saw Uma Thurman look directly into the camera's lens to explicitly promise us a "roaring rampage of REVENGE," and I failed to notice Uma Thurman kicking any bucket, but I did come up with my own theory of what *Kill Bill* is all about.

☆

It's about closure. It's about putting Bruce Lee's soul to rest. Through much of *Kill Bill* Uma Thurman wears a motorcyclist's jumpsuit, bright yellow with black stripes down the sides, that's an updated replica of the one Bruce Lee wore in *Game of Death,* his last movie, a ridiculous affair cobbled together by the studio after his untimely demise. So. Uma Thurman can be seen as a stand-in for Bruce Lee, his resurrection, even. Her goal in this most single-minded of films is to Kill Bill. Now Bill just happens to be played by David Carradine, who in the 1970s played Kwai Chang Caine, a Shaolin monk fighting his way across the Wild West, in the hit American television series *Kung Fu.* It might be hard to believe now, but Hollywood in the 1970s was too racist to hire a Chinese actor to play Caine. The idea for the *Kung Fu* series came from

Bruce Lee. The original title was *The Warrior,* and he saw himself in the lead role. But while Warner Brothers liked his idea enough to make a pilot episode for ABC, they hired Carradine, not Lee, to play the hero. Lee was devastated, then enraged. Carradine was awful in the role of Caine (he goes for the stereotypical "inscrutable" Chinaman shtick). Three decades later, in *Kill Bill,* he's equally awful in much the same way, wooden and monochromatic. Bruce Lee would have killed for the part of Caine, a part he invented, for chrissakes. So what *Kill Bill* represents is Lee's chance, channeled by Tarantino, to wreak revenge on Carradine.

☆

In the choreography of *Kill Bill,* we can also see the triumph of Bruce Lee in a wider sense. It's a triumph *owed to Bruce Lee,* the triumph of Asian sensibilities in world culture, specifically in the world's number one universally appreciated art form, the action movie. For example: what does *Kill Bill,* directed by America's leading (if I may dare) auteur, have in common with the *Matrix* trilogy, that hugely popular franchise directed by the Wachowski brothers? What does it share with *Crouching Tiger, Hidden Dragon,* Ang Lee's art house tribute to the "internal" martial artists of Wudang Mountain, and even with the aforementioned Jet Li vehicle, *Unleashed*? Answer: in all of them, the action sequences were choreographed by the same man, Hong Kong-based Yuen Wo-Ping, a top director in his own right. He directed Jackie Chan in the film that made Chan a star, 1978's *Drunken Master.* Chan took the persona he developed in that film—goofy, self-deprecating, and lethal—and turned it into the biggest box office draw in the world.

☆

The Rebel Sell, a recent book by Joseph Heath and Andrew Potter, describes how counterculturalism has become just another subset of consumerism, because mainstream culture, "the system," absorbs and adopts every critique the counterculture can throw at it, then sells a watered down version back to the next generation of kids who need to feel like they're rebelling. In a way, Bruce Lee was the public face of a similar phenomenon adopted toward Asia by the West. He exploded onto the world stage just as the Viet Cong, the wee pajama-clad fighting tigers of a tiny Asian nation called Vietnam, were kicking big bad John Wayne America's butt. The Americans armored themselves in tons of brawny gleaming steel, and their terrifying modern weaponry dropped megatons of munitions and chemicals like Agent Orange, but they still proved no match for a bunch of guys hiding out in caves dug by hand under their bamboo huts. The politics of "freedom" versus Communism became irrelevant in a mismatch like that—the underdog by default became the good guy. Then along came Bruce Lee, and suddenly every teenage North American boy with a testosterone-fueled fantasy of being tough, of righting the wrongs of the world with pugilistic powers, was identifying with a lithe, agile Chinese man, all fists and attitude, barely five-and-a-half feet tall. Millions of young people flooded into Kung Fu schools that suddenly appeared out of nowhere to teach the new fighting techniques. Overnight, Asian martial arts was mainstream. Can't beat the Asians? *Become* the Asians. Bruce Lee was the public face of that coping mechanism.

On the other side of the world, Bruce Lee was the public face of a rising Asian self-confidence, the ice-breaker who showed Asians they could compete, and win, on the world stage. Bruce Lee was their first champion, the David they shoved forward to face the best of the Philistines. He slew the Philistines, all right. They fell in love with him.

☆

One recent day I was stuck at the bank, feeling a slow boil start to percolate with impatience while it took forever for them to find someone to help me. Compulsive tapping of foot on floor. Deep breaths. Deep breaths. Finally, the name Preston was called, finally I was shaking hands with the guy who could get my paperwork done.

The guy was blind. He had a seeing eye dog curled up in the corner of his office. He had to wear a headset and use software that told him aurally what the various screens said on his computer, and what he typed on his keyboard. Naturally, this caused a radical change in my state of mind. I thought, Okay, I'm now thirty-six minutes and counting behind schedule for today, but at least I'm not blind. Count your blessings. Not that being blind is the end of the world, this guy seemed to be coping pretty good. But I wouldn't trade places.

We made small talk about me being a writer, then later, as I was leaving, he asked me what the title of this book would be. I told him *Me, Chi, and Bruce Lee,* and he got very excited; he said he was reading a book by Bruce Lee, a collection of aphorisms culled from his writings. "It's like having a thousand little fortune cookies all in one place, I read one every day," he said enthusiastically.

I respect Bruce Lee's place in martial arts. I respect the influence he has had on nearly every martial artist who came of age in the last thirty years. Without Bruce Lee, would East have met West? Certainly not as soon, or as spectacularly. The man was the catalyst, the spark, for a revolution in martial arts, give him credit for that. But I did want to make an editorial statement about the worst excesses of what I call "the Bruce Lee industry." I'll keep it short, because, considering the title of this book, it could be perceived as the pot getting snooty and calling the kettle sooty.

☆

It's one thing to be a fan, it's quite another to go completely over the top and turn the object of your worship into something he was not. Here are a couple of claims made in *Bruce Lee: A Warrior's Journey,* a book by John Little:

> Certainly the case can be made for Bruce Lee having "awakened" to his own Buddha nature and, perforce, having become enlightened, or a Buddha.

> It could be argued convincingly that Bruce Lee was not only one of the greatest martial artists of all time, but also, given the scope, breadth, depth, and enduring impact of his words on such matters, one of history's greatest spiritual teachers— or bodhisattvas.

Come on, John, get a grip. The impact of Bruce Lee's movies has been profound, but it's all based on the visuals. The impact of his words? Nil. Millions of people can imitate Bruce Lee's martial arts moves, or at least picture them in their minds. How many can quote him? Okay, maybe a few, like my blind banker. I've seen Bruce Lee's movies: they're not great, but his physical presence is unforgettable. I've read his collected writings: *snooooze!* They're mostly rehashes of Taoism and Buddhism 101, often lifted from youthful essays he wrote in his college days at the University of Washington in Seattle. Perhaps if he'd lived to a ripe age, if he were still alive today, he would have buttressed his physical reputation with a deeper philosophy, and evolved into some kind of sage. But he didn't. He died suddenly, at thirty-two, in the bed of a Hong Kong actress named Betty Ting Pei, while his wife and children waited for him across town. He died restless, unfulfilled, still consumed with worldly ambition, still driven by ego to become the biggest movie star on the planet, to taste sweet revenge against racist Hollywood for its initial rejection of him as a leading man. That's hardly the way a Bodhisattva bids goodbye to this earthly tumult.

10

☆

If You're Strong,
You're Wrong

A nd as I lay helpless on the floor, I saw his body lurch down toward me, his skull plummeting to earth like space junk about to blast a crater into the desert, only it crashed smack dab onto my ribs, and they popped in my chest like a bag of fluorescent tubes getting whacked with a hammer.

In the weeks after my return from Vanderhoof, my encounter with Gord was getting more elaborate and ornate with each retelling. And what's the harm? People like their truth adorned. The only persons to receive a sober, objective rendering of the incident were my doctor and Sifu Bob, when I went out to the Kung Fu Academy to let him know I'd be out of commission until my ribs fully healed.

"Did you wear your T-shirt?" Bob asked, meaning my regulation white Kung Fu Academy T-shirt, with a little logo on the chest of a yin–yang symbol topped by a scholar's mortarboard cap.

"I did wear it."

"He probably thought you were a Kung Fu Master," he said, smiling at the thought. "Regardless, they shouldn't have been practicing full throttle like that. Learning new stuff should be done as soft as possible. There's a saying: *Go Weak for Technique; If You're Strong, You're Wrong.* Strength is the wrong way to learn; you always need to practice as if your opponent is stronger than you. You need to be thinking, this is a technique by which I can beat a stronger man. If you're relying on strength in practice, that day that you come up against someone stronger and bigger than you, you'll actually have no technique against him. For sure you'll lose the battle. But if you train by picturing that people are always going to be physically stronger than you, then the opponent's strength doesn't matter.

"Now in a self-defense situation, when you start to apply power to your finesse and technique, then it becomes unstoppable, like Royce Gracie was. There is no way he can out-power anybody—he was fighting people that were three hundred pounds and beating them. He can't overpower people: he has to use technique with strength.

"We call it sticky hands. When you start practicing with someone, you're always feeling their energy, understanding where they're going, and later on, when you progress, you start to figure out how to manipulate somebody by feeling their energy, which way it's going, and letting them go that way, letting them do the technique for you."

"Sounds good," I said. "But does it work in grappling? I can't imagine redirecting someone's energy when they're sitting on me."

"Oh yeah, Royce Gracie is the proof that it totally works for grappling. When I teach grappling I get my students to close their eyes. When they close their eyes they become more aware of their bodies, with what's going on with their legs."

I told Bob I'd actually noticed that very thing about Royce. When he was sparring with some of the guys in the seminar, he'd be lying on the ground, limbs all intertwined with the opponent, and not moving, sussing them out, with his eyes closed. It almost looked like he was taking a nap. "I'm not sure closing my eyes would have helped me much in my situation, though," I said.

"Sounds like this Gord was very intense, very wound up," says Bob. "I find even in our school, in grappling, ego takes over. People find it very hard to settle down and figure out how it can be a learning process, rather than a test. People figure it has to be done really strong."

"It's more primal, more like basic schoolyard stuff we all went through as kids, and it triggers a lot of childhood stuff," I suggest. "You can feel the force of the other person, and you want to match whatever force he's trying to handle you with, and so you push back, and it escalates quickly."

"It's adrenaline, right," Bob says, "but the understanding of adrenaline, when it's just nerves, and when they are actually using strength—most people I get in here, the older they are, the more rigid they get. Like if I touch you, you tense, you become like a rock."

"It's true," I agree.

"So it's not a matter of you responding with strength, you just froze."

"That's exactly what I was doing."

"Yeah, you're not doing anything deliberately, the body just locks. And that sends a message to a practice partner that you're being strong on him, but really you're not trying to resist him, you're just tensed up. And people don't seem to understand how that works and how to feel the difference, so they have tunnel vision with one focal point in mind: to muscle through you until they get you in the lock, rather than adapting to the change. Grappling is by far where the highest number of injuries take place—we've never had a break, but people usually pull something in the neck, things like that."

"When do I get into grappling?"

"Next level. Orange belt. First you learn basics: when you're on top how to keep 'em on the bottom, and when you're on the bottom, how to get out. Then purple belt is locks, but we don't jump people into locks right away because it's way too easy for injuries."

11

☆

Like Chasing Water

One day I asked Bob, "How do you think your Master Don would fare against someone like Royce Gracie?"

He surprised me by saying, "There are nine levels to martial arts knowledge. Mastery of strength and technique puts you at the top end of level three. I put myself at the low end of level three. But Don is at level seven. When I spar with Don, I can't even touch him. He's on a completely different mental level. It's like a chess game and he's three moves ahead of me. He knows what I'm going to do before I do."

Really? Pudgy little Don the monk? The one trick he'd shown me had been impressive in its way, but it seemed almost like a novelty, like a card trick at a party. "What does his style look like when you're sparring, that you can't touch him?" I asked.

"He favors the monkey, which isn't one of our five animals we teach here. That comes later, after you've reached black belt and entered Shaolin."

☆

Afterward I couldn't get this image out of my head: big solid Bob plodding forward on the mat like a grounded, heavyweight horse, and balding, gap-toothed Don, prancing around him like a hyperactive little monkey, using his fingertips to poke him as if with a stick, giggling gleefully at his own cleverness.

I figured I'd better go talk to Don again, see if he would concur with Bob's rankings. When I caught up with him, he didn't quibble at all with being put on the lofty pedestal of level seven, but said, "Our art form has nine stages of training. Royce Gracie is probably about a four or five. The features that tell me that are, people who have worked with him directly, they say it was like chasing water. He was right there touching them, not actively resisting, but they couldn't ever get him. So that's a four, five, maybe even a six. I don't think you can get to a level higher than that if you plan to use it to compete. World champion kickboxers get stuck at three.

"That's not to slight them: they are impressively competent," Don continued. "But if they really knew what they were doing they wouldn't have to retire in their thirties, they could do it into their eighties and nineties and still be formidable competitors.

"But the attitude of competition forces the ego to stand its ground, and that works against Mixed Martial Arts fighters. It's still a sport, because there are things you can't do. Fishhook the mouth, gouge the eyes, for example. But there are other things that haven't happened because none of these professional fighters realize they can do it yet. Not to take anything away from them, but the internal styles supersede their knowledge."

"What do you mean?"

"They haven't studied the internal styles. They don't know. And that's a good thing. These people want to be powerful, and unique in an aggressive way. A person who does the soft style retrains their mind to think about it in different terms. The people who trained me are very good at looking after themselves, but it's for them a vehicle of expression and creativity. It's a way of life, because once you understand it, you make it a priority *not to be violent*. An internal martial art has as its priority not hitting, but *influencing*. That doesn't mean backpedaling on the use of force, because if you do *that*, sooner or later the person will overtake you. Being an internal martial artist doesn't mean you are nicer—killing or crippling injuries take very little effort to accomplish. But because the goal is *not* to hit them, it gives you the option of being gentle with them even as they are trying to hurt you. And in the true Shaolin art, there is a mind-training component that, if you pursue it, becomes a life-changing experience."

I listened with a healthy dose of skepticism, I have to say. I knew Don and Bob met once a week to train together as master and student, so I promised myself that I would get their permission to come and watch them. Ideally they would spar, and I'd get a sense if Don was for real, or if he was just blowing incense.

12

☆

Buddha Was a Deadbeat Dad

My progress in Kung Fu is not going as well as I'd hoped. First I broke my ribs, then I had a kid.

☆

My daughter, Grace Gitanjali Tahsis Preston, came into the world on _____, weighing seven pounds seven ounces. I was going to tell you her actual birth date, but there's so much identity theft around these days, if I print it in a book, next thing I know we'll get a bill in her name for a villa rental in Spain.

Birth is supposed to be a joyous occasion, and maybe it is if it all goes according to plan. But after thirteen hours of labor my wife and I were coaxed and prodded by half a dozen people in hospital uniforms to agree to a caesarean, which was presented to us as simply making a tiny neat little slit in mommy's abdomen for baby to slip out, a quick little procedure under local anesthetic. Next thing I know, my sweetie is strapped down tight to a T-shaped table like a horizontal crucified Christ, and they've draped a curtain at her neck to hide from her what a dozen masked strangers are doing. I'm led into the room and told to stroke her forehead soothingly and keep the curtain off her chin, and then suddenly, offstage as it were, there emerges the sound of a wailing baby, followed by a nurse saying, "Look at the size of her feet!" Then I'm encouraged to leave my wife and ceremonially cut the umbilical cord. Really all I do is clamp it, because it has already been severed, and the baby carried to the nearest sink, where after I do my bit she's quickly swaddled by three nurses who argue about how many blankets to use, and the proper way to do it, and then she's delivered to me, and I'm told to go sit with her in the room adjacent to the operating room where they store extra supplies, gurneys, and incubation trolleys.

My first sight of Grace she was naked and being carried across the operating room, and her body had looked spasmodic and shockingly purple, but now that she's swaddled she's looking better, she has big alert eyes even at ten minutes old, and when I look up beyond her I can see my darling wife through the operating room door vomiting into a bucket, still strapped down like horizontal Jesus while they sew her up and pump her full of painkillers. I actually start to cry, and then I sing to Grace the song that I will always and forevermore remind her was the first song she ever heard: "Don't Go To Strangers." "If I'm standing in a crowd, call my name, call it loud, Don't go to strangers, woman, call on me." It's not premeditated, I've just been listening to it on CD in the car a lot lately. J.J. Cale's album *Naturally*. A good one. Still holds up beautifully after thirty-five years.

☆

In preparation for baby's birth, I'd borrowed Ina May Gaskin's book *Spiritual Midwifery* from the library. My very practical and down-to-earth wife was having none of that hippie dippy birthing stuff, although after coming up against big bad impersonal institutionalized medicine she has now changed her tune. In her book, Ina May Gaskin describes how she once held a monkey's finger and found the monkey's touch to be "incredibly alive and electric." She writes, "I had a flash of realization then that my hand wasn't made any different from hers—same musculature, same bone structure, same nervous system. I knew that my hand, and everyone else's too, was potentially that powerful and sensitive.... I call this 'original touch' because it's something everybody has as a brand new baby, it's part of the kit."

I can see it in Grace: a tremendous pure physical presence. Later, when I've met plenty of martial arts masters, I'll call it unimpeded Chi. I wonder how long before self-consciousness and socialization will conspire to choke it off?

☆

So. She was born, then suddenly in the blink of an eye, she was one month old. Her one-month birthday got me wondering how many months the average person gets in a lifetime. Can you do the math that quick?

I'll tell you. A thousand.

If you live a thousand months, that's eighty-three years, four months. So next time a month goes by in the blink of an eye, remember you only get a thousand of them. A lifetime goes by in a thousand blinks of an eye.

Now, if you're like me, this kind of realization causes a momentary quickening of the pulse, and a resolve to *really do something* with your precious time. Then a couple of months slide by and, if you're like me, you haven't done anything different at all, so you just accept the fact you're on a certain trajectory through life, and it's not actually that bad: you're never going to be a superstar or a legend, famous or infamous, but what the hell, the only problem with life is that it goes by too fast, and there seems to be absolutely nothing you can do about that.

☆

Having a kid really takes it out of you, especially when you're closer to seventy than you are to twenty. Little brat is awfully cute, but she eats up my day. She keeps me up half the night, and then most days, from about six A.M. to about eight A.M. you'll find me swinging gently back and forth in a glider rocker in my living room with wee Gracie in my arms. Gracie? Gracie! Yes, she mostly gets called either Gigi or Gracie. When the name Grace first came up as a serious possibility, I honestly didn't even make the connection to Royce Gracie and Co. I still don't, even as I coo that name to her. Anyway, you'll find me in that very smooth-swaying glider rocker with contently comatose Gracie propped horizontally in the crook of one arm, the other arm free to handle a book. Today it was Jackie Chan's autobiography.

I am Jackie Chan—is that not the lamest title? The book's better than that, it's a good read. Born Chan Kong Sang ("Born in Hong Kong" Chan), young Jackie was dumped by his financially strapped parents to be raised in a highly abusive Chinese Opera training school in Hong Kong. Chinese Opera being a dying art, the school's master kept his operation afloat by renting the kids out to the film business as child actors or, as they grew through adolescence, as stuntmen in martial arts movies. Jackie Chan as a young man worked in several Bruce Lee films, playing just another of hundreds of anonymous evil guys getting knocked on their asses by Bruce Lee. Chan's insights into Lee are quite likely the most balanced, hagiography-free reminiscences around. The first time he ever lays eyes on Lee in person is while working as a stuntman on *Fist of Fury,* the follow-up to Bruce's massively successful first feature, *The Big Boss*. (The titles sometimes get confused. *The Big Boss* was released in North America as *Fists of Fury*. His second movie, *Fist of Fury*, was released in North America as *The Chinese Connection*.) Lee blows onto the set in a genuine fury and storms about, tailed by his director, Lo Wei, who is apologizing profusely for a quote in the morning newspaper to the effect that he taught Bruce how to fight. Bruce puts up his fists, seemingly ready to lay a beating on the overweight, out of shape Lo, until Lo's wife intervenes, and cooler heads prevail. Lee settles down, but not before issuing this threat: "If your husband ever talks about me to reporters again, I'll give *him* a lesson on how to fight!" Lee has undeniable personal charisma, Chan acknowledges, but he feels compelled to add that while Lee's punches and kicks were strong and skillful, "I knew people who were just as strong, or stronger, and just as skilled, or even more so."

☆

After watching a bunch of Jackie Chan films, I have to say that his loose, casual martial arts style appeals to me more than Bruce Lee's super-tense powder keg persona. I mean really, the very first lesson at the Kung Fu Academy, the absolute basic building block of the art, is one word: Relax. In the fight scenes of his movies, Bruce Lee never looks relaxed. His muscles look strung so tight they might at any moment snap like violin strings. His physique is so sculpted and taut on-screen he looks almost three-dimensional. It makes for good cinema, but is it good martial arts?

Some people don't think so. Another book I've been reading is Robert W. Smith's *Martial Musings*. Smith started out as a conventional boxer in the 1940s, became a Judo man in the 1950s, a Kung Fu specialist in the 1960s, and a Taiji proponent beyond that. He's undeniably expert, a grand old man with six decades of experience, and first-hand knowledge of many of the twentieth century's great-est practitioners. If I were to recommend any other martial arts book to you, it would be *Martial Musings*. In places it's beautiful and profound. In others it's abrupt and dismissive. For example, Smith has an extremely low opinion of Bruce Lee. "You can't fight without relaxing" if you believe in Chi, says Smith. Even Western boxers, at their best, display a "relaxed artistry." Then there's that "spoiled, pouting, adolescent brat," Bruce Lee. "He can't relax. Overfighting is as bad as overacting and Lee was guilty of both until the day he shuffled off this mortal coil."

☆

Blink of an eye, a month goes by. In my glider rocker with sleep-ing babe in arms I also have the TV on, sound muted and half-intelligible closed captions scrolling in fits and starts. Every once in a while I glance at the tube, and at my baby's sweet tabula rasa face, but mostly I'm trying to focus on getting some reading done, and right now the books are *Buddha: His Life and Teaching,* by Walter Henry Nelson, and *Buddha,* a "biography" by Karen Armstrong, which I'm making my way through for the second time. I read it just after Grace was born, in ten-minute snatches, but by the time I'd finished it, all that strange terminology—*annatta, samsera, dukkha, cito-vimutti,* etc., etc.—had run together like the colors of a child's finger-painting in my brain, addled as it was, and still is, with the sleeplessness and responsibilities of Dadhood. This time around, I'm getting it.

☆

Armstrong starts out by saying you can't really write a conventional biography of Buddha because once he had achieved enlighten-ment, once he *awakened,* he completely lost his ego, his individuality, his very self. He didn't have a personality anymore. This, apparently, is what we should all strive for. Buddha, being a man of his time and place, believed what everyone else believed in India twenty-five hundred years ago: that humans are condemned to a cycle of endlessly repeating reincarnations, unless they break the cycle by achieving complete enlightenment. By achieving Nibbana, or Nirvana, a state in which no suffering is felt, you stop being reincarnated. Buddha believed life is basically suffering, and delusion, and therefore not having to come back for another go-round is a great idea.

☆

I have trouble with that. I'd be only too happy to come back for another life similar to the one I'm having. Life's been pretty sweet to me: in the first two decades of adulthood I had some great travels, and now I've settled down on what amounts to a quiet, leafy little cul-de-sac on the streetmap of the world, far from war, famine, cruelty, and barbarism, and close to good libraries, quality marijuana, and decent wine shops. I occasionally feel guilty about that, and maybe I should feel guiltier than I do. The guilt of being lucky doesn't outweigh the pleasure of it, and in this I'm no different from most of the five hundred million or so souls out of the six billion huddling together on the hospitable slivers of this planet—the fortunate twelfth who share my level of affluence and comfort or better.

☆

Buddha was a deadbeat dad. I think that explains a lot. When he took off to seek enlightenment he was at exactly the point in his life that I'm at now: father of a newborn baby. He called his son Rahula, which means fetter. As in shackle. If he had fathered twins, I guess he would have named them Ball and Chain.

Domesticity was choking him. I bet every new dad has arched over the baby's crib, cooing soft persuasions to settle little Brendan, Emma, Grace, or Rahula to sleep, and realized with an emotion like regret or melancholy that this helpless little bundle of new life is also the death knell of an old lifestyle, the stopper on the bottle of those freewheeling, reckless, party-hearty, stay-out-all-night pre-Dadhood good times. As Donald Barthelme put it, "The world in the evening is fraught with the absence of promise, when you are a married man."

Not that I'm personally complaining. If I felt that way a little bit, I got over it quickly. I had another birthday, and now I'm forty-fucking-eight years old, after all. In other words, settling down and having a kid hasn't exactly pulled me from the game at my peak. But Buddha was twenty-nine, with a lot of dreams left unfulfilled. His ambitions weren't sensual or hedonistic, but spiritual. All the biographies of Buddha present the choice he made as terribly brave: the austere regimen of the ascetic over plush, easy domesticity. But the choice could just as easily be presented like this: vagabonding around, utterly carefree, with like-minded cerebral spiritual seekers, or staying home nights, changing diapers and listening to the wife complain. A no-brainer. He snuck off without even saying goodbye, and went to the woods to live a life without bills, deadlines, paydays, or duties. In other words he was free.

☆

Still, I consider Buddhism far superior to other organized religions, which require blind faith in a bunch of far-fetched fairytales and unprovable superstitions, the biggest being Almighty God Himself. In Buddhism there is no God, or as Don the monk puts it, "no universal big stick to punish you when you're bad." There is only the work you need to do through meditation to achieve a state beyond suffering. Don invited me to an open-house Sunday night Buddhist beginner's group, and I went several times. It was mostly tousle-haired twenty-somethings in mismatched socks lounging around on a cold carpeted floor, asking questions like, "Would an enlightened person be able to drink a cup of coffee and not be affected by caffeine?" while Don pontificated in that gentle monotone of his, saying things like, "I know from experience, it's possible to shut off the pain of an abscessed tooth, just by going into a meditation state," and "The Buddha is the awakened one. That means everyone else is walking around in trances. Hypnotized. If you have an attachment to a noun, that is a trance. Or to put it in Buddhist terms, a delusion. No person, place, or thing can impart any kind of experience to you. If I'm focused on an objective outcome, that is external, that describes *Samsara*. This wheel of suffering." Almost everyone in the room scribbled this pronouncement down into notebooks they'd brought, including me. The only person who didn't was the hippie dippy woman beside me, who was too busy bringing her ankle up to her nose to examine a bump on it. Excellent flexibility.

At the end there was lighting of incense and praying to a little Buddha statue. I can't say I go in for that, and told Don so, on the doorstep as I was leaving. He said it's only meant as a symbol, as a test of ego. "You're not expected to take anything here on blind faith," he said. "In fact you shouldn't take it on blind faith. It's not a religion, it's a philosophy. Buddha would ask, 'Is it useful?'"

At these Sunday night lectures there were only occasional martial arts references. Don mentioned that Morihei Ueshiba, the Japanese founder of the self-defense art Aikido, had been influenced by Christ's turn-the-other-cheek philosophy. "That's a good teaching, but I'd *move* the other cheek before he hit me. That way he avoids the karma of hitting me, and I avoid the pain." I have a notebook full of such Quotes from Nearly Enlightened Don (he doesn't claim to be *fully* there yet, although he believes his hundred-and-five-year-old master has made it). Stuff like "Anything that is *taking* is lust. Anything that is *giving* is love."

Then Gracie arrived in our household and I misplaced the will to leave the house and go listen to Don's weekly Buddha babblings. The will to do pretty much anything vanished, because our restless little newborn wailed herself awake every forty-five minutes all night long, and during the day the wife and I never recovered that lost sleep. While tending to baby I kept telling myself to set aside a couple of hours daily to practice my martial arts. I kept telling myself I should be *driven*; I should be like Mark Saltzman, author of *Iron and Silk,* a good book I consumed in my rocking chair with Gracie softly snoring as I turned the pages with one hand. Saltzman, an American, lived and worked in China in the 1980s and studied Kung Fu there. He practiced ten hours a day when he got the chance. Plenty of martial artists are like that. They live to practice, and the more they practice, the more they want to practice.

I hate practicing. Practicing is all about repetition, and to me repetition is excruciatingly boring. It would be like writing this book, then typing it out exactly the same again. Repetition to me is synonymous with tedium; the only exception I can think of is in music, especially blues music. Blues musicians all play essentially the same damn song, but somehow it never bores me. Not that I ever learned to *play* the Blues, or any music for that matter, for the same reason I'm having so much trouble mastering Kung Fu: it's boring to practice, doubly so when you know you're no damn good yet, and all you can do is run through the same old tedious little baby-step half-assed phrases over and over and over again.

Inside hooking, reverse hooking, rising block, downward block—sure, you can tell yourself you're going to practice for an hour, but after about five minutes the mind wanders, and next thing you know you're wondering what's for lunch, or who you need to phone or email, or you suddenly remember a time in grade ten when you should have said something clever to that girl with large breasts who smiled at you.

☆

Even if I couldn't seem to make time to practice at home, I continued to show up for Kung Fu class at least twice a week. Actually I have another confession to make: I mostly took the afternoon sessions, Tuesdays and Thursdays. These were lighter, less sparring-oriented classes that I came to think of as "Bob, Bert, the ladies, and me."

Bob was Sifu Bob, whom you already know. Then there was Bert, a silver-haired older gentleman, sixtyish, enthusiastic, keen to learn. We were inevitably paired off to work on techniques together, particularly techniques like elbow locks, and blocking–striking combination moves like triangular stepping, where you really need to have an opponent to practice on. Bert was a bit shorter than me, but well-muscled, strong, and way more flexible—he could bring his shin to his forehead when stretching out to practice high kicks—but I didn't feel out of my league working with him. The rest of the class I called "the ladies," a crew of half a dozen women, of whom four or so might show on any given day. I don't think of myself as a sexist person, but I'll say this: it's one thing to spar with a man like Bert and feel like he's continually getting the better of me, it's quite another to spar with a woman and feel that way. Jesus. It's all tied into childhood trauma, in my case when I was eleven and lost an arm-wrestling match to a girl, lying on the stage in the school auditorium, encircled by jeering class-mates. You never live that down. That's probably why I chose a wife who weighs a hundred pounds. I don't want to be out-muscled by the ol' lady.

Two ladies in particular at the Academy take their Kung Fu very seriously. They're sharp fighters. I shouldn't really call them ladies, they're women in their twenties with spiky post-punk hair. Brenda and Arlene practice a lot, so they've worked up the kind of muscle memory Sifu Bob expects us to build. One day we were doing an exercise where the two of them plus Bert were lined up to come at me continuously, throwing punches with either hand. I was supposed to respond with my choice of blocks and counterstrikes. Triangular stepping and another move I've forgotten the name of, an inverted backhand with a step to the side, were supposed to be the main items on the practice menu.

The three of them kept coming at me, and my brain locked up. There was no muscle memory to respond to the split-second decisions that needed to be made. So I froze. There's no other word for it. I just completely froze. I threw my arms up in front of my face, exactly like any fool would do who had never studied a day of martial arts in his life.

"Which one are you trying to do?" asked Brenda, trying to be helpful.

"I don't know," I said. I really didn't.

☆

For a few days after that I thought, maybe I should just accept that I might be the worst Kung Fu student ever, get a perverse kick out of it even, see how far I can go with it, before gracious, patient, unflappable Sifu Bob finally snaps, and stops being so fucking kindly and tolerant toward me. But our relationship was not like the traditional master–student relationship of old China. If it had been, he would have just kicked me out the door. Or beaten me with a stick until I improved. Nothing like that was going to happen, because our relationship was built around a mercantile core, essentially around me giving him eighty-five dollars a month. As long as I kept doing that, Bob would allow me to proceed at my own pace. I bet I could have stayed an orange belt forever.

But I didn't really want to be the worst Kung Fu student ever, so I went to talk to Bob. I like Bob a lot. When I came back from Vanderhoof and told him Royce Gracie was into hunting deer with rifles, and couldn't wait to go back there in the summer and shoot himself a moose, Bob had looked troubled, almost personally hurt. "Strange that a martial artist would be into that," he had said sadly. To him, emerging from a rough and tough boxer's youth into manhood, martial arts has been a doorway to a philosophy of non-violence.

I asked Bob, "How do you think I'm doing?"

"So far you're a typical, average student," he said. "Now, if you were to ask me, 'What do I need to do to enhance my training?' I'd say, 'Lower your stances.' Okay? Those are the types of questions you need to ask yourself, not just learn the technique, and then say 'I'm ready for the next.' You've got to refine the technique. You need to *experience* the technique. But a lot of people get stuck on the first level: they learn the basic mechanics of it, then they want new material."

"Well, you know, I find—listen, I'm forty-eight years old," I protested. "It's hard on my legs. I can't get low in my stances. I have very poor flexibility. Even Bert, who's way older than me, in the low-back stance, he gets right down there. He can put his knee to his chest."

"Again, everyone is different," Bob said.

"I'm not getting any more flexible, know what I mean?"

"There's the problem right there—"

"An attitude problem," I interrupted, knowing what was coming. Martial arts is full of aphorisms about the power of positive thinking. I'd come across one in a discussion forum (Topic: Is the UFC good for martial arts or not?) on the internet that very day: "If you think you can, you can. If you think you can't, you're right."

"Yeah. You never should say *can't*," Bob agreed. "It's like if you hand me something, and I say, 'I don't want this.' I'm thinking about what I don't want, and why did I get it. As opposed to just taking it from you, setting it aside, and having no thought to it. Then I'm still on track to get where I was going."

"Not so much I *can't*, but there are limits on how—"

"You will never be as flexible—"

"I was talking to this friend of my wife's, this Judo guy, and he told me for someone my age to take up martial arts, it's hopeless," I said.

"There was a fellow I used to teach who was seventy-nine years old when he joined," Bob replied. "He got a black belt when he was eighty-four. He is still my inspiration, that this is something you can do for the rest of your life. It was funny, he'd be in the back of the class warming up, and he'd be burping, farting—he was hard of hearing, so I don't think he could hear what he was actually doing. But that's one way to come to an understanding that movement and exercise releases all those toxins in your body, whereas sitting there, you build them up and promote sickness."

He wasn't cheering me up, comparing me to a flatulent eighty-four-year-old. "Can a geezer like that really be said to deserve a black belt?" I demanded.

"Every student is different. Certain martial arts like Tae Kwon Do, they tell you, 'This is the way it's done, this is the way you must do it.' So they have students who can never achieve a black belt. Whereas we believe everyone is different, and you work to your strengths. It's what your goals and expectations are: are you trying to do the splits, or are you just trying to get more limber? You have to have realistic goals. If you don't, you're shooting to the moon with an elastic band."

I was set to ask, "Okay, so, what should my goals be?" But Bob kept talking.

"At this beginning level all you're learning is the basics," he continued. "The basics are the entrance to Shaolin. You have to get a black belt to enter Shaolin. Right now you're learning tiger, you're training muscles, tendons, and bones for strengthening and conditioning the body. But only when you reach black belt do you start refining that: the *whys* of that: how a tiger fights, what the attributes of a tiger are, how to use a tiger for health benefits, for sparring skills and martial business. And that goes for the other four animals too. For example, at purple belt it's the leopard, it's all about movement, whereas the tiger is all power and in your face. It's only when you master the basics of all the animals that you can start to build the fighting style best suited to your body type, skills, and personality."

"So at this point, which of the animals would I be most suited to?"

"For your self and your body build, you'd be a crane," he answered. "Seeing as you have long limbs and you are tall, that would be a very versatile animal for you."

"What's associated with a crane?"

"Reach and no strength. Patience. Flow. As opposed to, say, a tiger, which would be straight in their face. A crane would outwait the opponent, stay still until they make their move, and at that point use an angle to step to the side, and use your reach to strike."

It sounded good to me. Kind of like a matador. Aloof, yet in control.

☆

Thereafter I embraced the idea that I might be working my way toward expressing my innate craneness. As species go, cranes do seem a good match for me. In this coastal town plenty of herons live along the shoreline, and herons are just a crane by any other name, so I see them often enough, I'm aware of how they move. They *don't,* a lot: they just stand around all day in ankle-deep water, waiting for little fishies to swim by, so they can snatch them and swallow them down like wriggling hors d'oeuvres. Being patient fishers doesn't qualify them in my mind as warriors worthy of emulating. Seashell-hunting children, frisbee-chasing dogs, or any other potential threat comes within thirty yards of them, and they spook, they unfold those big old wings and fly off to a place more solitary. Maybe Kung Fu is just teaching me what I already know about myself.

☆

In the weeks leading up to my departure for China we started seriously attempting some basic groundwork, or grappling. Some of the techniques, Bob said, were borrowed from the Gracies.

We were working on a move one Tuesday afternoon that is, in essence, the solution to a predicament that's forever linked in my mind to memories of roughhousing with my younger brother on the living room carpet as a kid: what do you do when someone is sitting on your chest, holding you by the wrists, and pinning your arms on either side of your head? If this happens to you as an adult, consider yourself in serious trouble. Here's your best option: without lifting your arms or hands off the ground, you stretch one arm up as far above your head as you can, to twelve o'clock, and bring the other down to your hip, which would describe, depending which hand you use, five or seven o'clock. This causes the opponent, the oaf on your chest, if he's intent on keeping hold of your wrists, to spread his arms wide too, until he no longer sits quite so well-balanced on your chest; he can be bucked off by thrusting your hips. That's the theory, anyway.

My usual partner, Bert, being absent that day, Bob paired me off with one of the ladies, in fact the oldest and least-fearsome of the ladies, Helen. I tried not to dwell on it, but this caused a disheartening suspicion that Bob's estimation of me was extremely low. Helen's age was tough to carbon date, because she dyed her hair the orangey-brown hue of a roast turkey, but I thought she must be about sixty. We started out with her on top and me underneath, trying to mimic the technique Bob had freshly demonstrated a moment earlier. She sank the full weight of her ass onto my chest, and it was quickly clear she had no concept of the ol' "Go Weak for Technique; If You're Strong, You're Wrong" adage. She snatched hold of my wrists, squeezed them vise-tight, leaned down close to me, and I was afforded a close-up view of multitudinous beads of perspiration emerging from the pores of her face. Likely my face was providing her a similar unpleasant vista. I was definitely breaking a nervous sweat. Undaunted, I tried to stick to the technique, spreading one hand as directed, upward toward high noon. She redoubled her effort, leaning forward, shifting her body weight ever more heavily onto my chest. My nose was now mashed into the nape of her neck, and at that moment a petit mal panic attack jumped out of nowhere and slapped me in the cerebellum.

It hit me—a frantic, desperate, overwhelming need to get granny off me, and I didn't care how. Technique? Forget it. I pushed straight up with my arms, with every ounce of my strength, as one might struggle against the rubble of an avalanche, or a car that suddenly tumbles off the jack. In panic there is a great rush of adrenaline—I felt like Hercules for a brief exhilarating moment as I sent Helen flying, and then the pain hit: something horrible tore

at my shoulder like the sharp teeth of a wolverine ripping my
tendons to shreds.

Bob, watching it all, tsk-tsked in that gently chiding way of his:
"Now that was nothing but brute strength. *That's not technique.*"

I got to my feet, clutched at my damaged shoulder, and said,
"That really hurt." What I meant was, "FUCK!!! That REALLY,
REALLY FUCKING HURT, and still REALLY REALLY REALLY
FUCKING HURTS!!!"

But I sucked it up, because I'd never heard anyone swear at the
club; it just didn't fit in with the whole respectful and honoring
"salute to past masters for knowledge received," a little recitation
we bowed in with before every class.

My shoulder was searing with pain, but like those Judo guys
grimacing their way to the toilet in that Vanderhoof bar, I toughed
it out. For the rest of the class, I was definitely not my usual sunny
self, but I went through the motions, at least. At the end, after we'd
bowed out, Bob said, "Have a great time in China. I guess I won't
see you before you go." Somehow he'd gotten my departure date
mixed up, when in fact there was a full week and at least two more
classes I'd thought I could fit in before leaving. But did I correct
him? Nope. "Ah yeah, that's right Bob, thanks, see ya!" I burbled,
feeling instantly like I'd lied, that I was using an untruth to slink
off into a hole to lick my wounds. My shoulder had spoken, and it
said, no more getting pinned by sixty-something women for a
good long while, Brian. Even now, three months later, typing this,
my shoulder is reminding me it's fucked up and I should treat it
tenderly, not sit hunched over this laptop for hours at a stretch.
It's telling me to take a break and do some of those exercises the
physiotherapist gave me, so cut me some slack if the prose doesn't
sing. *Suck it up, tough it out!*

Part 2

☆

CHINA

13

☆

His Essential Jarekhood

Early one morning I was flipping through the fifty-seven channels on our TV, taking care to keep Gracie's face turned away from the screen—the wife hates the kid watching TV, she thinks it'll rot or mutate all those delicate new brain cells. I have to sit on the couch holding Gigi under her armpits facing me, letting her use my abdomen as a trampoline to bounce up and down on, bending and straightening her little legs, while I peer over her shoulder and rot my brain cells staring at the TV. Unlike me, Gigi is overflowing with original Chi: she's a little ball of burbling optimism, she loves mindless repetition of the same physical action, and can perform her trampoline dance hundreds of times, but occasionally even she needs a break, and plops down on my belly for a wee rest, and I can free a hand to grab the remote and change channels. *Good Morning America* on channel 16: across the bottom of the screen the scroll says WHY YOU SHOULD CARE ABOUT CHINA. A guest expert is telling Jane Pauley, "All they really want is a better television, a nice car, and to get their kids into college."

"Just like America," she suggests.

"Just like America."

Then they cut to a commercial, and I'm thinking the scroll should have said, WHY YOU SHOULD NOT GIVE A SHIT ABOUT CHINA, THEY ARE JUST AS SHALLOW AND DELUDED AS US.

☆

I didn't really believe that China was "just like America," despite its white-hot capitalist economy. But when I read online about a booming homegrown hip-hop scene in the Middle Kingdom, I wasn't so sure anymore. From the very beginning of my martial arts training I'd had the idea that a pilgrimage to the Shaolin Temple would be essential for me. I was deep into reading up on China, and the more I read online the more bizarre the country seemed: there was the massive, garish faux-Rococo apartment building in Shanghai that housed nothing but nouveau riche businessmen's mistresses, for example. The Chinese had money to burn, and seemed hellbent on shedding Chinese traditions for Western fads. An article from the official Chinese press told me that "in their fierce competition for market share, the imported Tae Kwon Do, Karate and Thai boxing have taken the lead over traditional Kung Fu." The article claimed Tae Kwon Do has become "fashionable among young people" by updating its belt system to "meet market demand." These hideous capitalist public relations phrases jolted me: they made it seem urgent that I get over there and take the measure of Kung Fu in the land of its birth, before the land of its birth morphed into a wall-to-wall gargantuan sweatshop, meeting the entire world's needs for socks, snow peas, thirty-dollar DVD players, and every single item you buy at Wal-Mart. It would be like if you were a country music fan, and someone told you that the real thing is dying out, that in a few short decades the closest thing to authentic country music will be found in the karaoke bars of Tokyo. Wouldn't you head to the honkytonks of Tennessee today, to hear what's left before it vanishes?

☆

At a Vancouver agency specializing in travel to China, all the staff were Chinese, and I got passed along to Lily, the best English speaker and therefore the default agent for English customers. She booked me a ticket for Beijing, with a return date three weeks later. I was absolutely fine with three weeks, the maximum tolerable absence as negotiated with my wife, because I was worried if I went away for any longer Gracie would forget me. Plus if things went poorly, three weeks could turn into a nightmare of inadequate translation, cultural confusion, and homesickness, not to mention dubious restaurant meats, avian flu, and squat toilets. In any case, when I was giving Lily some numbers from my credit card there was a 444 in there, three straight fours, and I made a joke about how I'd heard fours are supposed to be very inauspicious to the Chinese. I'm not sure if in Mandarin or Cantonese, but the number four is pronounced like the word for death. She laughed about that and said actually, in North America, that superstition has been affected and altered by local conditions: the English word *four* sounds like the Chinese word *fa,* she said, "Like do re mi *fa*? And *fa* is meaning you will be wealthy." That fit with what I knew about the local Chinese, how they had all settled in a Vancouver suburb called Richmond because it sounds like Rich Man.

☆

My point here is that every language is subtle and fluid, and I was not highly confident that I could walk into downtown China and get the goods on a subject as esoteric and vocabulary-specialized as martial arts. Marrying a foreigner had really opened my eyes to the way translation often gets mangled even by the best writers—for example, the German scribe Günter Grass, who wrote a book about my wife's hometown, Calcutta. Calcutta these days is pretty much a forgotten backwater, although if the Buddha's dying words are anything to go by (his second last sentence was "Decay is inherent in all component things"), then Calcutta, the world capital of entropy and decay, should be considered the center of the universe. But lately writers have given it a wide berth, maybe because outside of dentistry, books on decay don't do well in the marketplace. Günter Grass pretty much has the recent field to himself, with a book called *Show Your Tongue*.

Now according to Grass, showing your tongue is a Bengali gesture expressing shame. I showed the book to my wife. "That's wrong," she said curtly. The gesture, *jeeb kata* in Bengali, means "cut the tongue." You stick out your tongue and then pretend to bite it, a gesture of inflicting pain upon yourself, punishing yourself. You clearly show your teeth biting it: that's totally different from just showing the tongue, which the Bengalis call *jeeb bhangano,* twisting the tongue. That gesture has the same meaning as here, "I'm mad at you." And like here, it's used mostly by children.

Anyway, by this example you can see that when it comes to translation, even the simplest gesture can open up a can of worms and words, and you can understand why I was not confident I could hit China at full speed and come away with the right terms for the million little techniques and movements that make up martial arts, things as simple as inside hooking, say, or open X stances, or spinning back kicks, not to mention the even more complex, invisible, and multitudinous ways Chi can be moved around a body. Günter Grass couldn't even get the title of his book right. What hope did I have?

☆

As a journalist and a generalist, there's one thing I know: if you can't be an expert, the best thing you can do is tag along with an expert.

Trolling around the internet trying to pick up some cues and clues about China, and especially the current state of martial arts in China, I came across a great website called China From Inside. It's produced by a guy in Shanghai named Jarek Szymanski. Jarek and I would eventually become buds, and bond for life, in part because we are probably the only two people ever brave or foolish enough to descend, on foot, in the pitch black of a moonless night, without the aid of flashlight, candle, or cigarette lighter, the long and serpentine stone staircase that flows down the steep slopes of Wudang Mountain from the Golden Temple, the sacred birthplace of Taoist Taiji.

Someday when Jarek has retired back to his native Poland to raise horses on a pretty acreage, I'll go visit and put Gracie on a pony in the daytime and drink beer with Jarek in the evening. It sounds great and I hope it comes to pass.

But at first Jarek was just a name on a website, a very good website about the "soft," "internal" Chinese martial arts, particularly Taiji, Bagua, and Xingyi. Jarek has lived in China for fifteen years, and his written and spoken Chinese are both excellent, although he's modest about that. On his website he has translated into English many rare, little-known, or ancient texts about Chinese martial arts, and also translated interviews he has conducted himself, in Chinese, with master practitioners of some increasingly rare and obscure martial arts styles. In this way he's like

an anthropologist who records the language of a rapidly assimilat-
ing tribe, before speakers of that language die out and the language
disappears altogether. He's a preservationist, a documentarian in
the best, strictest sense.

"Guo Weihan's Xinyiquan—Missing Link in the History of
Xinyiquan Found?" or "Fan Family Baguazhang," or excerpts from
the book *The True Teachings of Yang Jianhou's Secret Yang Style
Taijiquan*—these are the kinds of esoteric articles that can be found
on Jarek's website. As I browsed around it I had an effervescent
rush of "What If?" similar to the one I had when I first heard Royce
Gracie was coming to Vanderhoof. What if Jarek let me tag along
with him when he went out to record some exotic martial art style
in some remote corner of the Middle Kingdom? What if he let me
glom onto him like a sponge, soaking up his wisdom about martial
arts, his insights into China, and his essential Jarekhood?

Without sounding too much like an old fart stating the obvious,
let me say that the great gift the internet has delivered to
humankind is the means to make instant and affordable contact
with people halfway around the world. (I was one of the last people
in my profession to get online. When I finally did cave and
connect, I was thirty-nine years old, so I definitely know how life
was lived before the web and email and text messaging and all that
crap. To me, those days were better. Less to keep track of, fewer
strangers harassing you, and it was so much easier to establish who
your friends are—they're the people you're happy to see when they
drop by unannounced. No one drops by unannounced anymore.
Even a social occasion as simple as meeting a friend for a cup of
coffee takes six emails and seven cell phone calls to set up. A certain
kind of human interaction, which I would call spontaneous
conviviality *in person,* is in much shorter supply. Or maybe I'm just
pining for my undergraduate days, when my friends and I all lived

within walking distance in a student ghetto, and spent our days smoking weed and trying to wish a socialist Utopia into being.) There's already a generation of adults who take the internet for granted, but as someone who straddles before and after, its power to connect strangers still amazes me every time. Jarek amazed me. I sent him just a simple email explaining I was hoping to come to China; to his credit he responded with great openness. A few emails and a phone call later, I knew his life story.

☆

Jarek grew up in Poland, and at fifteen he got very excited about martial arts from seeing movies—Bruce Lee of course, but especially *Shaolin Temple,* the first major martial arts film made in mainland China. "It looked more real," he told me. "There were fewer special effects and more acrobatics. People in Hong Kong movies were always taking these incredible, preposterous jumps. I was never attracted to that. The other great thing about *Shaolin Temple* is it was shot on location at Shaolin Temple. It's on DVD, worth watching just to see how the Temple looked in the 1980s, before tourism really exploded there. It's quite different than now.

"Martial arts fever came to Poland at the end of the '70s and early '80s," Jarek remembers. "There were no computers, or video games, so it was like the best thing to do. A lot of people were attracted and did it for a few years, then fell into bodybuilding, or just simply gave it up. It was more like a fashion—when you're a teenager there's girls you want to show off to. You see people on TV breaking bricks and you think, 'Ooooh, that's nice! I wanna be able to do it! Yeah!' When you are fifteen or sixteen you see something, and you suddenly *really* like it and you just *go for it.* I started with Kyokushinkai Karate, then Kung Fu. Soon I was doing martial arts practice for five hours a day, and it became an important part of my life, and still is."

Much later, after we'd met up in person, while drinking beer in a deserted hotel on Wudang Mountain, Jarek would tell me another part of the story of his youth in Poland. An avid collector and lover of books, he had picked up a Russian–Chinese dictionary at a flea market. The Chinese characters fascinated him, and he started to teach himself Chinese. One day on the street a friend told him a nearby university was planning to open a "Sinology" department, and Jarek applied. Actually, he *meant* to apply—in the rush to get to a summer job in France, he left the application with his girlfriend, asking her to submit it for him. When he came back in the fall, she still had the papers: she had decided not to enroll him. Her rationale: if he enrolled in Chinese, *on top of* his final year of engineering, *on top of* his obsessive martial arts training, she would never get to see him.

Undeterred, Jarek went to the school and begged to be admitted, was granted probationary status, and on the strength of his self-taught ability to write characters, quickly established himself as one of the better students. All's well that ends well.

"Must have been the end of that girlfriend," I said.

Jarek said, "No. We're married."

☆

The first time we spoke on the phone I asked if it would be fair to say he had a lifelong love affair with China. "It was love at first sight, and not for a day or two," he conceded. "But it's dying out now. China is not the best place in the world anymore for me. The atmosphere in China has been changing very, very much over the last years, and people have also been changing. I'm not really happy about that."

"What kind of changes?"

He sighed heavily. "Well, when I first came to China in the early '90s people had less chance of making money. Most worked for a state-owned company, you know, they just lived their lives, pretty poor, but they could invest a lot of time into hobbies. So people were interested in martial arts, calligraphy, a lot of things.

"Lately people have been given the chance to become wealthy. They don't want to do martial arts anymore; they are just purely focused on making money. Year by year you can see it getting worse and worse. They want to buy a car, for example; that's their main focus now. You can't blame them, but the result is, the traditional martial arts in China are less and less popular. Some things are fashionable, but it's things like Japanese Karate and Korean Tae Kwon Do. They have many more followers than traditional Chinese martial arts. Young people see movies where yuppies practice Tae Kwon Do, so they get hooked on Tae Kwon Do." It doesn't help that the Chinese government puts the full weight of its support behind an official style of Wushu, taking the fighting applications out of Kung Fu and turning it into a more decorative, stylized individual routine similar to the floor exercises in competitive gymnastics, where contestants face no opponent, but simply perform a series of codified movements that are marked by judges. The Chinese are big on making Wushu a full-fledged Olympic sport, and lobbied successfully to gain it demonstration sport status for the 2008 Olympics in Beijing.

"The other thing is, in general, Chinese are not aggressive people. They refrain from fighting," Jarek continued. "There is no tradition of really practicing contact fighting, even within traditional martial arts circles. They don't have the equipment, like in Tae Kwon Do you get the gear and pads, and you can practice fighting relatively safely."

"So, are we seeing the demise of traditional martial arts in China? Or is interest in these arts cyclical anyway?"

"Just to give you an example, I would say this: people were attracted to martial arts here for hundreds of years, and nothing really changed in that, but now times are changing. You don't really need martial arts for protection. Plus, it was always considered low-class in China if you got into fights. You could study martial arts, but if you avoided fighting, you were much more respected. They even had this saying: 'A gentleman uses his mouth to resolve problems, instead of his hands.'

"The other thing is, many traditional arts require really strong basics," he went on. "You have to practice simple exercises for years before you are allowed to do anything else. Well, who nowadays can invest that much time into it? Many arts now have only a few old masters to practice them. The idea is supposed to be to pass the art on, but they can hardly find any students willing to spend as much time practicing as the teachers expect. Some masters are losing interest in teaching. They just practice by themselves."

"Are they bitter about that?"

"I don't know. Some try to find a shortcut, teaching just the basics, or not as many movements; some will even skip the basics to teach more 'entertaining' fighting applications. Students get only a fraction of the art, so this is actually hurting the art. People are learning the outside form, but there is nothing inside it."

"So how did you get started in your efforts to preserve and record these older arts?"

"In 1994 I went to Shanxi, a province not far from Beijing; I'd read this article about a rare style being practiced there, so I packed my stuff, got on the train, and went there. When I arrived I could feel that the old teachers were very conservative, they didn't really want to show much. Teaching basics took years, and young people weren't interested, so they were teaching simplified routines so students could take part in competitions. You see the old people practicing, then the younger ones, and there's such a huge difference. So that's the reason I decided to document various traditional styles, so that future generations have a chance to see the old skills and how they were done. There was one master in Hebei province I made a tape of, I was the only person who had ever done that, and then he died. This made me realize there's not much time left. The old generation of masters are passing away."

Many parts of rural China were only officially opened up to foreigners in the 1990s, and there were times when Jarek was the first Westerner to test the new policy of openness. Sometimes local police would insist on taking him to a village in a car with the curtains drawn. Other times they would refuse him permission to videotape. These days things are easier, he said, but "in some villages you're still the first foreigner they've ever seen. The whole place follows you and they yell, *Laowai*. Foreigner. But once you explain what you want to do, they are often moved that a person from a distant country finds things they consider common so valuable and important. China is a huge country with different dialects and ways of thinking. To me these travels are a great way of learning about the culture and the people. I find it really fascinating."

☆

Through the phone line I could hear periodic nasty, super-phlegmy eruptions of a child's chest cough; his four-year-old daughter sounded like she was really suffering, poor thing, and Jarek said he'd have to cut short our talk to attend to her. I wouldn't let him hang up until I'd pinned him down to a rough date for a face-to-face meeting while I was in China. "I may leave Shanghai," he warned. "I may go to Wudang Mountain on about October fifteenth or so."

"Wudang like in *Crouching Tiger, Hidden Dragon*?"

"That's right. There is a festival there, of a certain type of Taiji called Zhao Bao. My main goal in going is to study with a teacher I studied with many, many years ago, but at that time I was just too young for Taiji to understand it. I'm told he'll be there to give lectures and demonstrate. He's one of the best Taiji guys I've ever met. Just give me a call when you arrive in China, maybe you can also go."

"That sounds great," I said. "Maybe I could meet you in Shanghai and we could go up together."

"Sure. We could take the train, talk more about martial arts; you will see some of the countryside, see the sacred mountain, and meet some very good teachers."

14

☆

If I Kill You
I Am Not Responsible

The flight to Beijing is direct from Vancouver, eleven hours over the north Pacific. Judging from the Chinese men seated around me, especially the fleshy-faced guy in the muted gold blazer right next door, I'm flying to the last refuge of the middle-aged comb-over. Gluing a few sad strands across the skull is now a *verboten* hairstyle in the West, put to death by sarcasm. No one my age or younger would *dare*.

I was hoping to sit next to a fascinating person of the Asian persuasion, but Lady Luck has given me one who keeps slumping his knee against mine in sleep, like water seeking sea level, and all I can do is watch his thumbs twitch on his lap. Or watch Brad and Angelina in *Mr. and Mrs. Smith* on the TV monitors hanging above the aisles.

Ms. Jolie is mighty sexy in a black PVC suit with matching stockings. Early in the film some stooge allows her to handcuff him and whip him for the sexual thrill of it, but she gets carried away and kills him by snapping his defenseless neck. Apparently the ultraviolence of *Mr. and Mrs. Smith* is considered appropriate all-ages entertainment for a trans-Pacific flight. Bullets, blood, and dead bodies are fine, but language is trickier: Brad Pitt for some reason keeps saying "chickentwit," because to use the word *shit* would be like having a nipple pop out of Angie's rubbery recreational sex suit while she wields that whip. Whoa, hold on! That's *crossing the line*.

Bright yellow Chinese subtitles run across the bottom of the screen. I wonder if they have a word, a special Chinese character, for "chickentwit"?

I'll have to ask, and maybe even learn to say it. It pretty much describes how I'm feeling about myself. Eight days after Hurricane Helen pinned me to the floor, I still can't lift my hand above my head without a corkscrew of intense pain twisting deep into my shoulder. It never had a fighting chance to heal because that's the shoulder little Gracie likes to lay her head on while I walk a marathon coaxing her to sleep late into the evenings. Brat takes hours to settle.

Physical pain is depressing me psychologically. I'm doubting my self, my mission. I should be home inserting healthy doses of sex into middlebrow novels that make women cry in the bath.

☆

I've bought a Mandarin phrase book and I've been trying to figure out tones. I'm worried about them. Depending on your tone, apparently *ma* can mean "mother," "hemp," "horse," or "scold." Which, if anyone would bother to notice, serves to highlight the ancient and primal place cannabis had in Chinese culture—one of the most basic of human sounds got assigned to represent it. But that was my first book.

One of the books I'd been reading before coming to China I was afraid to bring on the plane with me. I'm sure it's banned over there. It was written by Zhang Boli, one of the main student leaders at Tiananmen Square. *Escape from China* describes the two years Zhang spent on the run from the Chinese police, skulking about the country posing as an itinerant farm worker, blending into the *mangliu,* a massive underclass numbering in the tens of millions. *Mangliu* translates as "outcasts," a group "generally treated as ill-behaved people of the lowest class, not protected by the law." The book is worth reading for one amazing, almost unbelievable tale, which begins with Zhang dragging himself across China's border with the Soviet Union in the dead of winter, and almost freezing to death in a blizzard before being picked up by the Russians. They quietly held him for two weeks, while they figured out what to do with him. This was during the Gorbachev era, and they faced a delicate diplomatic dilemma: let a pro-democracy leader seek asylum in the West, and alienate China, or hand him back to the Chinese, alienating the West. In the end they chose a third option: because they'd kept his arrival and detainment a secret, why not dump him back at the border? In a no-man's land between Chinese patrol posts, they gave him two packs of cigarettes, wished him the best of luck, and told him, "If you ever cross into Russia again, you *will* be handed over to the Chinese."

He seemed to have plenty of luck, eventually traversing the country north to south and sneaking into Hong Kong with the help of human traffickers, who waived their usual ten-thousand-dollar fee out of respect for his politics and bravery.

What surprised me most about Zhang's descriptions of daily life in China was how much alcohol people drank. They seemed to live for beer and *baijiu,* the cheap Chinese liqueur made from sorghum. The book's other effect was to prep me for China circa 1989, just after Tiananmen went down, a paranoid totalitarian state on high alert where anyone could be a member of the secret police. I imagined myself, the foreign journalist, continuously tailed and occasionally confronted and questioned by the police. What a laugh that turned out to be. In three weeks I met exactly one cop, and he wanted to practice his English.

☆

Geoff is an old friend of mine, a newspaper reporter based in Beijing. Someone once described him as a squinty bear, and that's about right. He's six foot six; in China that's tall, and Chinese taxis are small, so when we got a cab at Beijing airport I saw him do what he always does when he gets into a cab in China: he opens the front door, leans in and slides the passenger seat entirely forward, steps back out, slams the front door closed, opens the back door, and folds himself and his long gangly limbs in.

The line-up at the airport cab stand was very orderly and sedate, and the taxis were all shiny new, and the one we got played a cheery recorded message in English when we got out: "Please take your receipt and all your personal belongings." On the taxi ride to Geoff's place the driver drove sensibly and ably in a smooth river of cars and trucks. The highway was new, wide, and well-signed, the roadway lined with trees deep enough to give the impression of a forest. It was disappointing. I didn't come halfway around the world for clean highways and trouble-free driving. I wanted heaping dollops of weird chaotic foreignness. I wanted grannies smoking beedies on wobbly bicycles, balancing wicker baskets of live chickens on the handlebars, damn it!

Then we hit the city and saw the economic miracle of twenty-first-century China: massive construction everywhere, the old traditional neighborhoods—the *hutongs*—being levelled, erased, and replaced as far as the eye could see with shopping malls, apartment towers, and high-rise office buildings with ridiculous names like Dollar Mountain, or Success Village, or (honestly!) Elite's Dwelling. Names that cried out, "People obsessed with making money, come buy condos here!"

Geoff lives in an apartment reserved for diplomats and other foreigners across the road from a huge brand new mall with a Starbucks like a little mouse hole on an outer corner. The first floor of the mall is given over to display counters of all the major multinational cosmetics companies, and as I sat outside Starbucks I couldn't help appraising a constant stream of fashion model–type Chinese women heading past on their way to stock up on silkier-than-thou skin creams, and I got that slightly depressing globalization-has-robbed-the-world-of-unique-local-cultures feeling again. It reminded me of the time about seven years ago when I went to see *Abre los Ojos (Open Your Eyes)*, a Spanish film, thinking, "Oh, it'll be nice to see some Spanish culture," only the movie was entirely populated by people who looked and acted like they were on the American sitcom *Friends*. They all had *Friends* hair and went to *Friends* parties, except they lived in Madrid. Very depressing. On the upside, Penélope Cruz never looked better than in that movie, and she has an excellent nude scene.

☆

Andy Pi, who'd suggested we meet at the Starbucks, is part of this globalization phenomenon too. His grandfather was a general in Chiang Kai Shek's air force, and fled to Taiwan with most of the rest of the Nationalists when Mao and the Communists won China. Andy was born in Taiwan but raised in California, so he's got a real American go-getter, I-can-sell-you-anything edge to him. He runs the Beijing Brazilian Jiu Jitsu club, and is pumped about bringing the sport of Mixed Martial Arts to the attention of mainstream China.

"As a young, impressionable, and Chinese guy, my first exposure to martial arts was Bruce Lee. All Chinese boys love and idolize Bruce Lee, because he is everything you wanna be," Andy asserts. "So ever since I was a kid I had all kinds of interest in martial arts, and trained in Karate and Kung Fu, but nothing really serious, until 1994, when I was in college, and I saw a video of the Ultimate Fighting Championship, and I was like, wow, those guys are *really* fighting.

"All the fights ended up on the ground, and once they went to the ground there was one skinny Brazilian guy who would win all the fights. He was winning fights without hurting people. They would submit, give up, then just stand up and shake hands. It wasn't like other guys, who would have to bloody the guy to a total pulp to win. He was taking down big guys, making them give up, and not hurting them. Totally incredible."

Andy went to college in Riverside, California, about a two-hour drive from Royce Gracie's Jiu Jitsu school in Torrance. He signed up, and has been training for ten years now. The belt system goes white, blue, purple, brown, and black, and Andy is a purple. "Jiu Jitsu is weird," he says. "People are afraid of getting a black belt because you have to defend it. You have to prove you deserve it against the lower belts, who are hungry to test themselves, and there's constant sparring and competition."

In a month or so Andy's planning to fly four of the Chinese fighters he's training to Manila, in the Philippines, for their first pro bouts. As he trains his fighters he's also shooting a reality television show about it, which he says has been sold to eleven Chinese television channels with a potential audience of three hundred seventy million viewers. Big dreams.

I don't want to burst his bubble, but I start to tell him about Jarek's self-appointed mission to preserve some of the more rare and unorthodox styles of internal Chinese martial arts. And I suggest that these arts, based more on a Buddhist or Taoist philosophy of self-defense, have evolved into a way of cultivating Chi, and take years of practice to achieve deep results, but they're being lost in the rush of modern China to embrace a less complex, shortcut kind of fighting style, namely things like Tae Kwon Do and Brazilian Jiu Jitsu.

"I think it's a bunch of bullshit, to be honest," Andy says. "You are not going to learn how to fight unless you actually fight. You are not going to learn how to write unless you pick up a pen and write, so you won't learn to defend yourself until I come and try to beat the shit out of you, it's that simple. I don't care what style you train in or how many years you've been doing it, you have to defend yourself to be good at it. So when you train in class are you letting guys come at you? If you are sitting around holding one position for three hours, and another for three hours, that may be good for your health, but it's not going to teach you anything about sensitivity, timing, footwork, head movement, or responding to pain, or adrenaline. I think the traditional martial arts community in China is very threatened by Mixed Martial Arts, because you can no longer run your mouth."

"But Jarek bemoans the loss of the old styles, bemoans the fact kids just want to do Tae Kwon Do," I interject.

"I believe Taiji is incredibly helpful for health, but you have to look at why you are training in martial arts, what your purpose is. If I want to be a pro fighter, there is no way I want to do *this* three hours a day." He makes a dismissive floaty little parody of a Taiji movement with his hands, which looks doubly silly because he's sitting in a Starbucks chair. "I need to hit the bag and run."

Now he's warming to the subject: "There is a tendency in the traditional martial arts community to say Taiji used to be this or that, used to be great on the battlefield a thousand years ago. The problem is, that was a thousand years ago. It's the twenty-first century, things have changed. I'm not going to go back to a 486 computer if I have a Pentium 4, you know? Some people want to preserve things for the sake of preserving it, and that is fine. But movement is movement: you either move in a straight line or a curved line, that is all there is.

"For thousands of years the Chinese have had this closed door mentality," he continues. "The student is never taught everything the master knows, and then the student teaches what he knows, but not everything, so you have a level of technical knowledge decreasing and going down with every generation. It's understandable, this decline, given China's history in the last century. If you're worried about getting enough to eat, you're not worried about training. I believe Chinese martial arts is in dire need of revival."

I interrupt to suggest maybe he's bringing to China an attitude he learned in America: old is boring, it's always gotta be new.

"Mixed Martial Arts is not new to China, it's been here for thousands of years," he says adamantly. "Way back, if you were from the Black Dragon school and I'm from the White Crane school, how would we settle our differences? We would fight, and sometimes to the *death*. And it wasn't, 'Oh, wait, you can't use your black dragon tail whip, okay?' and then 'Okay, you can't use your white crane beak jab.' No. It was *anything goes*. We're just trying to give that ancient tradition a modern platform."

☆

Two nights later, under a framed poster of Helio Gracie, Andy's the master of ceremonies for a series of demonstration fights at his club. The main event was preceded by a series of submission wrestling bouts between club members, a little tournament to crown a champion for the night. There were four first-round fights, then semi-finals, then a final. I missed the first fight, and hence the announcement of the rules of engagement that would have preceded it, but it was basically no punching or kicking, just grappling, throwing, and groundwork.

Two of the toughest fighters were Mongolians, who have a long history of their own brand of wrestling called Boke, which along with horse races and archery is a major entertainment at the summer gatherings of their traditional nomadic "have-yurt-will-travel" lifestyle. These Mongolians were doing well in the evening's tournament, despite instincts from years of Boke that told them to never go down, to stay on their feet, and to throw the opponent to the ground for single or double points. Once they got pulled down to wrestle on the ground they were on less familiar terrain. In the semi-final the shorter of them—who looked well into his thirties and had cauliflower ears from a life-time of headlocks, but claimed to be twenty-six—ended up in a bad way when his opponent, a Westerner, got leverage on him from underneath and put him in a leg lock.

"That's bad, man," a voice in the crowd muttered.

"Call it, Andy," murmured several others. "Call it."

"He doesn't know it's going to snap," someone shouted with concern.

But Andy, who was refereeing, didn't call it, and the Westerner couldn't bring himself to break the Mongolian's leg, not in the thirty seconds before Andy called, "Time!" The fight was over and the Mongolian had won on points, but the Western contingent felt cheated a little. Jeez, in a friendly in-house club fight, if someone gets you in a spot where they *could* break your leg if they wanted to, you should submit. But those Mongolians don't like to lose. Especially the one with cauliflower ears, who went into the final against the other Mongolian, and won. Turns out he has won many horses in Mongolia, a horse being the big prize in Mongolian wrestling.

Afterward I try to grab a quick interview with him. Geoff and his Chinese girlfriend Dongdong have come along to watch, so I grab Dongdong to translate. She works for a big multinational consulting firm, so her English is functional. "What does he attribute his victory to?" is my first question.

Dongdong looks a bit perplexed.

Geoff interrupts, "Why does he think he won?" Gotta remember, keep the language simple.

Dongdong translates that and gets an answer: "He was very patient. This sport is actually a combination of wisdom and strength."

"Does he need to concentrate on wisdom because he is smaller than the other fighters?"

"Most important for him is, he should have courage to face the guys who are bigger than him. And second is, he trains nearly every day."

☆

So now it's time for the main event, a full-on Mixed Martial Arts bout. Andy has brought in an outsider to take on his boy. Where did he find him? "I've got my contacts," Andy says. "In martial arts there are always guys saying, 'Let me show you how great I am.' All you have to do is phone those guys, and butter them up, say 'Hey, you feel like coming down and breaking a sweat next week? Help us out, we need a good opponent.' You don't say, 'Want to come over and get your ass kicked?' No one wants to come and get beaten up. It should be interesting because this guy is in good shape. I don't even know what's going to happen. This guy has more experience on the ground, but my guy has been dedicated to ground work for the past sixty days, and he's hungry, he wants to taste blood. But it'll be a friendly thing."

The two fighters loosen up, each taking turns punching and kicking padded mitts held chest-high for them, and the tension begins to build.

Andy reverts to his role of master of ceremonies, and addresses the crowd, which has swelled until three walls are lined with people, and along the fourth, where there's a bit of room off the mat, they crouch or stand five deep. He explains he's taking fighters to Manila for a professional bout that'll be on Filipino television. "Before we go we need a few warm-up fights so they don't step in front of five or six thousand people without any experience. Tonight's match is a friendly non-professional fight, and we want it to be as safe as possible, so I'm going to go over the rules. No elbows. No elbows of any kind. No hitting to the back of the head. There will be no stomping of your opponent when he is on the ground. You can kick him but you cannot stomp him. No throat strikes of any kind. You can attack the throat with submissions, with chokes, but you cannot hit to the throat. There is no eye gouging, no fishhooking, no pulling the hair or the ears of any kind, okay? No attacks to the groin, no using your head to attack any part of the opponent's body. No head butting, no attacks to the spine, there will be no small joint manipulations, you will not see the fighters grabbing the fingers or toes, attacking the wrists is okay but not the fingers. There is no biting of any kind and on all throws, all takedowns, the head cannot touch the ground first. So you cannot pick the guy up and spike him in the ground head first. Okay, there will be two ten-minute rounds, with a two-minute rest in between. If the fight goes to the ground the fight will stay on the ground unless the fighters decide to stand up on their own. There will no stopping the fight for any reason other than either a submission, or when one opponent cannot intelligently defend himself, the referee will stop the fight. Okay?"

He repeats the whole thing in Chinese, then says in English, "Any questions?"

"Andy, can you use the wall?"

"Yes. No no no, no using the wall."

☆

The referee is dressed in a crisp white shirt and black Adidas stretch pants. He has the fighters touch their fingerless half-gloves, and then the fight is on. There are a couple of all-out strikes to the body by each fighter, punches that make you wince in a small room like this, and then in an instant Andy's man has the other guy down, and the two of them are suddenly surrounded by a crowd of aggressive gawkers; it seems like half the guys in the room want to get close enough to snap pics and vid with digital cameras, recorders, or cell phones. Reminds me of the way we watched schoolyard fights when I was a kid, elbowing each other for a spot on the inner ring. The crowd pulses fluidly around the fighters, expanding and contracting like a jellyfish. Barely two minutes in, Andy's boy wins the fight with a choke hold.

I ask Geoff's girlfriend Dongdong what she thought of it. "Horrifiring," she says. "I think the Chinese name doesn't tell the truth. It's called the tender art." *Rou Shu,* a direct translation of what Jiu Jitsu means in Japanese, is usually translated as "gentle art."

Andy asks the referee to explain "how the fight ended and what happened, because I think a lot of people don't know."

"The fight ended by submission," says the referee. "What's his name?" He points to one of the fighters from the earlier tournament.

"Wong Pau."

"Wong Pau, come over here and sit down."

So with Wong Pau as a dummy he demonstrates. "He had him like this, and his arm would pretty much break or be dislocated, so he tapped."

"He tapped," Andy reiterates.

☆

On our way out the door we meet Andy's dad, in his seventies but still working full-time in the information systems business. He declares proudly, "It took New York hundreds of years to become New York. It took twenty-five years for Beijing to become like New York." He admits to knowing nothing about wushu, except this: "The key here is, no one is trying to kill each other. This is entertainment. Because in old times, when two Chinese want to fight like this, if you kill me you are not responsible, if I kill you I am not responsible. That's not the right way."

15

☆

Like a Pig Fears Getting Fat

Coming down from Wudang Mountain, the minivan driver wants to haggle. It cost twenty to go up, so I'm not paying more to go down, and he wants sixty. Everyone in China—everyone, even this guy steering a beat-up piece of crap van with one hand—has a cell phone. His cell phone is as beat-up as his van; it makes me realize that I've never seen a really beat-up cell phone before. They love their cell phones here. On the twenty-hour train ride from Beijing the three Chinese who shared my sleeper compartment spent most of their waking hours compulsively fiddling with their phones, like Greeks or Turks with their worry beads, making and taking calls, sending and checking for text messages, playing games on them, and sometimes just staring at them, *willing* them to ring. Out the window there was unbroken flatness: fields of autumn cornstalks turning crisp and brown, interspersed with brickyards, and always a pall of smoky grey air. As we neared Wudang yesterday afternoon, hills and orange groves broke the monotony, but the air stayed dull and hazy. China is a twenty-first-century economic juggernaut powered by a nineteenth-century fuel, coal.

☆

In the town of Wudang, population maybe two hundred thousand, they're used to Taoist pilgrims piling off the train, eager to head straight up to the mountain, which is really a string of seventy peaks dotted here and there with Taoist temples. I arrived at Wudang unsure exactly where to find the Taiji festival, but imagining it would be up in the mountains somewhere. So I shared a minivan with a quartet of pilgrims loaded down with picnic sausages and incense, who got off at a small temple at a lower elevation. The van continued to climb to the end of the road, halfway up the mountains, at a little strip of hotels with ice cold lobbies and clerks wearing gloves with no fingers. It was pretty much deserted in the off season, and there was definitely no Taiji fest in the works. Also no one who spoke English, and no functioning telephones.

What to do? The festival wasn't due to start until the next day, so I wasn't quite in a panic yet. Seven shivering waitresses in dirty red jackets crowded around me in an otherwise empty dining room, and giggled and joked about me while I obtained a meal by pointing at my phrasebook's characters for tofu, green leafy vegetable, and rice. Afterward I figured a stroll in the hills would do me good. Along the major paths, whoever's in charge of making Wudang more attractive to tourists has hidden little loudspeakers in the woods every fifty yards or so, and strange, ethereal choral music was playing, like the soundtrack from some 1930s Hollywood movie about Shangri La. I came to a small temple with a sign in English on it. "No scribing," it said. Okay, no more scribing today.

☆

Next day, descending the winding mountain road in the dented van, still negotiating the fare—he's written "40" in my notebook, but I haven't budged from twenty yet—we rattle past the Purple Cloud Temple and Monastery. Below it, just outside the Academy of Wudang Daoism Martial Arts, eight young Westerners wait to catch a lift. (Can you make a Freudian slip on a keyboard? I just typed "waiting to catch a *life*." Which is pretty much the reason twenty-something Westerners travel abroad.) As they cram into the van one of them (sounds Scandinavian) is telling another (Australian), "You learn speed and you learn sensitivity, not to give it away." They continue to talk in that vein about various martial arts techniques on the trip down. They are going to the Taiji festival too. Perfect, now I don't have to look for it. They're excited and, like me, they have no idea what to expect. Joe, the Australian, says, "I hope we see some Taiji with real power."

☆

The van threads its way through the grim town and stops outside the Wudang Gong Fu Hall. The hall is not actually a hall, but a squat concrete outdoor stadium, fifteen rows of seats surrounding a basketball court. It's packed with spectators, both on the court and in the stands. A PA system is blaring music and commentary at headache decibel levels, and a wind is whipping multicolored bits of tissue paper all over the place. In the midst of this chaos a very somber-looking gentleman in glossy white silk pajamas and Chinese slippers is performing a Taiji routine that, on the surface (and let's face it, the surface is all anyone can see), looks like he's applying suntan oil to the back of an invisible stranger. Along the wall a forty-foot-long banner reads *First Friendship Meeting Wudang Zhao Bao Taiji Fist*.

I'm scanning the crowd, and while there seems to be a dozen or more foreigners here, most of them from Spain and France as it turns out, it's pretty obvious the guy with the digital video camera crouching at the front along the sidelines is Jarek. He's the most Slavic-looking guy in the whole stadium. Actually he looks half-Slav, half-German: tall, well-built, pink complexion, thick brown hair that stands up straight before it falls over into bangs, and the silver stubble of a three-day beard.

"So, at last I have a face to go with the name," he says when I introduce myself. Then we're distracted by some performers breaking concrete blocks with the blades of their palms. "This is fake stuff," Jarek says. "It's like a carnival act, or you'll see them on the street, passing the hat. I was last here in 1991, and one demonstration like this was really impressive, though. They put this concrete tablet on the ground, bound the head of the guy, turned him upside down, and they were pounding the tablet with his head. Three or four times. It didn't break, but you could hear this ugly, sickening sound. Everyone was pretty impressed."

☆

Whether he realizes it yet or not, I'm about to glom onto Jarek for a few days. We pass the morning watching entrants perform their Taiji routines for a panel of judges. This seems odd to me, that judges can score the subtle external movements of performers wearing loose, long-sleeved shiny silk shirts with matching baggy pajama-like pants, clothes that could only make it more difficult for judges to determine how exactly the body moves underneath. And it's doubly odd, since Taiji is all about moving Chi around your body *internally,* and there's really not much to see from the outside anyway. It's not full of flashy kicks and big gestures like the kind of Kung Fu I'm expecting to see practiced at Shaolin. Those at least have a gymnastic element, a physicality that can be assessed. How do you judge a guy waving his hands in front of his belly as if applying suntan oil to the back of an invisible stranger? I ask Jarek if the performers actually care about their scores.

"Unfortunately, many do care about it," he says, "though this is something Taoist ideas are against. Trying to be strong, trying to be first, trying to be best and so on—it's not what life is about. I mean, even if you are the best today you won't be tomorrow. It's like Lao Tzu was saying: softness is something you should look for, weakness is something you should look for. You should not go up. Go down, not up. Stay hidden, don't reveal yourself. Don't become famous. This is an idea that many Chinese follow and agree with."

Jarek, being Polish, is sympathetic to a philosophy of self-effacement. I've been to Poland, and I don't recall meeting a single ostentatious or self-aggrandizing person there. Maybe Poles worry that if they show up on the radar, the Germans or Russians will come back and stomp all over them again for the umpteenth time. Later, when I was joking with him that being in this book might make him famous, Jarek taught me a Chinese expression: "Human beings fear becoming famous like a pig fears getting fat."

☆

"But what are the judges looking for if it's so internal?"

"That's a good question. Because of competitions like this one, all these martial arts have been changing, becoming more demonstrational arts instead of internal fighting styles. They are degenerating, actually. This is the degeneration.

"People don't know what to look at when they watch martial arts," he continued. "What they want to see is something they cannot do themselves, something they think is extraordinary—high kicks, high jumps, whatever, something like acrobatics. So to meet those expectations, traditionalists begin to change the way they practice, to make it more appealing to ordinary people. And then it degenerates, the style. It shouldn't be about satisfying the crowd, it's about practicing your own skills. I don't know if you noticed this one expert who demonstrated in the morning, the one who did very slow, casual-looking movements, that's my teacher—*he doesn't show off!* You saw it. This is what real Taiji is all about. There is even this style that is called mind boxing, *Yiquan,* which is all about standing, there is almost no movement on the outside. It's movement coming from stillness, but it's all on the inside, always adjusting, always relaxing, you know? Just feeling the things going on inside your body, relaxing here and there. From the outside you would think, 'Oh, he's just standing there,' but a lot of things are going on inside. It really doesn't appeal to anybody to watch, but Yiquan practitioners are very powerful fighters."

A bit later Jarek asks, "See that girl performing, with the red ribbon in her hair? She's a student of my teacher; she demonstrates Hue style small frame Taijiquan, very small movements, extremely soft, high postures, to develop internal energy."

"A minimalist," I suggest.

"It's a very good style, but it's all from the internal, so there is not actually anything to see."

"What's the benefit of pursuing that style?"

"Benefit? It's for Neigong, for developing dantien and making energy flow freely in your body. When you practice it, you relax everything in your body. You lose all those muscles you get working out at the gym, so it's like there are no muscles after a certain period of practice, and then, they start to grow again, but very different."

"It's still hard for me to see how it would ever really relate to fighting," I say.

"Well, Chinese culture is very hidden. It's like when you enter a traditional Chinese garden, there's a wall: you can't see the whole garden, you have to walk around to see it all, and after each step is a new sight. It shows itself to you, but gradually. The same is true about Taijiquan, it's not shown on the outside. You don't show how powerfully you can hit. No. It's all inside."

☆

"When I was in Beijing," I say, "I met this guy, Andy Pi, he's into Brazilian Jiu Jitsu."

"Oh yeah."

"He said he knows you, said to say hello."

"Thank you. Thank you very much."

"I was talking to him about Taiji and all the internal arts, and he said, 'Oh, it's all bullshit. Any Brazilian Jiu Jitsu guy will beat the crap out of any Taiji guy no matter how skilled the Taiji guy.'"

"I will tell you something," Jarek says. He pauses for a long time to organize his thoughts. Then he says, "There are two different ways of practicing, two different ways of developing skills. Brazilian Jiu Jitsu is all about muscles—it's all about skill as well, but you build upon your Post-Heaven force, which is basically your muscles, tendons, your physical body. In Taiji, you don't develop any muscles; you don't develop any power; you're supposed to be completely *empty*. But Andy is right. How many people can use Taiji effectively? I don't know. Few, if any.

"The problem is this: Taiji is actually very difficult to master. There is a saying, you need ten years to have some skill in Taiji, and even then not everyone will have the skill. In Jiu Jitsu it's pretty easy, I think, for anybody to develop certain skills, I mean real fighting skills. In Taiji, first you have to change the whole idea of thinking, the whole idea of developing power. And it goes against human nature! From birth you are taught to develop strength, especially in the West, there's this whole idea of nice flat belly and muscles, this whole cultural thing about the V-shaped body. In Taiji, it's just the opposite.

"But to get back to the question," he continued, "I agree with Andy. In Taiji as a martial art there are very few people who can use it effectively. Few. Those Brazilian Jiu Jitsu guys practice professionally, full-time, and they have a lot of partner practice. While in Taiji, it's mainly some routines and gentle pushing hands. Few people go further into fighting."

"Do you think there was an era when Taiji Masters were unbeatable?" I ask.

"There was. There was. In the nineteenth century."

"Or is that just romantic fiction."

"Well, it's said that the Yang style creator, Yang Luchan, he was called Invincible, because he *was* invincible at that time. He was very, very good, but we don't know how he practiced, what his style looked like. Maybe it wasn't as internal as we think it was, maybe it was a mixture of some internal and external exercises. Hard to say. Actually, nowadays you still hear about pretty good people, but the problem is there are no competitions where you can see Taiji people using their skills, and if there are competitions, you don't see them participate. Taiji as a martial art is not supported by the government, so people just practice on their own time and support themselves in other ways. They have to work and think about other things, and they never reach the level they could. That ten years of practice I mentioned? That's hard practice. That means for us, that's more like fifty years."

A bit later Jarek introduces me to an unassuming guy named He Baoguo, who's notable for being one of the few practitioners I'm introduced to who doesn't have a business card. Everyone in China, everyone at this event anyway, has a cell phone and a business card. Except him. Afterward, Jarek says, "He's a peasant. He just stays in his home village, he has fields and crops, and he practices. His father was his teacher; his father was very, very good. He doesn't take part in competitions, he doesn't have the money to go to Beijing or somewhere for competitions, and even if he did, he doesn't have any experience. You need that, you have to get used to certain rules, because competitions are about rules. It's too bad we can't get some other Taiji Masters to go to his village, to spar with him, just for the exchange."

☆

At noon there's a break for lunch, and Jarek and I wander out of the stadium in search of a meal. Next door is the priciest hotel in town, the only one with a wrought iron gate and circular driveway. We wander in and get steered by staff to a large conference room where a banquet for festival participants is in full swing. Right on, free food! Two seats are found for us at a round table of twelve. Jarek is in his element—he's a social butterfly, glad-handing and making small talk with one and all. The meal consists of a great many dishes crowded onto the lazy Susan: a whole fish in a bright orange sauce, various meats and vegetables Chinese style. Everyone picks directly off the platters with their chopsticks, straight into their mouths and back for more. My phrasebook warns that this double-dipping is a cause of high transmission rates of hepatitis B in China, so I'm feeling mild paranoia about all these unknown mouths messing with my food. Jarek laughs at me and says, "Don't worry about it, just live it!" He's been here fifteen years and never caught anything.

"How come no one is touching the rice?" I ask. There's a big bowl of plain rice on the table but everyone ignores it to pick off the other dishes.

"You want rice? It's up to you," Jarek says. "The idea is you should feel comfortable at the table. But they all remember a time when all they had was rice, so they don't like to fill up on it now. They eat their fill of the other plates first."

Jarek translates our exchange to the guy sitting next to him, an accomplished Master of Wu style Taiji, and they have a discussion that he in turn translates back to me.

"He's saying kids today eat well; they get spoiled by their parents and grandparents, because previously China couldn't solve the simplest problems. People were dying of hunger in the late '50s, early '60s. Even as late as the '80s, they had these rationing systems so you could buy only a certain quantity of rice, meat, oil, or sugar. Now kids are getting lots of food, fast food is everywhere, so they're getting fat, and internally they have a lot of health problems."

"Did you offer any solutions?"

"No, he's just complaining, because he says it's like going from one extreme to the other, from not having enough food to *over-feeding* the next generation, which is going to be a problem."

"Exacerbated by the one child policy?"

"Absolutely, yes. When you only have one child, it receives everything."

The three youngish, thirty-something guys in track suits seated across the table are masters of three different Taiji styles, "all of them pretty rare," Jarek informs me. The moment they finish eating all three light up cigarettes, and two are having a shot of *baijiu,* the clear Chinese liqueur that comes in a bottle with a built-in plastic drip spout, so you have to turn it fully upside down over the glass to make it dribble out, like soy sauce. "I thought Taiji was all about 'My body is a temple,'" I say.

Jarek scoffs. "That's Westerners. Chinese don't worry so much about these things."

☆

Walking back to the hotel, I'm teasing Jarek that he's Mr. Popularity, totally articulate in the language, the friendly foreigner everyone wants a piece of.

"The various masters are not necessarily in good relations, so I have to find a way to stay on good terms with everybody, and at the same time not offend my teacher," he responds.

I tell him about the only internal stylist I know: tubby, unassuming Don the monk, Sifu Bob's teacher back home, who claims to be able to defeat any external fighter, even a recognized superstar like Royce Gracie, and that even Sifu Bob (a very practical guy, an ex-boxer—in other words, someone whose opinions in these matters I trust) insists Don's a seven and Royce Gracie is a five. "I'm going to watch the two of them work out together when I get back," I say. "At some point in my book I need to make a decision about whether I think he's got those kinds of world-beater chops or not, or is he just blowing smoke?"

"But you're writing a book about martial arts?" Jarek asks in a surprised tone, as if this is the first he's ever heard of it.

"Yeah."

"Martial arts??" He sounds totally shocked.

"Yeah. All kinds. Every kind."

"Have you been practicing any martial arts?"

"I've been going to this Kung Fu Academy, which is a basic kind of a, a Shaolin Wushu."

"How many years?"

"Eight months. It's kind of like I'm the neophyte going in with fresh eyes."

He smiles, and I worry that some sarcastic put-down will slip out of his mouth, but instead he says, "Good idea. This is a good idea. With all the infighting in martial arts I've seen over the years, it would take me a long time to write a good book. Maybe it's much better when you are fresh at it, you can write what you feel about it, so this is like a different ..." He pauses to seek the right words. Don't forget, English is his third language.

"Different take," I suggest.

"Yeah, a different take."

"I don't have any agenda of my own."

"Yeah, exactly."

"I actually make that comment near the start of my book," I tell him. "The zealousness of the new convert has a zest not found in the musty sermons of old masters."

☆

In the evening Jarek takes me to meet his master, a certain Mr. Liu Rui, from Xi'an, who is staying three doors down from my hotel room, in a suite wherein the living room and dining room are partially separated by glass shelves lit by strange blue tube lights. The whole place glows an eerie blue. We sit on leather couches around a coffee table littered with orange peels and empty one-serving yogurt containers, and copies of Mr. Liu's book on Taiji. Over a long-sleeved plaid shirt he wears a khaki vest with many pockets, like he's about to go fly fishing. He's ultra calm—it's impossible to imagine that serene face flustered. There are four Chinese guys who say little and seem quite deferential to the Master. Jarek and Mr. Liu babble away for ages, and then Jarek turns to me and says, "Sorry I'm not translating, but we haven't seen each other in years, and I'm just explaining why I think I'm ready to pursue his style now. It's a very soft style, doesn't look like much on the outside, but you wouldn't believe what you discover about yourself on the inside. It's like discovering your potential!"

In short order they are on their feet, and Mr. Liu, using only a single finger, demonstrates a technique that suddenly propels Jarek backwards, where he crashes *Bam!* against the wall, jolting some ceramic dolphins on the glass shelving into a rattling, clankity tap dance. Jarek looks startled at first, then flushes with excitement.

Mr. Liu has Jarek come close and stand behind him, then directs him to put his hands on Mr. Liu's hips. They look like a two-man conga line, as Jarek is encouraged to *feel* the technique as he hears it described verbally. Soon Jarek is nodding his head vigorously, blissfully. He's beaming.

Around the coffee table the others chat among themselves. Occasionally they smile at me sympathetically. We're oceans apart on account of the language barrier. They hold their cigarettes Chinese-style—hand low, palm up, thumb on top and two fingers below. One of them has a rough, beaten look, like maybe he's an addict or alcoholic; when Jarek returns from his lesson and there's an appropriate break in the conversation, I ask what the guy's story is. Jarek says he was an intellectual, banished to this backwater for re-education during the Cultural Revolution in 1968. "He was an urbanite forced to live like a peasant, with nothing," Jarek says. "Many people's lives were destroyed then."

"So what did your master teach you, just now?"

Jarek goes into a lengthy discourse on how the legs are conductors of power coming out of the earth, and how bending the legs disperses this power. Mr. Liu has lately decided it's better to keep the legs straight.

"So you hadn't heard that before?"

"No no no. This is pretty new to me. What he means by keeping the legs straight is to keep the shins vertical. Only then can the ground strength reach the hips. He's saying that when you move, you don't have to make a big movement: it's just enough that it's in your mind, or inside your body. You don't have to move your arms or legs. It's more about the *intent* than the actual physical movement."

Mr. Liu is making a point to the others with great conviction. They listen solemnly.

"What's he saying?"

"He says he won't take Japanese students, because his father was tortured to death by the Japanese. He had nails driven through his skull."

☆

When we leave it's only a dozen yards down the hall to my door, where Jarek and I stand talking for a moment. "That was pretty impressive, the way he threw you around with one finger," I say.

"Yeah. You would never take up Taiji to be a bodyguard, you would study other arts. But if you truly mastered Taiji, you could do anything with it, including be a great bodyguard. You can't give yourself a deadline to learn things in Taiji like you can in other martial arts. You cannot hurry things, it has to come naturally.

"The Master is such a nice guy," he continues. "Maybe I'm just superstitious, but I've never put him on my website. I have a special feeling about him. You know, there's more to his teaching than just giving instructions. More to it than just physical interaction, I would say." He pauses. "Maybe I'm just trying to …" He says something softly so that I can't catch a few words. Then he speaks loud and clear: "There are different kinds of teaching; we are so used to studying under pressure, working under pressure, living under pressure—this is a different way of studying, without pressure, and it works better. I like it. Okay Brian, I'll see you in the morning."

☆

A couple of hours later, in my hotel room, after watching television highlights of China's national games (amazing table tennis, and a funny moment in track and field, when Liu Xiang, the gold medallist hurdler from the Athens Olympics, is announced, and the stadium erupts with the high-pitched screams of teenage girls, like a Backstreet Boys concert), I'm lying in bed, trying to fall asleep, and I can feel a strange whirling sensation in my gut, energy of some kind is swirling around on a spin cycle. Very strange, and powerful, but not at all painful. I'd call it a friendly feeling, like a phantom puppy chasing its tail inside me. I've never felt anything like it, and have no context for it. Months later, sitting in a café in Olympia, Washington, waiting to meet the UFC fighter Jeff "The Snowman" Monson (for those readers who might be bored by placid Taiji and impatient for the crowd-pleasing blood, guts, and all-out war of the UFC—it's coming, my friends, it's coming), I would read Jennifer Oldstone-Moore's book *Understanding Taoism*, and learn that Taoists seek to bring together various bodily essences, such as "sexual fluids, saliva, and ch'i," into an *embryo of immortality*. "Also called the 'Red Child,' this 'holy embryo' was established in the belly of the adept, where, properly nourished, through correct practices, it would develop into a perfected body, an immortal, true, real self that would replace the adept's old, corruptible body…. Gymnastic exercises, such as *ch'i kung* [Qigong] and *t'ai ch'i ch'uan* [Taijiquan], both conserve essences and ensure the proper circulation for maximum strength and benefit."

Is that what I felt? The holy embryo stirring, awakened by the proximity to all these Chinese masters who have developed theirs to the max? Whatever it was, I felt it the next night too, and never again since.

16

☆

The More You Think,
the Worse You Understand

Next day there's a "push hands" competition on a canvas-floored wrestling platform, newly set up on risers at one end of the stadium. For push hands the two fighters begin by placing their hands loosely back to back against their opponent's, and making small circular motions in the space between their chests, feeling each other out. From there the idea is to either knock the opponent to the ground, or push him out of the ring. Many of the Taiji Masters on hand here are dismissive of it. One says it looks like "two hungry dogs fighting." The skills on display are not impressive—Andy Pi's Mongolians would undoubtedly kick ass here. What's interesting is the attitudes of the fighters, who all seem embarrassed to be performing in public. Win or lose, they shuffle offstage with goofy grins on their faces.

One of the Taiji performers introduces himself to me as Jack, and says he once worked as an English translator. He's been studying the art for eighteen years now. "I started at twenty-four," he says. "I just like fighting."

I tell him people in the West think of Taiji for health, not fighting.

"We have a conception of Chi. Ever heard of Chi?"

"I have. But I'd be interested to hear how you would explain it."

"Air. Not really air. Air or breath. Or how you say it? The baby comes into this world and first he must cry. This cry is breath. It's air. This kind of breath, we call it the common breath, but before the baby was born he or she has a kind of breath in his liver. Then this kind of breath we call the original Chi, and when baby grows up original Chi will be quite valuable in his health. The practice of Taiji is to cause this original Chi to stay in your body, and give you health. It's also useful in fighting."

"How does it help in fighting?"

"In that case, I have to show you with someone. You want to see the difference between Shaolin streetfighting and Taiji?"

With a shout he rounds up one of his master's younger students, an eighteen-year-old, and encourages him to punch him in the side of the belly repeatedly, as hard as he can. The kid is well-built, but Jack just smiles and takes the blows. "You turn," he says, exaggerating the way he is turning his body ever so slightly to deflect each blow. "After a period expires you find Chi is filled in the body. I use Chi and a little movement to—"

"To negate his power?"

"Yes. Can you see my movement? It's quite difficult for you to find. That's typical Taiji."

The kid shakes his wrist as if it's sore. "His wrist is hurt!" Jack says proudly. Then he tells me he's going to put all his Chi into one finger, holds his index finger in front of my chest, and asks me to take hold. "Try to defeat me," he says. I grab his finger and quickly find myself on my knees before him. He has subdued me with one finger, which might be impressive if you didn't know about

Hurricane Helen and the various other humiliations of my martial arts career.

"Tell me what you were doing. Is it a process in your mind?"

"No no no. Listen, Chi Gong is not in mind, we practice without any mind, just like water without wind is spread even, without any thought. In that case we call it original development. We can make this Chi come out, and practice with it. That's Taiji."

☆

In the evening Jarek and I wander into a banquet in a series of smaller dining rooms in my hotel, hosted by one of the masters. This time the waitresses demand we pay a small fee, as we don't have a ticket. Fine. The food is not as fancy as the previous day, more home-style cooking. There's a young woman at our table, a writer for a Chinese martial arts magazine. She's not a martial artist; for her it's just a job. After speaking with Jarek for a few minutes she gloms onto him the way I have, because he's a neutral, objective outsider, and capable of giving her the big picture, something she's having trouble piecing together from the subjective opinions of the various masters in attendance. They all have their own agendas. Jarek decides she needs to be educated about Zhao Bao style's place in Taiji. What it amounts to is this: the Chinese government has supported an origin theory that credits the invention of Taiji to a peasant turned rebel general named Chen Wangting, in the seventeenth century. Chen is associated with Chen style Taiji, which is associated with the village of Chenjiagou in Henan province, and the Chen family lineage. Zhao Bao is another village in Henan that has its own style of Taiji, with its own origin theory, widely accepted by Taoists: Taiji originated in the fifteenth century, in the mountains of Wudang, created by a semi-mythological priest named Zhang San Feng, who has now been elevated in the Taoist pantheon to the level of a minor deity. According to legend, Zhang came across a snake doing battle with a bird, possibly a crane. He liked the way the snake skillfully dodged the bird's beak and only struck when the bird had exhausted itself.

Since 1949 the Communist government in China has shown more sympathy to the peasant originator theory than the princely Taoist theory, so the Chen style has prospered under official approval. Lately, a loosening of government control over martial arts has mirrored the loosening of the economy. Now that China's booming, the local government of Wudang sees a lucrative angle to attract tourists, both Chinese and foreign, to their sacred Taoist mountains. Come to the sacred birthplace of Taiji! And the Zhao Bao practitioners, seeing how Chen village has prospered with flocks of foreign tourists coming to study there, are only too happy to have their creation theory legitimized.

☆

Also seated at our table are some young men imbibing *baijiu*. After accepting a couple of pours from them I can truthfully report that it's a god-awful sugary syrup with an aftertaste like industrial floor cleaner. The boys are eager to have us go back to their hotel and meet their master, a certain Mr. Wang Qing Sheng, a real tradition-alist direct from Zhao Bao village. Jarek declines the invitation; he wants to spend more time with his master, Mr. Liu, but suggests I go with the boys, who assure me one of Master Wang's students speaks very good English and will translate for me. Sounds good.

There's plenty of storefront neon reflected on the rainy main street of Wudang town, but only one business is open, a hair-dresser's, an enterprise that in China often does double duty as a whorehouse. This one looks strictly hair-centric, with swish men giving young women in tight punky jeans specialized cuts to make them look like Japanese heavy metal groupies. It's the hottest style in Wudang. Actually, all over China there are women who look like Japanese heavy metal groupies, in jean jackets and tight T-shirts emblazoned with English words like HYSTERICAL, or BITCH. We stop at a hotel to collect the translator, a guy from Hong Kong named William who lived in Canada for eight years, then proceed to another to meet Mr. Wang.

Mr. Wang's hotel room has gloomy wallpaper, probably golden thirty years ago, but now tarnished brown from cigarette smoke. He has white hair cut flat on top so that his head looks square. He looks like a tough old ex-boxer. He hands me a plastic laminated business card that says he is the Deputy President of the China Wenxian Zhaobao Taijiquan General Association, and also, in bold letters, that he is a **Tenth Era Descendibility Man**. In other words, he claims to be a tenth-generation master, and I make the mistake of asking a question that shows my ignorance, namely who the first-generation master was. William groans, rudely tells me I could get that from any book about Taiji, and says I'd better have better questions than that, for this is a great master.

I'm in an armchair; sitting cross-legged at my feet is a Frenchman named Jean-Thibaut Fouietier. The Chinese call him Tibo; he's the student of a former student of Mr. Wang who now lives and teaches in Paris, and he won first prize for his performance in the competition here in Wudang today. He's not impressed that I'm writing a book. He says, "People always ask me for a book so they can understand Taiji. I tell them, you don't need to understand it, you just need to *practice* it." He starts feeding me questions to ask the Master, questions he himself would like answered. "Does he think that the personality of the Master is different, or is it inside the Taiji, and the Taiji stays the same? Understand?"

Not really, but William says he does, and translates the question to the Master, who sits passively on the edge of his bed, both feet planted firmly on the floor. There follows a ten-minute discussion in Chinese before William reports back to us: "He said the whole Taiji is just one circle, a small circle just like a watch, a mechanical watch. You have different components: one helps the other to keep turning and that drives the thing around. Some of the masters, when they can't understand something, they change it, or if they are not up to that standard, they skip steps. So it seems to work, but all the inner workings aren't there. But Master Wang, he doesn't change it, he just keeps on searching, and searching, until he finds out, and understands the whole system. That is why he says his is the traditional Taiji."

Tibo makes weird grunting noises of approval throughout William's summation, which continues: "The other Zhao Bao styles have altered something; they change according to their own thinking, their own experience. But for Master Wang, it has stayed the same from generation to generation."

"But doesn't that place a huge responsibility on him, to find a student, and pass on the full extent of the knowledge he possesses?" I ask. "He's in his seventies, and no offense, but he's no spring chicken—he could die tomorrow. Has he found a student who is on the path to learning the whole system, fully and completely, so that he can die in peace, knowing it will continue into an eleventh generation?"

"It's easy to find a good master, hard to find a good student," is the beginning of William's translation of his answer, a martial arts cliché even Royce Gracie had fed me at one point. I try another tack. Mr. Wang has dedicated himself to his art for fifty years, even during the Cultural Revolution, when Taiji was treated as an illegal activity and he had to hide it from the authorities, practicing in secret, often in darkness. He had few students in those times. He worked days as a purchasing agent for a collective farm and spent long evenings at tedious, compulsory political meetings. So does that mean he hasn't had time to pass on some aspects of his system, and they will be lost when he dies? This question, which is a reworking of the last question, goes through William to the Master, turns into ten minutes of discussion in Chinese, and comes back with, "Hopefully, if his students practice, they will reach a level where he can pass on all the knowledge. But it hasn't happened yet. You have to find someone with good qualities, good virtues, and they have to spend time. Like, ten years of time. It's hard to find someone like that, and if he can't find someone like that, well forget it, because to pass the knowledge on to a bad guy, the guy could do a lot of bad things to society."

"So Taiji is a dangerous fighting art, is that why it shouldn't fall into the wrong hands?" Correct. I ask for a demonstration of the fighting aspect, and Master Wang rises from the bed, and bids me come at him, to try to push him over. I decide not to give him much, since Taiji is all about taking my energy and using it against me.

"You have to push him hard," William insists, but still I offer very little. We must look like indifferent partners paired off at a social dance, waiting for the music to start. He's standing so close to the bed his calves are almost touching it, so he can't step backward for balance. I figure if I push him, with luck he might topple back onto the bed. I go for it, make my move, give him a sudden push to knock him on his ass; he quickly steps to the side rather than back, and takes my lead arm and puts me in some kind of wrist lock that makes me drop to one knee. A murmur of satisfaction goes through the others in the room.

"The harder you push, the worse you get," Tibo says excitedly. "It's like the more you think, the worse you understand."

☆

Later I ask Jarek what happened to Taiji in China during the Cultural Revolution.

"A lot of things were lost," he says, "because with many teachers, the Red Guards came and destroyed all the materials. Now, you cannot destroy someone's skill unless you keep an eye on that person, not allow him to practice. There's a guy here at this festival, Zheng Jun, he had a Red Guard posted right in his house to prevent him from practicing. He lost a lot of his skill. Of course he remembers it, you cannot erase the memory, but his skill is not what it would have been if he could have practiced through the Cultural Revolution."

I express my skepticism about Master Wang's claims to possess the true Taiji, as invented all those centuries ago by Zhang San Feng, and passed down unchanged to the present day. "You meet all these masters, and they all have this idea that what they do is the only right, oldest, true, orthodox authentic style," Jarek says. "I don't want to follow those teachers who say they are doing it unchanged after generations. My teacher, Master Liu, is different. He says, 'I'm going down the path that my teacher gave me, I'm following his principles.' But it's not an exact copy of the outside form. Once you master the internal principles, you don't have to stick strictly to the outside shape. At a certain point you go into something without shape, without form."

☆

As the closing ceremonies of the *First Friendship Meeting Wudang Zhao Bao Taiji Fist* get underway, the wind comes up, a cold rain falls intermittently, and the push hands canvas gets sopping wet. A couple of kids wrestle on it anyway, until they're sopping wet and filthy dirty. I'm one of only a handful of spectators left in the stands. Two others, little girls, maybe six or seven years old, come over to look at the foreigner up close. "ABCDEFG," one of them says. That's more English than I've heard from any Wudang resident since I arrived. It's the future talking. In China, English has recently been made compulsory, from first to final school year. A dozen years from now there'll be a whole generation who know the basics, and some will be fluent. By then China will own the world, and knowing English will make it much more convenient for them to give us orders.

17

☆

Fancy Smell

The next day, before we set out to ascend the sacred mountain, Jarek orders us up some lunch in a little curbside restaurant in Wudang town. I'd noticed at the banquets how he'd fastidiously avoided pork dishes, and now he's getting even more hardcore about it, insisting to the waitress that he wants no food that can be traced back to a pig: no pork, no ham, no bacon, no sausage, no cooking oils containing pork fat, nothing. "Sometimes I tell them I'm Muslim," he says. The waitress is peeved. She's not into it, sees no reason she should shoulder the responsibility of *guaranteeing* a pork-free dining experience. Her shrug creates a standoff, a stalemate. So Jarek demands to see the cook. While we wait for that, he tells me the story of his first visit to a rural village in China. His host's latrine was nothing but a hole in the ground, surrounded by inadequate rattan walls, where local kids gathered to peek through the gaps and play Spot the Foreign Devil's Dangly Bit. So there's Jarek squatting, trying to relax his inhibited sphincter, when to his ears comes an impatient grunting noise, and he looks down through the hole, and meets the eyes of a pig looking up at him. "That was the last straw," he says. "You become what you eat, and the pig was made of shit!"

In a filthy apron, and smoking a cigarette, a twentyish guy sidles to our table, and listens to Jarek rerun the list of disallowed pork and pork byproducts. The chef pledges his culinary word, the ordering of lunch can proceed, and in short order four ample plates are plopped before us: fungus and egg, spicy tofu, your basic fried greens, and "is this potato?"

"I think so," Jarek says.

"I'm worried for you. Seems to have bits of pork in it."

Jarek gets his nose up close to a sample. "No, it can't be pork, has too small a smell." We decide it's ginger.

☆

On our way to the mountain we stop at an abandoned Taoist temple on a flat valley floor. Soon to be submerged by a hydro-electric dam under construction nearby, it's set among small-plot vegetable farms, but we see no farmers, only their dogs, who bark at us but keep their distance, as Jarek stops to read a plaque in Chinese by the gate. "This place is called Yu Zhen Gong, Palace of Meeting the Immortals," Jarek reads. "Construction was started by Zhang San Feng himself in 1312, and it took five years."

The place is ghostly and more beautiful for being uncared for, not like the temples of Beijing, which are maintained for tourists and end up feeling fake. In faded white paint, four-foot-tall Chinese characters cover the inner courtyard walls with slogans: "We closely follow Chairman Mao. We closely follow the Central Committee of the Party. Educate the working people, and teach the intellectuals labor."

"Ridiculous," I say, after Jarek translates them.

He disagrees. "Sometimes people were writing these slogans on the walls to protect them. Many temples were destroyed at that time. But no Red Guard would destroy them if they had these slogans written on."

☆

Halfway up the mountain we stop at the Purple Cloud Temple, which is well-preserved, meaning it's mostly a reconstruction of the original, is kept freshly painted, and sells camera film and "Wudang Kung Fu" DVDs in a gift shop manned by Taoist monks. One of the monks complains to Jarek that they are so busy with tourists they have little time to meditate. The complex is built into the side of a mountain, with a bare cliff face hanging ominously hundreds of feet above. You climb a series of stone staircases, each one leading to a temple. There are plaques in English; for example, outside Shi Fung Hall, the Praying Temple: *The sitting statue is Zhenwu in the middle with Lu Dong Bing on his left and Zhang San Feng on his right. Lu lived in the Tang dynasty, he once met an immortal called Han Zhongli, and was enlightened by his magic Golden Mallet Dream.*

Zhang San Feng established the Wudang school of Taoism. He created the arts of Taiji Quan and Wudang school of Kung Fu, the internal school based on the law of Taiji. The creator of Taiji Quan advocated that Confucianism, Taoism, and Buddhism should all be blessed religions which are totally different from evil sects. Although each has different origins and separate founders, the three have the same purpose, which is to improve personal character and be altruistic. Confucians tend to benefit social order, Buddhists try to enlighten people, and Taoists focus on longevity. Zhang also insisted that benevolence and the practice of qigong makes one immortal.

☆

There's a Taoist nun practicing a Taiji form while tourists take pictures. Turns out she's not a nun, she just borrowed the black hat, blue coat, and white leg wraps from a nun. She's a Taiji instructor, here to provide a beginners' lesson to a busload of British tourists who came through this morning. Now she's just hanging out, playing around with the real monks and nuns. I ask Jarek if her form is any good. "Her postures are nice," he says. "But looking nice isn't necessarily good. I'm sure the English people thought they were getting the real Taoist Taiji from a real Taoist nun."

Down below we can see the parking lot is filling with tour buses, and loads of Chinese tourists are pouring out. Each busload wears matching baseball caps of a bright color, so they don't stray from their flock and get lost. The hats come in every possible shade except green. Apparently in China the expression "to wear a green hat" means you've been cuckolded, so you never see a green hat. The tour guides are all chattering away into competing battery-powered megaphones, and the resulting goddamn racket is the opposite of what you hope for in a visit to a working monastery. Up at the highest temple it's not so bad, it's one too many staircases for most of the tourists to climb. This one is called Parents Hall, and the plaque there says Wudang Taoism "emphasizes loyal to the nation and filial to the parents."

On the right there are seven goddesses. The goddess with the tablet is the Goddess of Childbearing, Infantile Health, Agriculture, Marriage, and Travelling. The goddess with the eye is the Goddess of Eyes who is said to be able to enlighten children and make them bright.

The four goddesses beside her are the Goddess of Pregnancy, the Goddess of Vaccination, the Goddess of Midwifery, and the Goddess of Preventing Miscarriages.

☆

This is the day back home when Gracie is scheduled to get her four-month vaccination set, so I ask the appropriate statue to keep a kindly eye on her. Can't hurt.

Here at the top level, one of the young Westerners from the martial arts school, a twentyish Dutch woman, is trying to shoot a documentary on a palm-sized digital camera. Using hand signals and pantomime, she's directing the oldest, most photogenic of the monks, a grey-haired gent who looks positively wisdom-soaked, to walk as naturally as possible out through the doors of the temple and stroll across the stone courtyard. But even this simple scene is proving tough to pull off; Chinese tourists with their cell phones held in front of their faces in snapshot-taking mode keep coming around the corner and wandering into the shot. Poor kid. She's trying to capture an image of a quiet monastery, where the monks pad serenely in slippers as they have for centuries, but reality keeps intruding into her documentary.

☆

Later we wander down to the martial arts school, where outdoor training is in full session. The air is heavy and wet and there are puddles on the cracked concrete plaza. Eight Westerners practice under the watchful eye of an instructor named Zhong Xuechao, whom they all call Bim. I can see Joe the Australian doing a sword form, and that Scandinavian guy walking a Bagua circle. The Chinese students are mostly young boys, practicing short forms and tumbling routines under the stern gaze of masters who don't look all that much older, except that they've perfected an air of strictness.

The kids live here in dorms, a young woman who works here tells us. "Are they here by choice?" I get Jarek to find out for me. Some, yes, but others weren't good in school and were sent here by their parents to get skills and discipline.

"And what will happen to them when they leave here?"

Some will take part in a troupe, performing martial arts shows, some will work as teachers. But most will have to learn some trade, or work in construction. "In China, there are three hundred million people coming from the countryside, in the same boat," Jarek says.

"Are the kids Taoists?"

No they're just students, says the young woman.

"I'm beginning to doubt the Taoist roots of this place," Jarek says.

The kids are performing a complicated form that involves a lot of crouching and kicking. When their instructors call for a break they gasp for breath, clutching the metal handrail that separates two levels of concrete.

"They look like they're being worked to exhaustion."

"This is the way you practice external martial arts," Jarek says. "You push it to the limit."

☆

When the session is over Bim the teacher, who wears his hair in a weird topknot, invites us up to a lounge where he works on the computer and shows off their website. He and Jarek get into a highly animated discussion. "Sorry, Brian," Jarek says eventually. "I'm just telling him my belief that Xingyi and Bagua were only taught at Wudang since the 1920s, they are not ancient traditions here."

I wander off to talk to the students. On the fourth floor, the top floor, the room where they all congregate belongs to a guy named Arec from L.A. His translucent Apple laptop glows seductively, and everyone is entitled to come use it, as they all pitched in to pay the twenty bucks a month internet fee. The roof has been leaking and there is a serious black mold problem on the ceiling that needs addressing pronto. Arec doesn't seem too worried. He's twenty-one and two hundred forty pounds. Like most men that age and size, he thinks he's invincible.

Joe asks him, "Did you shave your head again?"

"Yeah, I Bic it," he says, using his disposable razor's brand name as a verb. "For me it means a fresh start."

"What brought you here?" I ask.

"I felt compelled to come here, like a divine force drew me here," he says. "I found Zen. I learned to use Zen playing poker. I always kind of applied life to poker and then I started to apply *Zen* to poker, and started kicking butt at poker! Then I applied Zen to life, and now everything is just going great, one thing leads to another and I'm here."

"How do you apply Zen to poker?"

"Well basically you're very detached from the cards, okay? You learn to let them go, and not play every hand, and just find the flow of the game. You're not really concerned with anyone else at the table, it's like the game is a joke at some point, because you know everything that is going to happen, and every card that's going to hit, and you're only playing perfect hands, and it's amazing—I swear, I picked this book up in my brother's room, I don't know how it got there, I picked it up and in two days I changed my whole playing game, I was just *kicking butt* at poker. It's called *Zen and the Art of Poker,* it was pretty cool."

"So that got you into Zen?"

"Yeah, it opened me up and it led me here. I've been around martial arts my whole life, so Wudang is the best place to learn Kung Fu. I prefer Wudang Kung Fu to Shaolin. My mom owns a Karate dojo—I've been in it since I was three, travelling and competing in the States—but I don't really have a love for Karate anymore. For me, I want something more, I want something divine, I want to—I have these feelings inside, and with Kung Fu everything I want to be true is possible, and there is this point where everything that is divine and everything that is tangible just kind of interlocks."

"Good stuff. How's that going?"

"Great. I'm exactly where God wants me. Spiritually I'm a Christian. Jesus Christ is my idol!" He laughs heartily at himself. "The sword form I'm learning is over three hundred years old. It's called Eight Immortals Sword, and a lot of people know about it, but not that many know the form itself and, um, forty years ago it was almost lost and only one dude knew it, now they've taught each other, and it's really advanced, and it's cool that I'm learning it but I don't know if I'm ready for it yet. It's a lot more difficult than Japanese sword forms that I do know, it's very cool to learn something that is that old and has got moves from all these different Immortals that live on the mountain.

"And I'm learning Five Animal Qi Gong, which is required by all the Taoist priests to learn, and that is just cool because if they make all the Taoist priests learn it you know there is something to it and I love it. When you get your breathing going in motion with the movements and then all of a sudden you are like, just ONE, it flows very well with nature and you feel crazy sensations you have never felt, and *this* guy"—he points to Joe, who wears a beatific grin sitting on the bed listening to his buddy's gloriously upbeat riffing monologue—"we go out on the roof at night and meditate and practice our Qi Gong and I am having the time of my life, and I'm going to stay here as long as I can, I've got money to stay till about my visa runs out, I've only been here three weeks so we'll see how I feel after three months."

Whew. The kid's enthusiasm makes me feel I need to catch my

breath. I ask, "Do you ever imagine you could end up staying here in a monk's robe?"

"Yeah, that is what I wanted. I have a great life for a twenty-one-year-old back home. I have been so blessed. I've owned my own home. I have a forty-thousand-dollar car at home, I have great things going for me, but I almost feel like throwing that all away and staying here in these beautiful mountains. My car is in storage right now."

He stops to light a cigarette, which seems a good time to turn to Joe the Australian. "Why are *you* here, Joe?"

"One reason is like a pilgrimage," he begins. Back in Australia, his Kung Fu school was visited by a high-ranking Chinese Wushu official, who was also a Yang style Taiji adept. "The way this man held himself left quite an impression on me, and at the end of the weeks that I spent with him he said to me, out of the whole class, that he felt like he was talking to an old friend. People come across on different levels, you know, but I could really feel what he was saying in my whole body. Then he said to me, if you ever get a chance, go to Wudang Mountain, and you will feel the spirit that the people have cultivated there. And when I arrived I could really feel it pulsating through my whole body, just the majesty of the peaks and … being in China!"

"What about the Chinese kids who study here? I was told some of them aren't here by choice."

Arec speaks up. "Whether they really wanted to be here at the start, when you see them practicing, they really put all their heart into it. They love it, dude. I think they love it."

"They impress the tourists that come up here, so that's gotta give them a good feeling," Joe adds.

Arec says, "The thing about the students is all the stuff we are learning in school was secret until about twelve years ago, so they are getting a chance to pass on these historical, Wudang styles, these styles haven't been exposed, they are living history, and they don't realize how everyone back home would *die* to be here."

"Back in Australia I was doing Shaolin Kung Fu, more of an external style, but the Shaolin Masters have internal power that is second to none," Joe says. "The flow of the moves is different, maybe you could say that Shaolin is a little bit more static, and Zen is the heavy influence on Shaolin, and Taoism is what resonates over here, with the Taiji."

"Nice, bro," Arec tells him. "Dude, I love it, we have so much in common, that's why it's just so awesome that we both came here, I really believe it's through fate!"

☆

Meantime, Jarek's been drinking tea with the owner of the place, who has driven up from town on hearing we're snooping around. In a grand office with an enormous desk and a big yin–yang symbol painted around the bare light bulb in the ceiling, they sit on comfortable chairs in the corner of the room while the owner performs the tea ritual on a portable wooden tea-making tray. They're deep into a conversation that's often close to out and out argument, from what I can read of body language. Jarek is practically shouting at times. At one point he turns to me and says, "He's afraid I'm going to tell the truth about this place on my website."

"You don't think there's anything wrong, do you?"

"Not wrong, but when you write the truth, people get hurt."

"He's young," I observe.

"He's thirty-three."

When it's time to leave it's pitch black outside. The owner offers us a ride in the school van, but Jarek insists we will walk the couple of kilometers up the road to our hotel in the dark.

The sky is overcast so there is no light to guide us, although the white stripe painted along the shoulder of the road glows faintly luminescent. Without it we'd be lost, or at least stumbling into the stone-lined drainage ditches. As we make our way uphill Jarek complains that the owner has turned out not to be a Wudang adept, but a businessman who studied his martial arts in Shaolin, so he's more familiar with the hard, external Kung Fu taught there, not the soft, Taiji-influenced Wudang stuff.

"I was asking tough questions, and you could feel the atmosphere was getting tense in some moments," Jarek says. "I was asking, 'What do you teach in the school? Are *real* Wudang martial arts being represented in your school? We came and we saw what you are teaching here and there is a lot of modern Wushu being taught.' And he got defensive: 'Well, you can't stop them if they want to learn that.'"

A dog barks close by in the darkness, maybe twenty feet away, and scares the hell out of us. But Jarek picks up the thread once we've passed by and all is quiet again. "I told him, foreigners want to come to Wudang and learn the real, original Wudang martial arts and they pay money, quite a lot of money—he was telling me how much, nine hundred American dollars for a month, eight hundred a month if they stay a full year. And I said, we have the example of Shaolin Temple, and look how bad its reputation has gotten in the last ten years or even more, the performing monks showing acrobatics is like a circus! It's not martial arts at all. And now you have this Wudang martial arts coming up, and what I am afraid of is you are teaching similar stuff and just giving it another name."

"This is an amazing way to walk through the mountains," I say. Far below we can see the headlights of a single vehicle slowly snaking up the switchbacks toward us, but otherwise there is only that faint white line at our feet, and a black void around.

"Yeah, I just wanted to tell you all this stuff because you were sitting there getting pissed off."

"I was not. I'm very patient."

"I wouldn't mind just walking and shutting up," he says. So we ascend silently in the void, but Jarek can't keep quiet for long and starts complaining again about the quality of the school. "My main concern about Wudang martial arts nowadays is that what has been preserved up to now are just empty routines, without content. Not *systems,* not complete systems that would allow you to develop for your whole life, you know what I mean?"

"That is what you think is happening here?"

"Yes."

The headlights that have been snaking up the mountain finally reach us, and the driver stops to offer us a lift. Two crazy foreigners wandering like ghosts in the dark, we just wave him on.

"But they are learning some internal arts here," I suggest to Jarek. Back at the school I'd also talked with a kid named Anders, a Norwegian who had been studying in Wudang for seven months. Anders had been attracted to Wudang in part through the movie *Crouching Tiger, Hidden Dragon.* "I didn't know much about it apart from that film, because all you hear about in the West is Shaolin," he said. Anders told me a story about how Bim, the teacher with the topknot, had a great pile of various Taiji style forms written out on paper, and that an American student who had been here for awhile, a Hawaiian, looking through them, had discovered the Five Animal Qi Gong, "something all Taoists need to know, it works the body and breathing," as Anders had put it. The Hawaiian had "jumped up and said, 'What is this shit, why aren't we learning this?'" Bim had replied, "Oh yeah, we can do that."

"So now, almost every class, we do one or two of the animals as a warm-up. Because they are Qi Gong, they don't have a combat element, but besides that it looks like Taiji. Like, turtle works the kidney, there's a lot of body twisting. Crane works the heart, snake is breathing, tiger is strength, and dragon is intestines. Dragon looks like Bagua, it's very coiling."

So I relay this to Jarek, but he's not impressed. "Studying a martial art is not about memorizing a routine—the routine is just a method that helps your body to reshape, to re-pattern. Basically what I'm afraid of is, someone has some basics in one style of modern Wushu and then they learn a lot of routines, and then they teach them, and don't go any further. The guy from Norway, he's here learning a lot of routines, which is fine for a guy in his twenties, but when you get to your thirties you decide on a *path,* on a style that you really want to *master,* and to do it you need a teacher who has been on this path for longer than you, and knows all the stages."

"Kind of like Master Wang's Zhao Bao," I suggest.

"Exactly. He doesn't need to know a million routines. He knows *one complete system,* and he's been focusing on that system for fifty years. He's an authentic teacher."

☆

The next day our plan is to climb to the Golden Temple that crowns the highest peak at Wudang. First we rouse the grumpy staff of the hotel to unpadlock the restaurant and fix us breakfast. Inside it's too cold to sit; we can see our breath as we wander around the room looking for interesting distractions while we await our chow. The best is a big glass jar of alcohol on the bar that contains a snake coiled on a bed of pickled ginseng. "In China they say it'll improve your health, but what they really mean is it will boost your sex life," Jarek says. While the women have gone off to cook us up a couple of big soupy bowls of greens, eggs, and noodles, the only man of the place sits behind the bar reading a book called *Raising Standards in the Food and Drink Industry*.

Having slurped down our soup, we begin the long climb, accompanied by that ethereal Shangri La muzak floating mysteriously out of the flora. It's driving me nuts, and Jarek even more so. A detour to a cave to see Yellow Dragon God and God of Medicine is no respite from the God of Running Speaker Wires Up a Cliff.

To reach the Golden Temple you must climb thousands of stone steps; I don't actually count them but it *feels* like thousands, and the flabbier Chinese tourists hire locals with palanquins to carry them for stretches. Jarek trucks on ahead and is quickly out of sight, while I wheeze and gasp and take plenty of breaks to look at little birdies in the woods, or read the English signs at one of the many small temples along the stairway. One translates a "couplet" thus: "You dear devil vermin, stop your wrongdoings." It'll stick in my mind and, when I get home, become one of my favorite things to yell at Gigi when she misbehaves.

☆

About a third of the way up, the Shangri La music stops. The path forks, and we take the less travelled route. It's almost deserted. Jarek is nowhere to be seen, so the climb becomes a serenely lonely (and sweaty) meditation, built around the repetitive act of placing one foot ten inches higher than the other. When I get to the top, feeling that giddy sense of accomplishment and altitude lightheadedness all trekkers know, there's still no Jarek, but there are a million Chinese tourists snapping photos with their cell phones and yelling out from the summit to check for echo. Turns out there is a modern and efficient electric cable car running up the other side of the mountain. I even recognize one of the tour guides from yester-day at the Purple Cloud Temple, barking through her megaphone at her yellow-capped coven. I'm feeling cheated because I just walked up about six thousand steps like a good Taoist is supposed to, my clothes are soaked through with sweat, and Chinese tourist girls in high heels with tinny iPod pop songs dribbling out through their ear gristle are looking at me like *I'm* the freak. Then I enter the temple complex and feel even more cheated because the first monk I see is selling me my admission ticket, and the second is chattering into his cell phone.

Waiting for Jarek to show, I hang out at the Imperial Scripture Hall, where the monks do their incantations of Taoist scripture, accompanied by flute and gong. It's a beautiful sound, and right across the cobblestone path from it there's a big stone oven where incense is burned, and I can stand close to it and dry out my sweat-soaked back that turned ice cold as soon as I stopped climbing. The wind is very cold up here, especially as evening starts to come on, and still no sign of Jarek. A Beijing businessman buttonholes me and says in broken English the mountains that circle us are like the circle of Taiji. He demonstrates some Xingyi for me, and his punches look lightning quick. But he's forty-four; he says he's too old for Xingyi now and has switched to Taiji. He tells me that likewise I am too long in the tooth for my Shaolin Kung Fu and should take up Taiji. That's exactly what I'm thinking. But when I imagine breaking the news to Sifu Bob back home, I feel like I'd be letting him down.

☆

Light is beginning to fade, and the crowds are all making their way to the cable car station, a couple of hundred feet down the moun-tainside. Finally I find Jarek, on a wide concrete platform big enough to land a helicopter on, where earlier in the day tourists had scarfed down disposable Styrofoam bowls of instant noodles. Now some of the monks are practicing their martial arts forms. The tourists are almost entirely gone, and the girls who sell noodles are closing up shop. Jarek tells me he's just been teasing one of the younger monks, accusing him of using his martial arts prowess to impress one of the girls, and threatening to report him to his master. The kid seems to be taking the threat seriously, and has gone all self-conscious in his practice, his face a mask of diligence.

The vice-abbot of the place, a thirty-five-year-old with a baby face, a topknot, and a down-filled vest, is telling Jarek about a celebrated Taoist martial artist from his hometown who was a bodyguard for the last emperor. He used to meditate for months, drinking only water. Even into his eighties, he liked to sleep in trees and other uncomfortable places. When he died, they opened the coffin two days later and there was nothing inside. Is it possible this man had achieved the Immortality so prized by Taoists?

"Have you seen any Immortals on Wudang Mountain?" Jarek asks him excitedly. The best the vice-abbot can come up with is a young monk, in his thirties, who goes barefoot here, even in the damp snowy winters. As the last light of day fades, an icy cold wind is whipping across this exposed platform. Jarek's impervious. This is exactly where he wants to be. Some of the monks are performing some Taiji routines, or some fairly straightforward official-style Wushu. One of them has a sword, intending to practice a Wudang sword form, but now that foreigners are watching, he's gotten stagefright and can't be cajoled. All in all, Jarek's a little saddened at the lack of systemic skill on display this afternoon. Here at the apex, Wudang martial arts are not being preserved.

I tell Jarek if we don't take the cable car right now we'll be walking down those thousands of steps in the darkness. Exactly, he replies. That's his intention, his desire. Soon the cable car closes, and we have no choice. But even this dim twilight is not dark enough for my dear Polish madman, he wants pitch black. It's some kind of semi-mystical rite for him, I reckon, to descend from the sacred home of Taiji guided only by the touch of the mountain through the soles of his shoes. The abbot invites us to a dining hall built beneath the concrete platform. Under a low ceiling there's room for three booth-style tables, and the rest is crammed with instant noodle boxes. On a television in the corner, some soap opera set in olden days shows a lovely young mother frantically running, baby in her arms, from some evil warlord's relentless troopers. The vice-abbot lights up a cigarette and offers me one. Why not share the peace pipe? Seventy percent of Chinese men smoke. What's that—three hundred million maybe? He's a bit embarrassed about smoking, being a Taoist abbot and all; he blames it on stress, on the assault of tourists arriving in waves off the cable car every single day. But when he's seriously meditating, he assures us, he stops smoking and eating meat.

He and Jarek get into a discussion of whether the Tao follows nature or nature follows the Tao. The lady with the baby escapes the evil troopers by hiding in the reeds, and then the show degenerates into conspiring courtiers' talking heads. I've got talking heads on the television and talking heads at my table, all in Chinese. Also a steaming bowl of instant noodles offered free of charge. I didn't realize how hungry I was. It's warm and cozy in here, compared with outside, where it's now dark and a freezing wind howls. Since it's already dark, my panic to get down the mountain has left me. I'm still worried, but there's no hurry now, dark is dark. Belly full of warm noodles, there's time to cadge another cigarette, and ask Jarek, "So, what is Taoism all about, anyway?"

☆

"The whole idea in Taoism is to become immortal, and the whole process of achieving this goal is called internal alchemy," he begins. "There is a branch of Taoism called Complete Reality, which the monks here follow, which is a mixture of Taoism, Buddhism, and Confucianism, and it's all about meditation. Taoists consider meditation to be the true and only path to understanding what is Tao. Taoism is not about empty slogans, or reading books and showing off by quoting this, that, or the other thing.

"It's about understanding with your *body*, it's internal alchemy, it's about your body and mind. Both! You cannot just have it in your mind, you have to have certain feelings in your body. Taoists consider that each of us has three treasures: Jing, Chi, and Shen. Jing is like vital energy. It's the energy that is in your kidneys. This is the life energy! This is the vital energy you get from your parents when they make love and you are being procreated. It all comes to you in that moment of conception. It's like all the money you have for your life. You spend it, you die.

"Then there is Chi, also energy, which makes your blood flow. It's a very vague thing, actually. It's about breath, also. And the third one is Shen, spirit. You know, related to your mind. The vital energy is related to your body, and Shen is related to your mind, and Chi is something in between, you could say.

"And so you have these three treasures, and you go through the process of internal alchemy. And what is it about? It's about changing this vital energy into Chi, which is a different Chi, it's written with two characters, one means nothing or not existing, and below it is four drops, which means fire. No fire. What is fire? They say, in Chinese thinking, fire is your thoughts in your heart, *xin*, your emotions, feelings that are going on in your heart, so you have to get rid of all this garbage. They call it *qing jing*, which means purity and stillness. Not only of your posture when you practice, but the main thing is stillness of your mind. Which means no thinking. There is even this saying: When the human mind dies, the mind of Tao becomes alive. You have to die to really live. On a basic level you have to stop thinking to be able to see. You have to kill your own thinking to be able to see things as they really are. You are not subjective anymore. There's no 'this is wrong' or 'this is good,' there is no judgment, there is no emotion. This is what I'm saying, but it sounds like from a book. You have to have the experience of it. There is no understanding if there is no practice. There is no real Taoism without meditation.

"So most of the Taoist classics can't just be studied; you have to combine it with practice, otherwise it's all empty intellectual talk. And the basic idea of alchemy is using this fire of your heart. You know, kidneys are the place where the water is, they belong to water in Chinese medicine, the heart is hot so you heat the water of your kidneys with the fire of the heart—in other words—"

Suddenly he laughs.

"I don't want to go too much into details; I'm not really sure you should put it in your book. The idea is when you meditate you have to have true intent. This is important, this is the Shen part, the spirit part. You observe a certain place in your body; you just focus on a certain point and look for stillness, complete stillness, no emotions. They even say in Taoism that in this state if you see somebody really ugly beating up a little child or torturing an animal you shouldn't move in any way. If you are in the perfect state, you shouldn't care about anything."

He sees a reflex to protest rise in my eyes and cuts me short before I open my mouth. "No no no no, don't get me wrong, I'm talking about meditation, not about living in society. I'm just showing how extreme this stillness should be. Your eyes, they look, but they do not see. You listen but you do not hear. It's about emptiness—a lot of people practice meditation by doing visualizations; in Taoism this is the last thing you should do. You just find a certain point in your body, and you just leave your attention, but not like active attention, just leave it there. And through this process you can take the vital energy from your body, you can feel it come out of the kidneys, and then you use it on the Small Heaven circuit, which goes down your body, but the energy doesn't move because you want it to move, you just observe it—a lot of people imagine energy flowing in this channel and that channel, it's not the true movement of the energy, ah? This is Chi, the vital energy that comes from your kidneys, you know? It's already kind of transformed, but the full transformation needs a certain number, Taoist classics mention three thousand circulations along this microcosmic orbit, because the idea is, human beings are a microcosm of nature around us, we are a microcosm of the world outside.

"This kind of practice has been basically kept secret and taught only to disciples by masters. I've been through certain stages of it, and I don't know what's really going on, from a scientific point of view, probably you could measure certain things, I don't know how to say them in Western terms, but certain things are happening, and you need a master to supervise you. It's really easy to go astray, because it's about mind, but the good thing is you don't think about it, you are not supposed to visualize anything, so it's not like some other meditation systems where you should imagine this, or imagine that, and so on, you end up completely messed up. You know, I'm not really sure you should put all this in your book. Or if you don't mind I would like to have a look. Okay? Can we have this agreement?"

"Sure."

☆

We bid our farewells to the vice-abbot and set off into the gloom. It's not bad here at the very top, there are no trees to block whatever tiny vestige of light lingers in the clouds. I'm dreading this descent. I have poor night vision to begin with, the result of being stung in the eyeball by an insect in the Philippines when I was twenty. So I'm a bit of a one-eyed stumbler. I'm also thinking about a friend of mine who once slipped and lost four teeth clambering over rocks on an English seashore, and that was in broad daylight. If I tumble headfirst down a stone staircase in the dark, four teeth will be the least of my worries. Worse than the pain or panic would be the kind of sympathy I could expect from my wife: *You decided to walk down a mountain at night with no light? How old are you, fifteen?*

Jarek, meanwhile, is chattering away, oblivious to the peril ahead. "What's really interesting for me now, visiting here again, after so many years—because before when I was here I was a real, true believer, fascinated and excited with the place, kind of like those young guys we met yesterday at the Wudang Martial Arts School. Now I'm a cynic in a way, but I can still see a lot of good things and real good stuff. That vice-abbot is a good guy, he's 'on the way,' they are really on the Taoist path, they really want to be Taoists. They had to prove themselves to be here."

"What about when it comes to martial arts?"

"It's so humid here, you have to practice, you have to move, otherwise you can get sick. It's so cold and humid."

"Damp is the word, cold and damp."

"Yeah, damp. You can get rheumatism. And he was complaining there's no time, during the tourist season, for meditation. He was saying, 'Sometimes I smoke and eat meat, it just happens.' This guy was not bullshitting, he was open and honest. I liked this idea he had, that they should standardize the martial arts they study on the mountain."

"What did you think of what they're currently doing?"

"It was okay, but a lot of it was just demonstrational stuff, to perform for people. It's always a question how legitimate are the styles, and at this point it's more to do with keeping feet and body warm than to develop real skills, you know?"

We're feeling our way with our feet, edging our toes over a thousand ten-inch precipices. It's not like it's one continuous straight line of staircase. There are left turns, right turns, small landings, meanderingly rising and falling footpaths, all kinds of complications that can't be seen, only felt with the feet. Jarek goes in front, and he's good to me, he calls out directions when the path turns, and when the next set of stairs begins. I'm discovering something: all that practice Sifu Bob put me through, those hundreds of shuffles up and down the padded mats of the Kung Fu Academy, slithering along in the basic slide-stepping bow, are now paying off big-time. I'm keeping my center of gravity low, breathing from the dantien, barely lifting my feet off the ground as I slide forward. I'm joined to Taiji mountain, and it's coming up through my feet to join with me.

Along the way, in one of the few spots where a stone handrail supports the steps, you could say I'm practicing external alchemy as my wedding ring scrapes along the stone in the dark. Undoubtedly I'm leaving minute trace shavings behind, a sprinkle of true golden molecules on the Golden Temple's mountain. I share with Jarek some digestive biscuits called Fancy Smell; they're a little bit savory because they contain "onionwater." Balancing the crinkly-stiff cellophane cookie tray in one outstretched hand, I'm inventing a new Taiji form: Crane Descends from Golden Temple with Fancy Smell. Eventually, as we reach lower altitudes, Jarek and I start getting giddy because we now believe we will make it unscathed. I start getting overconfident, then we hit a scary patch where the path is all torn up from a reconstruction job, and the stone steps lie strewn about like suitcases spilled from a bus crash. At least that's how I visualize them, remembering them from the climb up. I can't actually see them now. It's extremely hard to negotiate the way down a steep slope in pitch black, let me re-emphasize that. I catch a toe and almost trip a couple of times, go weightless in the dark, but always find my feet, noisily, clumsily, so that Jarek calls out, "You all right?" I am. I am. This is fantastic. Then at last we hit a long winding stretch of uniform and uneventful pavement five feet wide with little houses alongside it, and women stepping out of shuttered shops to greet us with the Chinese equivalent of "How ya doin'?" which translates literally as "Have you eaten?" Of course you must always say yes, because they are not really offering you food.

"It's funny there's no dogs barking," I say.

"They ate them all," Jarek says.

I'm feeling like if martial arts has taught me one thing, it's balance, and I've been brought to a time and place where I needed exactly that. My chest swells with the pride of accomplishment, and it only diminishes slightly when we arrive at the last temple of the descent. During daylight hours the path passes right through the middle of the temple courtyard, but now the gates are all locked up for the night. Jarek yells for the caretaker, who emerges at a high corner window and shouts that we need to back up and find a dirt path that goes around, which is what the locals do at night. The locals use flashlights; we won't be able to find it in the dark. Jarek pulls out his cell phone (it's his sixteen-year-old son's, actually, he's just borrowing it), and for the first and only time he resorts to a tool of illumination to guide our way. Does that ruin everything? My body tells me, No, something great was accomplished, now relax and drink beer on your laurels. But the mind says, It was almost perfect, but in the end it wasn't. It could have been perfect.

18

☆

Harmony of the Outside and the Inside

It's very depressing to come down off the mountain and back into that grim little city called Wudang. Nature took millions of years to make those mountains aesthetically perfect, humanity made Wudang polluted and ugly in a couple of decades. Now that the Taiji festival is over, there's absolutely no reason to stick around. Quick as we can we catch a bus to Shyan, an hour away, where we can get a train to Zheng Zhou, and Jarek will arrange for me to meet Madame Lü, a respected Master of an internal martial art called Xingyi. Then we will part, and I'll go on to Shaolin alone.

On the bus to Shyan the TV screens play music videos, Bollywood and Björk mixed with Sino-pop knock-offs of Avril Lavigne and Will Smith. Shyan is the truck-building capital of China. Through a bus window at night it looks big, industrial, and prosperous. The bus drops us on a busy street, and friendly fellow passengers point us toward the train station, a ten-minute walk past the red-lit parlous of little storefront whorehouses. Sometimes you can see an entire novel, an opera, in a glimpse through a doorway: a pretty teenage girl on the furthest corner of a couch, struggling to hide her repulsion as an old leering drunk with bad teeth leans toward her. It tugs the heartstrings. You want to rush in and save her, pull her out of there and get her enrolled in a dental hygienist course at community college, but what would your wife think? The other scarlet ladies have submitted to fate, watching TV, ignoring the street, their body language saying I'm numb, bored, and only grudgingly available. There's one exception, one aggressive chattery femme fatale, who races out to the sidewalk at the sight of us, all strutting hips and exaggerated lips. Drag queen? She's way too over the top to be an actual woman.

☆

Our train started in the Gobi desert, or the Afghan border, some-place as far west as you can go in China; it left days back headed for Beijing and still has nineteen hours to go. Climb the stairs, step inside, and the humidity hits, a sauna warmed slowly to ninety-eight degrees by a hundred human bodies. It reeks of orange peels, armpits, stale breath and green tea, a modern railcar jammed with sunburned frontier people who settled into the high-backed seats and made themselves comfortable days ago. There's no room for us. Jarek starts begging for a sleeper, and the brusque, no-nonsense woman who handles it says there are a couple of empty berths, kept aside for the drivers to use; if we take them and they want them later we'll have to give them back. Fine. We'll take our chances. So she leads us to the sleeper car, and then, in the cool air between cars, she changes personalities and becomes sweet and kindly, telling us she made up the stuff about the drivers, just so the other passengers wouldn't get jealous she was giving the foreign visitors the last bunks left. Oh. Thank you thank you thank you.

In the morning Jarek looks extremely grumpy, he had a snorer in his compartment. He kept nudging him awake but the guy would just apologize and fall right back into it. They should have snoring and non-snoring sections in the sleeper cars, like smoking, non-smoking. I slept fine on my top shelf, my nose six inches from the ceiling. Now it's daylight, the sun is throwing horizontal beams through the windows, and I'm stretching in the hallway, watching a fellow passenger hork a big gob up his throat, spit it on the carpet, and casually rub it in with his shoe. Glad I didn't see him doing that last night, I wouldn't have slept so freely. Would have been sniffing my pillow and wondering who the hell used it last.

☆

Zhen Zhou is a huge city of four to seven million people, depending who you ask. We arrived at seven in the morning and by ten I had a room at the Greenland Hotel kitty corner to the train station. Jarek went off to buy a bunch of martial arts DVDs for his mail order business and I tried to sleep a bit. The phone rang. Some woman said a bunch of stuff in Chinese. *Wor boo ming bai,* I said, one of my five Chinese phrases. It means I don't understand.

There was a long pause. Then, "Massagey?"

"No. No massagey."

"No massagey?"

"No."

She hung up.

Five minutes later, the phone rang again. Another woman, same deal, again I said, *Wor boo ming bai.* Then this one cooed, "Mek looooove?" No. No mek love.

Ten minutes later there's a girl at my door. Fluffy fake feathers border her cleavage; with lovely delicate hands she's demonstrating the international symbol of copulation, index finger through the doughnut. Chinese sex trade workers are a persistent bunch.

"What's a guy have to do to get some peace and quiet around here?" I ask her. *Wor boo ming bai,* she says.

☆

In the afternoon we head out to a martial arts school run by Madame Lü, who teaches an art called Xingyi, old school spelling Hsing I. She's a member of the Hue minority, the Muslims of China. The Muslims developed their own branch of Xingyi, which they sometimes call Jaio Men Quan, "righteous boxing." For centuries knowledge of this style, referred to as Henan Xingyi (after the province in which it was created), was limited to Muslims; it was jealously guarded as an effective self-defense tool against the lesser skills of the Han majority.

Madame Lü's school is way out of town, in the countryside. When we arrive she's not available—she's praying, one of her five times a day, so one of her sons sits with us and argues good-naturedly with Jarek about the history and lineages of various branches of the art. Jarek translates only occasionally. "We're talking about Mai Zhuangtu," he says at one point. "He was very famous for his leaping skills; he could get up a tree with the power of dantien, with the foot strength you develop in Xingyi."

☆

Madame Lü appears, dressed in a track suit and possessing a saintly charisma. Jarek last saw her five or six years ago, and she still remembers a question he asked then, about the difference between two related martial arts styles, Xingyi, which translates as "Shape and Intent," and Xinyi, or "Heart/Mind and Intent." According to Jarek, the style she teaches is a mix of the two and has shaded closer to Xinyi. The subtlety is lost on me, but she's been thinking of his question ever since he asked it, and wants to answer it by writing two lines of Chinese characters in chalk on the concrete floor. Jarek translates: "This is a philosophical idea. Your heart is inside, but the principles are in all shapes around you. They're all around and in your heart. The subjective perception of things, right?" Hmmm. Okay. I take a picture of her and her floor writing, and much later I'll email it to Jarek, to let him take another shot at translation, at his leisure. He will email back:

"Mind is inside while the principles are carved in Things. Things are outside but their principles are gathered in mind."

"In Martial Arts there has to be full mind control over your movements, and … it should be subconscious, without any forced intent," Jarek will write. "This is what they call the Harmony of the Outside and the Inside."

☆

"She's welcoming you to China and is happy you will be adding to the popularity of martial arts in the world," Jarek translates. I feel like I'm in the presence of someone special. Her father was a legendary Xingyi Master; she herself was seventeen and a martial arts master in 1949, the year the Communists took over. I hardly know where to start with the questions. She tells me that as a child she learned her martial art "without realizing I was learning anything, it was just play. Then one day I realized I knew it."

I'd noticed some girl students at the school, and I ask whether the techniques change when taught to boys or girls. It depends more on the individual than their gender, "on the personal under-standing of boxing principles," Jarek translates. "She quotes a classic: chopping like lightning striking the ground, or moving

upward like a dragon getting out of the water. Your own understanding of these descriptions will make your way of practicing
different. When you practice you should be as big as heaven. It
may be a little bit hard to understand, or mysterious, but when you
practice, it's almost like forgetting yourself and becoming part of
nature. Not completely, but you can get close."

She calls three of her students to demonstrate: two boys sixteen
and ten years old, and a girl, six. Xingyi is all about lightning-quick
movements; it seems like the oldest boy is just out for a stroll,
minding his own business, then suddenly he's combining a block
with a simultaneous counterstrike and straight-line full-forward
attack on an imaginary opponent. "This is a martial art that uses
speed to overcome an opponent," she points out.

The two younger kids perform the forms with less power, more
fluidity, so it's almost like dance. "You shouldn't use power when
you are just beginning practice," she explains. "A beginner doesn't
know how to release power, so it will be incorrect, and harmful for
your body."

I ask how it compares with Taiji, which can be practiced into old
age, with slow movements meant to move Chi around the body. She
says her father was practicing in his nineties, still doing the Santi
stance, the basic stance of Xingyi, which is said to link heaven,
earth, and humankind together. "He was doing it slowly, all the
movements, the linked fists and chopping, it was very relaxed and
casual—if the intent is there, you don't have to show the speed on
the outside. There is no reason why old people can't do this style."

Madame Lü announces that she would be very pleased to see
some of our martial arts skills, to see what foreigners can do with a
Chinese art. I blush and refuse at first, but Jarek joins the chorus
of encouragement. Okay. I do the first bit of Kempo One, carrying
the ancient knowledge back to China, halfway around the world

from the Kung Fu Academy in Colwood, Canada. I worry it's a lame-ass performance, and hope they're not too embarrassed for me. But they applaud freely. I'm not sure what Jarek thinks. He spares me that. For some reason he who could actually impress them declines to show them anything. Maybe he's taken to heart that Taoist mantra: It's not about showing off. Go down, not up. Stay hidden.

☆

We head outside, to the hard-packed earth of the training area, where the kids run through various routines for our benefit. Jarek bids farewell, hopping into the school's minivan to be delivered to a nearby bus stop and his own separate adventure. I really can't thank him enough, and then suddenly he's gone, and there's a huge void. Now I'm alone in a foreign land, and communication becomes a series of gestures, smiles, and fruitless searches in the phrasebook. Madame Lü has a strong sharp voice as she critiques the kids. I tape some of it and get it translated later in Beijing. Here's what her patter sounds like:

"How come you put your head this way?

"Ta-ta-ta-ta-ta-tak!

"You were *just taught* this! Why can't you do it well?

"Use your dantien to make the Chi come up into quick action!

"You should stare at the opponent, and be fast!

"practice with your heart, with your mind!"

I'm really enjoying sitting on a little plastic stool in the sun watching the kids perform. On the edge of the bare dirt field, there's a row of concrete table tennis tables with metal nets, where a gaggle of middle school girls watch the martial arts boys. Behind them the fence is painted with the slogan, "Bitter hard training improves the spirit."

☆

For dinner Madame Lü, a devout Muslim, puts on a black head scarf, and I hardly recognize her. She looks so much older and more severe, for a moment I think this woman must be her mother. But it is her, the lime green Adidas shoes give it away. The cafeteria has rough concrete walls and odd shadows from fluorescent lights that hang irregularly from beams that are nothing more than logs skinned of their bark. Money is obviously tight, but the spirit is good. When kids approach Madame Lü she wraps an arm around their shoulders affectionately. When the girl beside Madame Lü finishes and stands up to leave, she's gently ordered to sit back down and eat every single grain of rice left on her plate. The kids are not allowed to talk while eating, but you can see them mouthing words to each other, communicating silently under the clickity-clack of fifty metal spoons on metal trays.

☆

In the evening, another of Madame Lü's sons arrives. He speaks a tiny bit of English and has a Chinese–English dictionary he can use. I tell him I'm headed to Shaolin next, and he says, "Shaolin Kung Fu is," and then thumbs through his book until he finds the appropriate Chinese character, which translates as "bold, vigorous, sturdy." Then he says, "I love," and points to the character for "Allah," then quickly flips to the character for "creed."

I love Allah creed. Got it.

He gives me a ride all the way back to the heart of the city in the school minivan. On the way we stop to get a tire fixed at a repair shop with no sign, just a hundred feet of air hose snaking out and looping over itself, from a concrete shack to the road. He offers the repairman a cigarette, then one to me. I accept, and with the peace pipe shared, the sacred passing of flame, we bond. He suddenly gets much more articulate. As we drive past massive new high-rise apartment towers, he says, "Now in China there are rich and poor. A few rich have a lot of money and many poor have none. The rich send their children to college and the poor can't feed their children."

I have a feeling that twenty years ago he memorized these phrases in English class, but at that time the lesson began, "In America." In other words, it was meant to denigrate the exploitative, capitalist West. Now it applies equally to China. When he continues, the words are his own, and sound very heartfelt. "It's unfair. It was better before. But still I love my country."

19

☆

Diligent, Hardworking, and Affectionate in Networking

The bus to Shaolin is full of young Chinese army recruits in uniform, plus three tattooed Australians, two guys and a girl, lounging in the back, looking like punk extras from *Romper Stomper,* the ultraviolent skinhead movie that launched Russell Crowe to stardom. As endless blocks of brand new pastel-painted apartments roll past out the window, the bus's television plays *Ong-Bak: The Thai Warrior,* a recent martial arts movie that has led many to predict that Tony Jaa will be moviedom's next big martial arts superstar. He'll need to learn English, though. *Ong-Bak* is about a kid who perfects a lethal style of Muay Thai, the Thai indigenous kickboxing, at a Buddhist temple. When he graduates he promises the abbot that he will be a good peace-loving Buddhist and never, ever employ these bone-crushing talents he's worked so diligently to acquire. So he leaves his village and heads to the decadent, corrupt city, where he's continually thrust into predicaments that leave him no option but to kick the shit out of evildoers. It's reminiscent of Bruce Lee in all his movies, especially the way young Mr. Jaa seems so lean and *tight,* so totally tense and wound up, even when he's just practicing, like when he shows off his command of the basic Muay Thai moves at the start of the movie. The best thing about *Ong Bak* is the built-in instant replays: the stunts are shown again and again, in slow motion from different angles, to prove it's all real. No wires, tricks, or special effects.

☆

The Australians have done their homework: they've arranged themselves a stay at a Kung Fu school listed in that obese brick of a book, *Lonely Planet's Guide to China*. Me, I'm never that organized. I'll just wing it, see what's there when I get there. Before that, the bus stops on the edge of the town of Deng Feng, below Shaolin, where there's a Place of Historical Interest for us tourists to pile out and visit. It's Song Yang Academy, the site of a university dating back to 484 AD. The best feature is two gnarled and balding cypress trees, "General 1 and General 2," planted in 100 BC and still alive. But the Aussies can't be bothered to go in and tour the place, they sit in the shade at a canteen outside and get hustled by a poacher from another Kung Fu school, trying to get them to switch to his school instead. He's even brought along an exhibit, a big goofy friendly American in short tight gym shorts like people wore in the '70s, who signed up yesterday and has no clue why he's now here and not at the school. He's never done any martial arts in his life but sure enjoyed this morning. "Learned some cool stuff!" he barks cheerfully. For some reason the salesman ignores me, which is fine. I'm hoping for a school a bit more legit than one that hustles people at tour bus pit stops.

When we get to Shaolin the road ends at a massive parking lot full of buses like ours, and a brand new courtyard surrounded by modern shops selling swords and tourist trinkets, Buddhas and DVDs. The soldiers file off, and then the Aussies stumble out with all their gear. Whoever was supposed to meet them is not here. They're trying to find a phone. I'm wandering around hoping a martial arts school will magically pop into view, when three local guys start waving a martial arts school contract in my face. The contract is in English but it's not informative, it just has spaces for name, passport number, and all that. I'd like to ask a few questions before I sign anything, but my spoken Chinese amounts to five phrases, and their spoken English zero. Suddenly two tough-looking aggressive dudes in black leather jackets come up and growl something at the other three, who back off. One of the dudes makes the international gesture for "Do you need a place to sleep?" (Make to pray with the hands, then turn them and lay your head on them.) Yes, I do need a place to sleep. He points toward his car, which has black tinted windows and is the first souped-up muscle car I have seen in all of China. These guys definitely come across like thugs, but what the hell. Take me to your leader.

So we pile in the car and I look up the word for school in my phrasebook: the pronunciation is something like *shwair syao*. So I start saying "Kung Fu *shwair syao*? Kung Fu *shwair syao*?" And they answer back, "Kung Fu? Kung Fu?" Now we're getting somewhere. We stop at their hotel, which is really a restaurant. Behind it maybe three extended families live in a warren of rooms, and two of the rooms are set up to rent out to tourists. The place is full of kids, and wives all dolled up in tight black slutty clothes even though they're home looking after kids and babies, and the bathroom tiles have pictures of naked ladies on them. The whole place just feels weird. I haggle a little and feel I got a deal, about eighty yuan, or eight U.S. dollars, and then the next thing I know I'm in the back seat of the car again, heading into the hills over a bumpy half-washed-out dirt road with jolting knee-deep potholes, and one of the leather dudes passes me back a cigarette and I'm hoping they are not as thuggish as they look. Otherwise this is my last smoke, and I'm about to disappear into a shallow grave in some lonely, rocky ravine. But soon there's a big three-story white building in the distance that must be a Kung Fu school.

When we get there, two hundred and fifty Chinese boys come over to check me and the car out, plus one giant German kid named Jan, who is seventeen years old. He's the only foreigner at this school, and he's able to explain to me that this is the best school at Shaolin, because it's owned and overseen by the guy who teaches martial arts to the Shaolin monks at the temple, a guy who is renowned in China for his Seven Star Form. "He's like a celebrity in Chinese martial arts," says Jan. "I've got his DVD." Perfect. I'm brought to an office where one entire wall is a twenty-foot-by-ten-foot larger-than-life color photo of him performing the Seven Star Form for the president of China (not the current one, but the previous one, with the bad posture and big glasses), and I sign up for two days, starting tomorrow. Jan the German sits in on the negotiations and helps me explain to the school officials that after my training, on the third morning, Geoff the foreign correspondent and his translator (actually Dongdong, his girlfriend) will come down from Beijing, so he and I will want to interview the Master. Ten o'clock Saturday morning. Agreed.

☆

Then it's back into the blackmobile, back to the restaurant for dinner. Little kids in China don't wear diapers, there's just an open slit in their pants that lets them squat and pee and poo wherever. When I come out of my room one of the women of the place is wiping her toddler's ass through that gap with a filthy bit of cloth that's totally inadequate to the task. A minute later she's my waitress, handing me a menu that's all Chinese. Did she wash her hands? I doubt it. I point in my phrasebook to steamed green vegetables, eggs, and rice.

There are only four tables in the place. At one of them pretty much the entire contingent of foreigners studying at Shaolin are dining out together. Since it's off-season, late October, there are only six of them (in summer there are more than a hundred), all in their twenties: one Brit, two Americans, and three Mexicans. I invite myself over to do whatever the Chinese equivalent of breaking bread is. Suck noodles? There's Joshua from England, Bournemouth to be precise, he's twenty-three, with a degree in physics. Impressions of China? "It's cool. The Chinese way of life takes some getting used to."

What aspect?

"Everything is filthy," says a fat kid with thick red hair tied back in a ponytail.

"Yeah, they have medieval hygiene habits here, that's one of the main things," Josh says.

"Here everyone cheats you out of your money and does it with a smile and sees nothing wrong with it," says the fat kid, an American named Page.

How did you choose your school?

"I chose the one with the Western toilet," says Josh. "*Your* school just has a long trough to shit in, no separate compartments, no doors."

"And the Chinese are very curious about Western plumbing," adds Page. "A dozen of 'em will gather 'round to have a look."

☆

A few years ago the area around the Temple was a crazy mishmash of trinket shops and competing privately owned martial arts schools, but the Buddhist monks of Shaolin have been getting more business savvy lately, more proactive in ridding the vicinity of tacky tourist traps. They've also trademarked the name "Shaolin." Most of the schools and all the shops have been levelled, and the two-kilometer walk from the bus parking lot to the Temple is now a stroll along a wooded path, or at least it will be wooded when the trees grow up. (Maybe it's appropriate that the trees are young: in Mandarin the name Shaolin means small forest, in the sense of young trees.) To take the stroll and enter the Temple complex you have to pay a hundred and ten yuan at the gate. Twelve U.S. dollars, which is pretty steep for the average Chinese. But plenty seem happy to pay up. Judging by the number of tour buses in the parking lot, the monks are making a killing.

One major school still operates inside the gates, called Tagou Wushu School. It has three thousand students, on top of the ten thousand at its main school down the hill in Deng Feng. In all, there are seventy thousand students studying Kung Fu in Deng Feng. The guys at the table all study at Tagou because you can live there in Western university dorm-style rooms with television and flush toilets.

Joshua says they're learning "Shaolin Wushu," which is a contemporary version of the traditional Shaolin style. "The Temple was destroyed in the late 1920s, and it's never really recovered its Kung Fu since then. The forms practiced now are the old forms—they have the same stances and the same movements—but people in most of the schools don't really know what they mean. And they've changed the forms to make them look a little flashier. Only a few schools still practice the old style. Your school, in fact, is the best for that. But for me Tagou is fine. My teacher in England is Chinese and trained in China for fifteen years, so this is exactly the way I trained at home."

You might be surprised to learn that three of the six young men at this table had zero martial arts experience when they arrived at Shaolin. "I'm doing mainly Taiji because it's easier for a fatty," says Page. "It's slow, but it's hard to move *that* slow. I always get yelled at for moving too fast."

I turn to the three Mexicans. One says, "I can't talk about it, I hurt my knee." And the other two don't speak English.

The other American, Dave, who appears to be of Chinese descent, is a more serious student. He says, regarding motivation, "It's not that you want to be the best, you just find it beautiful and you can't stop training once you start. That's it, you know? When you train Kung Fu there are steps to achieve but there is no end. Kung Fu is for life. When you're younger you want acrobatics, you want power in middle age, and in old age you want to know your body better."

"That captures it so well," says Josh. "It's the training, the doing it day by day. You feel yourself get a little bit better and you want more. That's what the words Kung Fu mean: hard work. It never finishes."

"We train six hours a day, six days a week," says Dave. "We try to train with the Chinese, but that's not possible, they do eight hours a day and then have regular school in the evening. And the teachers are much less patient with them."

"They kick 'em, and treat 'em like animals," says Josh, and then everyone is talking at once.

"They have a special room in our school for beating people, or so I was told, beating people with sticks," says Page. "They'll say like, 'Oh yeah I had three sticks,' and it means they broke three sticks on them before they stopped hitting them, and the sticks are the staffs we use for training; they're more than an inch thick."

"It's really hard to break those sticks, these are not little sticks, these are weapons," says Dave.

"It makes them tougher," says Page. They all agree on that.

Josh says, "Jan, the German guy at your school, has a harder training. He does a few exercises that are extreme, you could say. He does Iron Palm, hitting his palms against bags and posts for half an hour without stopping, doing push-ups on fingertips, and plunging his hands into boiling water."

☆

When I get up to my school the next morning, I'm assigned to Shu, a twenty-one-year-old kid who's in charge of training the school's six best Sanda fighters. Sanda is a sport art, basically kick-boxing with throws. It's generally about scoring points, there are few knock-outs. Shu gets his six-man team to set up some mats in the sunshine, and while they proceed to thoroughly exhaust themselves sparring, he teaches me the Tiger form, and works on a form of his own, using a beautiful old sword with antique characters on it he can't read. The blade isn't super sharp but the point could easily kill. It's impressive to watch the way he can wave it in a figure eight around his ears. When he sets it down to continue my instruction, I eagerly offer to show him what I already know, basically the two forms I've learned from Sifu Bob, but Shu waves me off, he has zero curiosity about that. I feel a bit hurt. The Tiger form he teaches me, also called Small Frame Hong Quan, is not terribly different from what I'm used to, except the hands never form fists, even when striking, and there's one move—where you keep your feet together, your back straight, one arm straight down your side, and you kneel down as low as you can get—that's a killer on the knees. The school kids in their burgundy track suits and dusty canvas shoes who gather to watch can't be impressed by my struggle to raise my sorry ass back to standing. Shu keeps asking me how to say in English the moves he's teaching me, for each of which there is usually a simple Chinese word. I haven't a clue. He gets frustrated and wanders off, telling me to just sit in the shade and visualize what I've learned. Less work for him—since he can't see my thoughts he doesn't have to critique me.

☆

They assign me to share a room with Jan, the seventeen-year-old German. It's right on the main floor, across from the canteen that sells soft drinks, snacks, beer (!), and cheap canvas Kung Fu shoes. On the wall next to my bed some previous occupant has marked off the days in pen, eighty-eight in all, grouped in little blocks of five, four with a slash through. Is this a prison? In some ways it feels like it: there's that common trough to squat over and shit into in the bathroom, and the beds have no mattresses—each is just a wooden platform with a blanket over it. Even Jan, who claims to love it here, crosses out each day with a big X on his wall calendar. He first studied Kung Fu when he was eight, from a Frenchman in India, where he spent much of his childhood; his mother is an artist and writer, deeply into Indian mythology. He shows me a book she wrote and illustrated, all about dragons in various cultures, but mostly Chinese, Indian, and Celtic.

He's lonely here, obviously. One time I come back to our room to find him sitting on his bed leafing through a photo album his friends in Germany made for him. "I haven't looked at it for three, four weeks," he says, "because it's not good to see that book too often, to remind you of all the good times you were having."

So why did he come here to learn Kung Fu?

"I just love it, I don't know why. And this is the best place to learn, the best school. They're teaching the old style here, where you don't often hit clearly, it's more hidden attack. You don't hit with the fist, you more hit with the palm, not like at Tagou, where they got really many many students, and they change the style to make it easier to do and easier to teach. Everyone can do it there, but not here."

"Are you getting the philosophy? Because you don't speak the language, and no one here speaks English or German."

"I learn the forms and everything and all the Chinese names of every step, and my teacher tries to tell me the meanings, and I understand a few, like the tiger opening his mouth. For all sixty movements of the Tiger I know the Chinese names for it, but not always what they mean."

He shows me an oversized notebook he keeps, wherein he has mapped out each routine he's learned with little drawings of stickmen, and written descriptions in German underneath of what's going on, and an attempt at spelling the Chinese word for it. One of the forms uses his weapon of choice, the crescent spade. It's a long pole with a deadly crescent-shaped blade at one end, and a square metal blade like a shovel at the other. (You can see it in the film *Crouching Tiger, Hidden Dragon*: Michelle Yeoh picks one from a rack of weapons during her protracted battle with Zhang Ziyi, but for some reason she decides it's too heavy and drops it immediately, shattering the floor tiles.) "It's a really famous weapon because it's a symbol of Buddhism as well," Jan says.

"How does that work?"

"The crescent shape is the moon, symbolizing the sky, or heaven, and the spade down here symbolizes the earth, and the stick symbolizes the people connecting the earth and heaven. Combining all of those in one weapon, it's a really powerful weapon, and it's also good luck."

☆

I have a brief meeting with the Master, dressed in the orange robes of a monk, and thereafter catch occasional glimpses of him coming and going in a chauffeured car, in Western clothes, usually a black turtleneck sweater, or coming down from his office to greet high-roller business types who pull through the gates in massive SUVs. His Buddhist name is Shi Yongzhi, and he is bald, with an unkempt salt and pepper beard. He seems dour and preoccupied. Jan tells me that in the four months he's been here, he's never seen the Master smile. He doesn't come across as very Buddhist, I have to say. He should be meditating most of the time, shouldn't he? And another non-Buddhist activity goes on around here: according to Jan, the school is like Tagou—the kids take a beating when they get out of line. He promises to show me the pile of broken sticks as evidence, but I never see any sticks, or any beatings, maybe because I've made it so clear I'm a journalist. But I'm going to ask the Master about it when "my translator" gets here.

Meanwhile Shu's handing me off to other guys to guide me deeper into the Tiger form. There is no shortage of young men hanging around the school, working for peanuts probably. One of them I call Mr. Wrong, because his only word of English is "Wrong!" I try to get into my routine, and he's shouting, "Wrong, wrong, wrong!" There's another I call Dr. No, because *his* sole word is "No." Dr. No is amazing to watch; his version of the Tiger is markedly different from Shu's and Mr. Wrong's. His has no soft edges of flow—it's all a crazed high-voltage explosion of abrupt strikes. He'll rip through it, giving it everything he has, then prompt me to imitate. "No no no no no NO!"

☆

At meal times Jan and I go to the cafeteria, push aside a filthy curtain of heavy plastic strips to enter the kitchen, and pick up our meal, pretty much always the same food. Rice or bread (the bread is steamed, not baked, so it has no crust and is damp and doughy), bean sprouts, scrambled egg, and a steamed vegetable like cabbage or pumpkin. You can see old grease marks on the bowls, like they'd just been rinsed in cold water rather than properly cleaned. I feel like gagging just thinking about it. On day two I have my chopsticks in my hand when I pass through that filthy curtain, and the plastic strips fall against me like giant hungry tongues. I put out my hand to ward them off, and a tongue licks my chopsticks. I think about washing them again—there's a single tap outside with warm water where I could rinse them—but decide I'm being too paranoid. A couple of hours later I start to feel queasy; I can tell from the way saliva's pooling in my mouth that soon I'll be barfing. I just pray it comes back up the throat and not out the other end: if I get the runs there is no way I could face the common trough and the giggling kiddies that inevitably, unselfconsciously gather to catch a glimpse of my dinky there. So I go for a walk. I'm wearing my white polyester training pants from the Kung Fu Academy, and no underwear. That's because yesterday I tried to wash my clothes for the first time since I left Beijing. Every piece of clothing I had was dirty because I was travelling light, with just one small backpack like a schoolboy would use to carry books to school. So I washed almost everything I had, including all five pairs of underwear, and hung it all out to dry on some metal lines at the side of the school. There were no clothes pegs so I just draped everything over. Then the wind picked up and all my clothes fell in the dirt, then a sudden rainstorm hit, they got soaked, the dirt stuck to them, and they were worse than ever. When I went to pick them up I had to shoo away a flea-bitten half-wild dog sniffing at them. So now, with the runs about to hit, I'm getting really worried about a worst-case scenario of anal leaking with only one layer of white polyester between me and humiliation, so I go marching out the gates as fast as I can while holding my sphincter tight, and waddle up the road like a penguin on fast forward, and turn into some dry, cropless terraced fields, where I puke up a semi-solid lunch and shit out breakfast in a pure liquid. I feel much better immediately. Then I check my white pants and they're mercifully stain-free, and I feel even better.

☆

But I skip my afternoon workout, and can't face dinner, taking just a tiny bit of rice and some rosehip tea Jan made for me. What a sweet kid he is. We're sitting around his room when the door opens and in walks the English teacher. I forgot to mention I'd gone up to the classrooms, where the kids had regular school in the evening on top of their Kung Fu all day, and I'd dropped in on the English class, where a tiny woman in a man's black suit tried to tell me things in English but I couldn't make any sense out of her garble of syllables, which the kids picked up on ("Teacher can't speak English!!") and became rowdy as hell. I drew the five interlocking Olympic rings on the chalkboard and told them Beijing was getting the 2008 summer games, and my country, Canada, was getting the 2010 winter games. Then they said, "Sing a song!" so I sang "Oh Canada" loudly and with feeling, which always feels good, not that I'm super-patriotic or anything. Canadians are too smug and persnickety.

(In a few days when Geoff arrives with Dongdong, at some point I'll ask her, what three words would you use to describe the Chinese national character? She'll say, "Diligent, hardworking, and affectionate in networking.'" The last one has something to do with *guanxi,* that Chinese term for both a circle of friends and essential connections in business and in life. Actually, in China the two are the same. Dongdong will immediately turn the question around and ask Geoff and me for three words to describe our quaint little nation's citizens. You guessed it. "Smug and persnickety." I know that's only two, and we'll fail to come up with a third, so I guess it should be "unimaginative.")

Anyway, this English teacher comes in Jan's room uninvited and sits herself down, wanting to talk. She hadn't realized Jan spoke good English until she'd seen him talking to me, so now she wants to make up for lost opportunities.

"Miss English Teacher, I need to ask you a question," I say.

"Yongtai Temple is very near," she replies.

"No, I need to ask you something."

"Only five hundred meters."

"No, I want to ask you a question."

"Question? What is your daughter's name?"

"Grace."

"What is meaning?"

Grace is not in my phrasebook, so we use Jan's dictionaries to go from English to German, then German to Chinese.

"Yu May," I say. That's grace in the sense of gracefulness. Not in the sense of God's grace.

"Oh, beautiful."

"Yu May go now," I joke. But she doesn't. In that case I'll ask my question: "Do you hit the students, when they misbehave? When they are bad. Do you hit them?"

After a few more rephrasings she seems to get what I'm asking.

"Yes," she says.

"Like this?" I make a slapping gesture.

"Yes."

She hangs around until the bell rings, causing her to jump up, shouting unhappily, "Oh, crass!" And she's out the door at a run.

☆

The next day I get up at five thirty, along with the two hundred and fifty kids in the school, for the morning assembly, and listen to them chant part of the Heart Sutra, the most famously poetical bit of Buddhist instruction, as they stand in the dark in a light drizzling rain. The rain means Shu's six-man Sanda team will set up their mats and train in the cafeteria today. The smallest of them is assigned to teach me. He takes it very seriously, like he fears he might be punished if I don't learn. "He has a hard life, I think," Jan says later when I tell him about it. "The other kids beat on him when the teacher's not around, because he's the smallest and came later than the others."

At breakfast rosehip tea is again all I can handle. Then it's time to watch Jan go through his Iron Fist training. He has a heavy canvas bag about the size of an airline pillow, packed full of some kind of dried black beans, like peppercorns. When I go out to the hard-packed dirt courtyard to watch him, he has set the bag on a concrete bench, and from a low horse stance he's pounding away on it, alternating the front and back of his hands. His training also involves punching a wooden pole, and remaining in push-up position on the fingertips of one hand for as long as he can stand it. Then he shifts to push-up position on one fist. Between exercises he spends a lot of time clapping his hands together, "with power, so they get really red and everything, so you rub them really hot," he says. "If you don't rub them then your skin dies and falls off, but if you rub them it stays alive but gets really hard. And you have to slap the wooden pole with power so it really hurts, it should hurt, and then you rub your hands again."

Likely he has the most swollen, calloused knuckles of any seventeen-year-old kid in the world. It seems crazy to me. It's supposed to turn his fists into club-like weapons, hard as rock and deadened to pain, but probably all it will do is lead to a nasty case of arthritis in old age. How often is he really going to use those fists anyway? He's not the type to get into Mixed Martial Arts–type fighting; he's more the sweet-natured gentle giant type. Jan's teacher is only in his late thirties, I would guess, and the first two fingers of his right hand are like fat sausages, completely misshapen lumps of scar tissue. His specialty is doing a one-armed hand stand on those two fingers, and his ultimate goal is to do a hand stand on one finger. I'm not sure why. To me that spells Freak Show, not Kung Fu.

☆

Outside the gates there's a big stack of red bricks, twenty feet long by four feet high and wide. Jan's teacher selects a dozen or so good ones, and brings them over to a concrete bench, where Jan is expected to break two at once with the blade of his palm. Eventually he wants Jan to be capable of breaking three with one blow. It's tough because Jan must hold the bricks off the edge of the bench with one hand, and break the overhang off with the other. Physics is not helping. If both ends were on benches, with a gap in the middle, it would be a snap. Today every time Jan strikes, only one brick breaks. Sometimes it's the top one, sometimes the bottom. He's seriously hurting the blade of his hand, you can see it swelling. Some of the other teachers gather around to watch. Everyone has an opinion, but no one is testing their theory on themselves. It's all talk, only Jan is whapping those bricks.

We go up to his teacher's room, furnished sparsely with a bed and a desk, where a big pot of water simmers on a hotplate. A cloth bag of Chinese roots and herbs soaking in the pot has turned the water deep purple. The teacher takes it off the element and places it before Jan, who sits crosslegged on the floor. Steam meanders up toward the ceiling. I stick my hand in, and declare that it's not as

unbearable as I was expecting. This causes Jan's teacher to put it
back on the hotplate and crank the heat. When he decides it's truly
hot Jan is instructed to plunge his hands in. He balls them into fists
first, hesitates to summon courage, and finally thrusts them into
the pot. He leans back and away, twisting his face in agony, his
arms stretched, putting maximum distance between brain and
pain. His hands stay submerged in the hot purple liquid. One of
the school's vice-headmasters and another teacher wander in
through the open door, sit themselves down on the bed, and watch.
The vice-headmaster smokes a cigarette, letting the ash grow an
inch long. Beads of sweat break out on Jan's forehead, and occasionally he makes a quiet gasp of pain, but Jan's Master and the two
Chinese gentlemen ignore him as they banter among themselves.
Through clenched teeth he tells me, "It's okay as long as I don't
move my hands, or open my fists. The medicine is supposed to
make your bones really strong, so they don't break. I got hurt in my
palms from hitting the bricks, but when you put it in the water, it's
okay."

Jan's teacher gives him the afternoon off, for the first time ever.
It seems like everyone at the school has things to do. A barber has
come up from town, and all the kids are getting their heads freshly
shaven. New uniforms are being given to the most poorly dressed.
Rumor has it that tomorrow the entire school will head up to the
Temple to be extras in a film or television shoot. The Shaolin
Temple has recently announced plans to make a twenty-million-
dollar Kung Fu movie of its own, based on the true story of a band
of Shaolin monks who were hired by an emperor to fight Japanese
pirates in the sixteenth century. The Temple presents this not as a
money grab but an attempt to reclaim their name and heritage
from a thousand Chop Socky movies that have used the word
Shaolin in their titles without permission. Finally a movie will be

made that does justice to the Shaolin tradition. Chan Buddhism was born here, after all, and later spread to Japan, where it is called Zen. Shaolin is not just about Kung Fu, it's a philosophy of life.

☆

Liberated for the afternoon, Jan wants to head to Tagou and hang out with the Westerners there. It's maybe a kilometer's walk up over a rock outcrop and then along a dusty ravine to the main road, where we flag down a bus for a quick five-minute ride up to the Temple parking lot. We skirt the gates and head over to Tagou. A big banner in Chinese and English proclaims that the school's women's Sanda team won gold in the recent National Games, the same ones I'd been watching on TV in Wudang. I did see some Sanda, but it was dull: the contestants wore headgear and chest pads, and it seemed like you scored points for touches, so the punches and kicks didn't need great force.

We weave our way through hundreds of boys in bright red sweat suits, plus one six-year-old still in civvies, bawling his eyes out, clinging to his mother's hip. He's about to be left here, poor little guy. Torn from mommy's loving arms to regular beatings with inch-thick sticks. Jan leads me up several flights of stairs to Page the fat redhead's room, where the guys I met the other night are splayed out on chairs and beds watching *Training Day* with Denzel Washington on DVD. Somehow a classic indolent North American undergraduate's dorm room has been meticulously re-created in the heart of China: ashtrays full of butts, candy bar wrappers and dirty clothes all over. Plus guns and ammo: the boys are all deeply into life-sized plastic assault rifles, complete with scopes and lasers, that shoot little red plastic bullets the size of Tic Tacs. Page says, "Since we got these guns, we gotta sleep next to 'em, cause we just be poppin' in, shootin' each other."

Today Josh the Englishman is in extreme pain—one of the Mexicans, a skilled fighter with a baby face, caught him with a kick up under the rib cage while sparring this morning, and damaged cartilage or something. Page the fat boy has scrapped all plans to work out today, he's thinking of heading to Zheng Zhou just to buy some decent Western whiskey. I don't know why he thinks he needs Western alcohol, everywhere I've been in China the local beer has always been satisfactory, and often excellent. An Australian named Nick drops by with a liter of Vietnamese snake liquor. "It's good for rheumatism, good for bones and kidneys, good for sexual function," he claims. "I even saw the bottle it came out of: the snake was coiled in it, set up so he looked poised to strike." Peer pressure forces everyone to take a swig; only Jan refuses. It's not bad, definitely better than *baijiu*.

In the end only four of the eight guys in the room can summon the energy to go down for the afternoon's three-hour Kung Fu session. Page isn't one of them. "I'm taking my last week slow," he says.

"Don't you want to go out with a bang?" asks Nick.

"Yeah. A slow bang."

I'm having trouble getting my mind around the idea that people could come halfway around the world to learn Kung Fu and then wimp out like Page and two of the Mexicans, glumly sitting in a half-dark dorm room watching Hollywood movies on a sunny afternoon in the symbolic birthplace of Chinese martial arts. Since they're paying six hundred U.S. dollars a month, I guess they—and Tagou school's administrators—figure they can do what they please. Wouldn't want to push them too hard and send them scurrying off home. But pushing might be the best thing for these young dudes. No one has ever pushed them to accomplish anything, so they haven't. The threat of a light beating would do them a world of good. It would certainly get them up off their asses.

☆

Because the day has turned sunny and shirt-sleeves warm, the training session takes place on a hill above the school, on the site of another school that was torn down a few years back. Small cypress trees have been planted here, but in one place there's a tile floor twenty yards square, still intact, an indoor floor outdoors, perfect for practice. The instruction is one-on-one, and the four Kung Fu teachers are younger than their students. Teaching foreigners is a plum job for recent graduates of the school. Besides teaching they're expected to keep improving their own Kung Fu, and are tested twice a year to make sure their technique is tops. They drive their students hard, but take no pleasure in it. It's just the way it's done here. Kung Fu means results achieved through hard work, after all. I ask Nick if he's seen the younger Chinese students beaten.

"Yeah, it's always a bit of a shock when you see a six-year-old being kicked in the chest and whipped with a stick," he says. "Shocking at first, but that's how they discipline the students, and it works, it's effective. You don't make the same mistake twice if the punishment is that severe. And it doesn't kill you, a bit of pain, a bit of humiliation. You do feel sorry for them, but that's what they're used to, they've grown up here, that's their reality."

☆

Afterward I head down to the town of Deng Feng, where Geoff has booked me into a room in the best hotel in town. I have some time to wander around before he and Dongdong arrive, and come across a Chinese opera presented outdoors on a stage set up in a vacant lot (the crowd is mostly grannies and babies), then walk the streets trying to decipher the strange English on shop signs. Sugar Wine The Non-staple Foodstuff Criticize The Zero. What could that mean? Is it like, Sugar Wine for Special Occasions, Nothing Else Will Do? Gotta have *some* meaning. Life is a search for meaning, mostly fruitless. When Geoff and Dongdong arrive in the evening we party in their room. Not really *party* party, because Geoff is a teetotaler, has been all his life. I'm the only one drinking beer, and then I get an urge to light up one of those cigarettes Madame Lü's son gave me.

"Can I smoke?"

"Yes," says Geoff.

"Yes?!!!" cries Dongdong. "How come in cabs, if the driver smokes, you roll down window and tell him to stop?"

"Because Brian asked. Canadians ask! Chinese never ask."

"He is one man. Taxi driver is one man. Why you say Canadian and Chinese? Some Chinese ask."

"No Chinese ask!" Geoff says, quite venomously. I've touched a nerve.

Now it degenerates into a domestic spat. Dongdong has a deep resentment of the way Geoff dismisses Chinese patriotism as propaganda. "It's okay to love your country but they ram it down your throat," he says. Dongdong does love her country. When someone sings a beautiful patriotic song on TV, it touches her, and she's not about to apologize for it. On the other hand, Geoff's been working on a story about how the Chinese use psychiatric hospitals to lock up pro-democracy dissidents without trial. The term *dissident* can sound grandiose, like a person who has made a lifelong commitment to challenging the one-party monolith that runs China, but often a dissident here is just a regular guy filing a specific, legitimate complaint about local government corruption. Next thing he knows he's imprisoned with violent psychotics and at the mercy of sadistic guards. Of course you don't hear about that on television here, which infuriates Geoff even more when some TV crooner starts warbling some state-supported song about how great the country is.

I excuse myself to get my cigarettes. By the time I'm back, the air has cleared a little. A cease fire is in effect. They're in bed together, under the covers but with all their clothes on, watching the Miss Chinese Cosmo beauty pageant. The six finalists include an American with a California Valley Girl accent who keeps apologizing for not speaking Chinese well, and a Malaysian whose specialty is salsa dancing. So contestants from any country can enter, except they gotta be ethnically pure Chinese. It's racist, essentially. "Up until three years ago beauty pageants weren't allowed in China. Now they've exploded," Geoff says.

"You can't suppress the worship of youth and beauty," I say. "Even at the Wudang Taiji fest, when the awards were given at the end, it was cold and rainy, but a bunch of tall beauties in slinky red dresses materialized out of nowhere to hand them out."

☆

Next morning we pull up in a taxi at the gates of the school, in bright sunshine. We're escorted up to the Master's office, an even more impressive office than the one with the giant photo of the Master and the president. Instead of a desk there is a giant tree root that has been carved and polished to serve as a multilevelled platform for making and serving tea. This one is particularly impressive, especially the carvings of two dragons the size of house cats pushing a giant pearl with their tongues. I've seen lesser tea ceremony tree roots all over China—the first was in a department store across the street from Geoff's place in Beijing, losing business to the Starbucks. My first few days in China I went there every afternoon and used my phrasebook to have nonsensical conversations with a young man in a wrinkled white shirt who sold the tea. He was always brewing up another pot, which involves adding boiling water to a porcelain cup crammed full of leaves, straining it through a stainless steel sieve into a tiny glass tea pot, and pouring it out into dainty little one-slurp cups hardly bigger than thimbles. The first soak of the leaves in boiling water is quickly discarded, that's just washing the leaves. Then each succeeding soak requires a slightly longer time to steep, so that the same strength of flavor is achieved each time. It keeps the tea maker busy with a little ritual, but not so preoccupied that he can't happily sit and chat.

The Master sits behind his giant polished tree root in a black turtleneck sweater that says Vasco Yachts. We arrange ourselves on little stools across from him, but he's not satisfied and commands us to shift to the empty stools at the end, so that we're within easy serving reach for him. Time for tea and talk.

Things get off to a shaky start when I ask whether Shaolin monks can be married. I've noticed an attractive thirtyish woman around the school who doesn't seem to be doing much as far as work goes, and who dresses to the nines in tight sequined sweaters, designer jeans, and black high heels. It's like she's acting in the wrong movie: she should be starring in a Hong Kong gangster flick, not *Shaolin Schoolkids.* Someone told me she was the Master's wife, but the language barrier made me less than certain I'd understood. But as it turns out, yes, he is married, because he became a monk later in life. If you join the Temple as a boy and take your monk's vows as a young man, then you can never marry. But if you already have a wife, you don't have to renounce her when you join the Temple. He explains this quite curtly, then tells me it was very rude to ask a monk this question. Dongdong, the translator, is caught in the crossfire.

"Now, Dongdong," I ask her. "He is famous for his Seven Star Form, okay? Did he choose that form, or how did he come to specialize in that form?"

"You cannot say he specialized, he just practiced it in recent years—it's internal, its movements are more delicate than most Shaolin Kung Fu. It's very ancient, it's from the Sung dynasty, the twelfth century."

"Internal, like Taiji?"

"Quite different thing, actually." Dongdong laughs nervously, which makes me laugh nervously. The Master scowls and goes about the business of preparing more tea. He talks at the same time, then Dongdong translates, "Actually Seven Star Form is similar to the movements of the constellation of the sky, which has seven stars. Its movements are limited to what is in the atmosphere."

Time to shift gears. "The children training here, are they also receiving training in Buddhist concepts and practices?"

"Actually the students are learning Buddhism now," Dongdong dutifully translates. "Shaolin is closely related to Chan Buddhism. Every morning they have to recite a sutra, about merciful Buddha helping people. You have to be merciful, and kind, and understand the suffering of people."

Oh yeah? And still beat the living shit out of the kids, eh? The time has come to ask that question. Of course I phrase it more delicately than that, and probably in translation Dongdong rephrases it even more delicately. "On that issue of suffering," I begin, "the training here by our standards seems quite tough, and also we think of Buddhism as a very peace-loving religion, like in other countries there are Buddhists who won't even kill a fly—"

"Fly?" Dongdong interrupts.

"Like an insect, a bug."

"Oh. Oh."

"Here it seems they discipline the students quite hard, even to the point of hitting them with thick sticks, which seems to be against Buddhist practice. So I'm wondering if he sees a contradiction in that, or how he justifies that?"

Dongdong looks unhappy. I think she was expecting a nice friendly chat over tea with a nice mellow Buddhist monk, who would talk about the unconditional love for humankind all Buddhists are supposed to cultivate, and instead the questions are tough and the monk is unfriendly. She's just Geoff's girlfriend, for God's sake.

"We are very strict with students because in order to learn martial arts, strictness is inevitable," she translates. "When people are young, they don't have the awareness or sense to treat themselves harshly; you have to push them to learn things. So it's reasonable to be very strict. Also you should show them by actions, and treat yourself very strictly too, so the students will be impressed and learn quickly with better effects."

☆

I really don't like this man. His covering an entire wall with a larger-than-life photo of himself put me off before I ever met him. He does seem awfully vain for a Buddhist, and I'm not the only one who thinks so. Dongdong says as much herself, after listening to him take a tangent and veer off-subject to tell us about the big Wushu convention they'd had here a few years back, where competitors came from fifty-eight countries around the world. He had practiced very hard for it, and when he competed, the judges were so flabbergasted by his brilliance that they stopped cold, they just didn't know how to score him. They had to have a meeting, right then and there, really just to confirm what they all felt: that he deserved a score much higher than all the others. Just in case we're still not impressed, he adds, "I was the only one doing traditional Shaolin Kung Fu, and I faced greater pressure at that moment because *everyone* was watching. And then the judges gave me the highest score."

"How often does he practice?"

"He says he is always practicing: when he is drinking tea with us he is practicing, and when he does calligraphy, he is practicing martial arts."

This reminds me of a story I'd been told in Wudang, about a Taiji Master who once spent a whole morning in bed, until his wife yelled at him to get up and do something constructive. "I am, I've just done my form eight times," he answered. So I pass that story along to the Shaolin Master, and without cracking a smile, he tells me I've failed to understand his point. "Because it's very mysterious," Dongdong translates. "Later he will practice calligraphy for us, using martial arts techniques, and you will see it's different. If you want to do one movement well, you have to practice every day for a year. Martial arts and calligraphy are the same that way."

He continues to make pot after pot of tea, letting us sample a variety of leaves. "To study martial arts is like making tea, it's particular and delicate," he tells us. "You need to understand what kind of tea leaves to use, and a certain temperature of water. The first time, you steep it five seconds, the second time seven seconds, and the third time nine seconds, and in this way the tea will taste the same for the guests every time. Recently I wrote an article about tea, calligraphy, and martial arts. It took three days to write," he says. He swivels in his chair and makes a pretense of searching on the shelf behind him, even though the paper is right on top of the pile. He hands it to Dongdong. "It's not very good," he says. False modesty, I suppose. Here's a snippet of his essay, translated by

Geoff's secretary back in Beijing: "In tea ceremony, we sit respect-fully, wash hands, burn incense, clean pot and cups. It's just like the breathing control before practicing the quan (Chinese boxing) that one prepares himself for burst-out. The water pouring into cups is like the smooth and integrated actions of Shaolin quan, for example to give out like releasing a strong tiger, and to withdraw like a swift cat."

The Master leads us up to the top floor, to a sunlit room set up as a calligraphy studio. He's going to demonstrate his Kung Fu-influenced brush strokes for us. He's extremely solemn about it, and to me the whole exercise comes across as merely an extension of his vanity, but maybe I'm being too hard on him. He says it's good to cultivate this kind of artistic interest, or hobby. "Understand delicacy and your martial arts will improve." Through Dongdong we learn that his writing style is very fast and full of power, compared with most calligraphers. He writes two characters, side by side, filling a two-foot-square piece of beige practice paper. One is *Ch'en tao,* the way of the sword. He dips his inch-wide brush into a beautiful little ink pot; it has a water buffalo reclining comfortably in the middle of it, so when you pour black ink to cover the bottom, it looks like the beast is wallowing in a mud hole. I comment on it, ask why a water buffalo. He says, "Writing is like plowing. It's to remind you you are working hard."

☆

As we make our way out to the car, the vice-headmaster recruits some of the younger kids to perform for us. I ask to see the Tiger form, the one I was learning. Although they are only eight years old, these little guys in torn canvas sneakers perform a complicated and highly demanding routine flawlessly, right down to those movements where they are called upon to growl like tigers. I never got that far. These cute wee boys show such focus, discipline, and self-control that my eyes start to get wet with tears. I'm not crying, but I'm choked up. These kids are so amazing, I want to give them all a hug and tell them just how fantastic I think they are. At the same time, some cynical (realistic) little voice in my mind is whispering, isn't it incredible what a kid that age can accomplish if he's beaten regularly?

☆

After four days at Shaolin, I finally get around to entering the gates of the Temple proper. Of course it's crawling with tourists. Ten thousand a day at fifteen bucks a head, that's a cool fifty-four million dollars a year. Not bad when the staff is unsalaried. We wander around and see the famous sights, like the widely reproduced mural showing Kung Fu training as practiced centuries ago, with chubby little monks in loose robes paired off and sparring around the Temple's courtyard. Then there's the floor in the Pilu Pavilion, where generations of monks pounding with their feet have worn deep bowl-like indentations into the floor. The sign says, "On the brick floor are left 48 footprint depressions, which have resulted from the monks' arduous pugilistic practice in the past several centuries. These depressions are popularly known as 'Foot' Kung Fu Depressions."

Geoff is skeptical. "Maybe that's just some naturally occurring depression in the earth," he says.

"No way, that's centuries of stomping!"

We're not sure who to approach about seeing the abbot. His office is right in the middle of the Temple complex, but it's padlocked shut. One of the monks shouts to us, "Jian-a-DAH?" which is how they say Canada, and someone fetches the key to the office and escorts us inside. There's an imposing wooden chair with a plush red seat like a throne, and off to the side there are stacks of boxes of bottled water. We sit in little fold-up chairs around a table near the boxes and wait for him. There are some ancient Buddhist statues of arhats or avatars on the other side of the room, but on our side it's storage space, although I do notice a funny plastic wastebasket with eyes, a beak, and the jagged top of an eggshell for a hat. The abbot, a short, chubby guy in a bright orange robe, comes in and sits with us at our little side table, very casually and informally, and orders an underling to boil some water for tea. When the water's ready, we find that his tea ceremony skills are definitely lacking; the tea is not of the sublime quality we experienced from the Kung Fu Master. In fact there is nothing to suggest "the sublime" in the abbot's manner, or in his answers to our questions: overall he seems grounded in the material world, more the slightly harried executive than someone who has put in the long hours of deep, rigorous meditation needed to get you far along the path to Nibbana. But maybe I'm just too eager to project my own fantasies onto him, romanticizing what a Buddhist abbot should be. At least he's not smoking cigarettes like the Taoist abbot we met at the top of Wudang Mountain. But he's extremely worldly in other ways: his cell phone vibrates loudly enough that we can hear it under the folds of his orange robe (only once does he take the call), and his assistants keep handing him handwritten notes that he immediately reads and responds to. He's a decision maker. Geoff and I have already agreed that he probably pulled some major Vatican-level maneuvering and manipulating to get this job, and that he's likely a master of political intrigue; he does nothing to disabuse us of our prejudice when he tells us in the middle of the interview that he's been de facto abbot since 1987, and official abbot since 1999, and that his title is dependent upon approval "from the National Religious Bureau and other agencies."

In other words, he's Communist Party-approved and seems proud that he passed their test.

He tells us that one hundred and sixty monks live at the monastery, of whom sixty practice martial arts. Are they going to star in the upcoming movie you're planning, where the monks do battle with marauding Japanese pirates? That depends on the director, he says. Then he goes into a short history of the portrayal of Shaolin in the movies, ending with more recent films like *Hero* and *Crouching Tiger, Hidden Dragon*. "The image of martial arts in these movies is quite far from the real one," he says. "They use a lot of stunts in pursuit of profits, they don't concentrate on the real movements."

"What will you do differently, can you give an example?" Geoff wants to know.

"We will represent the spirit, the truth of martial arts, but as to detailed plans that's for the director and actors to represent." Then the conversation degenerates into a discussion of how to get approval from the government film commission, how to attract investors, and Dongdong, translating, gets to use the word *leverage* a lot. Normally she works translating documents for the Beijing office of a Western business consulting firm, so she's very comfortable with the word *leverage*.

☆

Back in our hotel in the evening Geoff already has his laptop set up and is tippity-tapping out the Shaolin story. "How's this for the lead?" he asks, then reads from the screen.

The scene in the Shaolin martial arts school is as timeless as the sacred Buddhist mountains behind it. With swift jabs of controlled power, the warrior monk is perfecting his ancient technique.

But when he's finished, no enemy is prone on the floor. The only outcome is an immaculate sheet of Chinese calligraphy in black ink.

It's a nice set-up, a natural lead-in to the monks' contention that a quarter-century of Shaolin movies have exploited and distorted their message, and that their philosophy applies just as much to tea and calligraphy as to kicking aggressors in the throat.

"Great," I say. "You've already drawn a moral from the day."

He thinks I'm being sarcastic, and gets a bit testy. "That's the difference between you and me," says my big squinty-eyed fellow scribe. "You present life as messy and chaotic, and expect readers to make their own sense of it. I write for a daily; readers expect me to look at reality and try to organize it for them, so they can get meaning from it."

"That's fine if you get it right," I say. Personally, I do write pretty much what I see, and try not to draw big unproven inferences from it. I hate journalists who fly in and out of some place in a couple of days, then pretend to write the definitive, authoritative, objective story about what's *really* going on there. I'm not talking about Geoff: he's good, he's a workaholic, he researches his ass off, and generally presents just the facts, straight up.

So take my conclusions about China with a grain of salt: "It's degenerating," said Jarek about the Taiji we saw at Wudang, and I took him at his word. As for Shaolin Kung Fu, I came back from China feeling that what Don, my local Buddhist monk, had predicted before I left was true: Shaolin Kung Fu as practiced in China has lost much of the internal secrets of the art, and become almost purely external, almost purely flashy Wushu acrobatics, the kind of sport art the Chinese government hopes to lobby straight into full standing at the Olympics, where it can join the other subjectively judged events that periodically fall prey to scandal. "He raised his knee too high on that back kick, and should only have gotten a 3.7, but the Korean judge inexplicably awarded 3.9." That kind of nonsense.

Shaolin Temple was destroyed in 1928 and the monks dispersed. The Communists rounded up and shot any monks they could find after they won the country in 1949. The lucky ones got out before that, and as Don put it, "Nobody who knew what they were doing ever went back to China. It wouldn't be skillful to go back to help a regime that basically wiped out the Buddhism that was once there. The monks performing there now are basically demonstrating Wushu, an art that's beautiful to look at but has nothing to do with real Shaolin. They are not the same." If you want the real art, you'd be better off studying in the West, from teachers who learned from teachers who got out before the Communists came to power, adepts who fled to Taiwan or other countries, where they could live undisturbed, perfecting and passing on the art freely. That's what people told me before I went, and I saw nothing at Shaolin to dissuade me from accepting their view. If I needed any further confirmation, it came a few days after I got home from China, in an email press release forwarded by Geoff: the television series planned by the Shaolin Temple was going to be a reality show, where martial artists from across China would compete to win the chance to become a "real" Shaolin monk.

Part 3

☆

THE ETERNAL
SPRING PATH

20

☆

Let's Face Facts

A young man
Does not usually understand Tao
If he hears of Tao
He won't fully believe
Or practice it
But when he reaches
Fragile old age
He understands the importance of Tao
By then it's too late
He lacks the vitality
Needed to cultivate Tao

—ADAPTED FROM SUN SIMIAO'S
PRESCRIPTIONS WORTH A THOUSAND OUNCES OF GOLD
(SEVENTH CENTURY AD)

When I first got back from China, I presented Sifu Bob with a nice pirated Chinese boxed set edition of the complete works of Bruce Lee, seven discs in all, pretty good considering the man only starred in five movies. Then it was back to class, after more than a month's lay-off. One week a month at the Kung Fu Academy is devoted to grappling, and the very week I chose to return was grappling week. No choice but to get back down on the mat, to be straddled by a partner, then attempt to reverse the mount. This time it wasn't Hurricane Helen on top of me, it was a big barrel-chested dude named Barry, who toyed with me like a kitty cat clawing a crippled sparrow. I fluttered my wings, twitched and turned and struggled to get out from under him, but it was hopeless. At one point he said, "I just want to see how good your technique is," and offered close to zero resistance, just rolled over and *let me* reverse him, the inference being my technique was lousy, which it was. Even when he was letting me, it was a monumental struggle, and later my shoulder felt like it had suffered a definite setback in healing. I think it was trying to tell me Kung Fu wasn't the art for me.

☆

One day in class Bob made us do a drill where we had to present our forms to him, each in turn. He watched like a drill sergeant, but being Bob, his admonishments came across more like gentle, whispered cheerleading. "You can do better!" There was a new kid, Cameron, a psych major at college, a borderline blowhard, brimming with loud opinions about inconsequential matters, but still sweet and well-meaning enough to avoid fully qualifying as a total pain in the ass. Young Cam whizzed mistake-free through the whole of Kempo Two with power and confidence. His strikes looked real, like they would hurt if they landed. When it was my turn I got all self-conscious and teetery in my cat stances, screwing up the Stance Form, a form stressing balance, a form we learned *before* Kempo Two. As a result, Bob never gave me permission to attempt Kempo Two, and I felt a little blood rush of shame. Loss of face. At session's end Bob made a speech, criticizing our collective work ethic, not singling anyone out, although I felt his eyes lock on mine as he made a key point: "A goal is something you are in the process of working hard toward. If you are not working hard to get it, then it's only a wish, or a dream."

Well, it's true, my black belt fantasy has remained a wish. I'm still just Bri, the soft, indolent guy who wouldn't hurt a fly 'cause he *couldn't* hurt a fly.

☆

China had opened my eyes to the idea that other martial arts might be more suitable for my age and temperament. I started looking around. On a snowy evening during a trip to Ontario, I spent a few hours with Steve Higgins, who runs a Taiji school in Kitchener called Cold Mountain Internal Arts. (His website is the clearest, most succinct presentation of the benefits of Taiji I've come across.) A buddy of mine in Victoria had studied Taiji with Steve for years, and insisted I simply had to meet the man—he assured me Steve was not only a genuine scholar and a fabulous raconteur, but also a lover of ale, all of which added up to ideal company on a snowy evening far from home. When I reached Steve's home the ale failed to materialize; instead he brought me herbal tea in his cozy living room, and while we slurped and chatted his little lapdog jumped up and settled in the trough of my thighs. A disciple of Dr. Shen Zaiwen, Steve also studied "Cannon Fist" under Jou Tsung Hwa, until that grandmaster's untimely death in a car accident in 1998. He was full of stories of these great men, but it was a story he told about one of his own students, a seventy-year-old German woman, that really stuck with me afterward.

One day the lady in question had gone down to the basement laundry room of her apartment building, only to find two fuming young punks, quite possibly drunk, angrily cursing each other out. Being German, she had no hesitation in telling them to watch their tongues and improve their public comportment, which infuriated one of the punks so much that he charged at her with the intention of knocking her on her ass. The lady instinctively struck a grounded, stable Taiji posture. The kid tried to push her, she shed the blow, and it was he who found himself on the ground. Disconcerted, and more than a little embarrassed, he'd hastily picked himself up and fled.

Afterward I thought, and I still think, that's really all I need, that's a much more realistic goal to aim for: enough skill in self-defense to repel a punk in a laundromat. There's no way I'll ever be driven to perpetrate Kung Fu revenge, there'll never be a Bill I'll want to Kill. I'll settle for the more humble, simple confidence that I can keep my feet in a shoving match. Taiji can deliver that much. I want a martial art I can practice when I'm eighty. More and more, an internal art—like Taiji, Bagua, or Xingyi—is looking like the best route for me.

But even thinking these thoughts makes me feel like a two-timer, a traitor to Sifu Bob.

21

☆

Stress Inoculation

Kase, one of my wife's colleagues, is driving his minivan to the Judo Club. I'm up front, in the back are his daughters Micah, thirteen, and Emma, nine. Kase has been bugging me to go play Judo with him ever since he heard about this book. Yesterday afternoon we were over at his house for a Sunday afternoon pre-Christmas party, and he said, "You've got to come to Judo tomorrow night. There's a guy who lives in Japan, one of the top foreign Judokas ever, he's won some of the top tournaments, and he's going to give a seminar."

That sounded good. So now we're driving there together in his van, and Kase is telling me that at fifty-four, he still likes to get in there and play Judo, and he thinks it's a great sport for his daughters to learn. Why? "For two reasons: one is fitness, and the other is it's good for them to know how to defend themselves, and nothing's going to give them that better than Judo."

"Why's that?"

"Micah grapples with men—you know what a man feels like, how strong he is, what he can do to you, and you know the only thing you can rely on is your technique—*boom!*—to get out of there. Men aren't going to stand there and punch a woman, that's very rare. Men tend to grope, right?"

"So women don't need any striking skills."

"Right. Judo's all a woman needs to stop a man from grabbing her."

His girls both started at seven, and love it. I ask them if they've ever used it outside the club, for example fighting boys in the schoolyard.

"I'm not really allowed to use it," says nine-year-old Emma.

"No one says you're not allowed," her dad tells her.

☆

"Judo's a martial art, but it's a sport art, right?" says Kase. "The rules were introduced for safety. That's why I don't understand this Ultimate Fighting stuff. Too dangerous. You know, Judo rose from Jiu Jitsu, and the reason it did is because Jiu Jitsu at that time was getting too violent." I know a bit about that. Dr. Jigoru Kano founded the original Judo school, the Kodokan in Tokyo, with nine students in 1882, first and foremost as a place to practice a clean, respectful sport, a response to the dirty Jiu Jitsu of the day, which had been taken over by gangsters and street fighters. Dr. Kano stressed an ethical component and banned techniques that could cause severe injury. "About ten years later they had a big showdown between the Judo guys and the Jiu Jitsu guys," Kase continues. "And the Judo guys won, hands down. They had better fitness, better technique, because they weren't getting hurt as much."

Kase is a loyal Judo man. "The last twenty years there's been such a proliferation of martial arts, I can't keep track of them all. I've never heard of some of them. We get guys come into our club doing Ultimate Fighting or Brazilian Jiu Jitsu or something, young guys in their twenties, trying to hone their skills with the groundwork. And those guys can't touch some of our guys who are in their forties!"

☆

The club is up on the top floor of an old building that runs back a long way from a narrow street frontage. On a whiteboard in the corner of the main room it says

Keith Durrant, 6th Dan Kodokan, will be here Monday 6:30–9:00.

1. Keith started Judo at this club in 1977.
2. Keith went to Japan with M. Fitzgerald in 1980 and has been there ever since.
3. He is 5'5" in height and weighs "roughly" 80 kg.
4. He is the first Canadian Judoka to receive all six black belts at the Kodokan.
5. On a couple of occasions he has received "the outstanding fighter," for his technique and fighting spirit.
6. Keith loves fighting/Randori and is known for his tenacious spirit + the fact he will not give up!!

Keith Durrant turns out to be a bulldog with severe cauliflower ears and an essentially Japanese manner: soft-spoken and formal. He even does the little Japanese bow and two-handed presentation when he offers his business card. His Judo session is a dizzying array of specialty moves, including a couple of takedowns that won him "technique of the tournament" awards in Japan, a rare honor for a foreigner. At the end he announces, "This is the first Judo class I've ever taught." In Japan there are so many excellent Judokas that his expertise is not sought.

☆

Afterward in the storage room/clubhouse, a classic men's retreat replete with two ratty couches and a beer fridge, there's talk of the good old days. Mickey Fitzgerald, who went to Japan with Keith but came back after six years, is remembering training at the Kodokan, still the Mecca of Judo a hundred and twenty-four years after its founding. "It was the center of the universe for me, a huge dojo with five hundred mats on seven floors. I walked in: 'My God, I'm here!' And Komata Sensei, who's a legendary fighter in Japan, famous for his springing neck throw, he just grabbed a-hold of me and threw me, fifteen or twenty times. I couldn't even feel it! Before I knew it I was flying through the air. It wasn't powerful like Western Judo, it was just clean and fast and pure, and that was my introduction to Japanese Judo."

He remembers another Japanese master getting hold of Keith and choking him out repeatedly, then letting him come back to consciousness, to the point where he would begin to struggle to get free again, then choking him out again. And again, and again. "You know those dolls with the weighted bottom, you knock it down and it springs right back up? A lot of guys would get hurt— shoulder, knee—and not get back up. The Japanese wouldn't train you unless you got back up. Keith's not a quitter. He's not a quitter! That's the key to martial arts, and to life."

Kase introduces me to another Judoka, Wayne Unger, who's been training at this club for thirty years, since he was thirteen. "His Judo is beautiful," Kase proclaims. I recognize Wayne: he's a cop who was profiled recently in the local newspaper. He trains the rest of the department in "use of force" techniques for dealing with violent confrontations. For cops, he says, it basically comes down to this: make sure you win every fight you're in.

"So how do you teach that?"

"I teach really simple techniques, gross motor skills that will work under stress," he says. "We know that when you're under stress, blood flows to the major muscle groups, so using the major muscle groups is good. Knee strikes, elbow strikes, palm strikes are good. You start getting into complicated wrist locks, it may work if the officer is skilled, but very few train on the side.

"A regular person, seeing violence escalate, will leave," he continues. "Run away. We don't have that option. We go *toward* the danger, *toward* the gunfire. If you can't leave, then use extreme violence. You have ten seconds to end it, and you need to train like that. So you have to work with ten seconds of panic, with the over-rush of adrenaline. We run them through scenarios that simulate that critical incident, so you're not as stressed. You've been there, done that. Stress inoculation. That's the state-of-the-art training."

I ask if he does other martial arts besides Judo, and Wayne says, "Yeah, I do something called Ma Gui Bagua; it's a circle walking art I try to practice daily."

That piques my interest. Bagua was Jarek's art of choice too, one he also practiced daily, but I'd never gotten a chance to see it in China. "So, is Bagua part of the natural fighter's arc for you, like the way people who trained in the harder arts in their youth switch to Taiji in their old age?"

"I don't know if that pattern is typical for Judo," he says. "Judokas tend to do it until they can't do it anymore, then they do nothing. Over the years I've practiced Taiji, and now Bagua with my teacher, Andrea Falk. She's a scholar and an academic, she's fluent in Mandarin, and she travels to Beijing every year to learn from the great masters. You can check her website, lots of reading in there. I met her three years ago because I wanted to learn Bagua; I'd done a lot of reading about it. She likes to train serious martial

artists: she doesn't want to train people who are just casually interested. I got an introduction, and I met her, and she began showing
me the basic techniques of circle walking, which is the foundation
of Bagua, for leg training and core strength training. I've been
doing that for two and a half years now pretty well every day. Not
as a hobby, as a discipline. It's actually hard work: you're gripping
the ground as hard as you can with your feet, you're dragging your
body along, dropping your center as low as possible. It's physically
demanding. I've noticed a tremendous amount of strength gain in
the body, I can't tell you why. I'd almost quit Judo at one point; one
of the reasons I'm back here at Judo is I'm generating so much
power in my body, Bagua has made me much stronger in the Judo.
It's not mysterious, you have to practice every day. The Chinese are
funny, they're not like us: 'Oh, three times a week is enough.' It has
to be every single day. I like that."

"Are you into internal alchemy, and cultivating Chi?"

"I just feel stronger. The Chi thing, I don't feel that. Well, maybe
I do. I'm a skeptical person. I'd like to believe it. I'd say that these
Bagua Masters are very efficient bio-mechanically. As for Chi? The
Indians call it Prana. I've been doing yoga for twelve years now. It's
beneficial to move Prana around your body."

22

☆

Unimpeded Chi

Wayne's enthusiasm for Bagua inspired me to check out his master, Andrea Falk. Look at her website and you'll see that she lives beside an isolated lake in the forest north of Montreal. Six months of the year, when the snow buries their driveway, she and her husband have to walk a mile through the woods, from the main road to their house, packing all their food and supplies on their backs. Year-round they draw water from a source half a mile away. She carries it Shaolin-style, arms outstretched, in two-liter bottles. She owns three pairs of snowshoes: two long pairs like the traditional trappers wear, and one short pair to do her Bagua circle walk in the snow. There's a beautiful photo on her site of a perfect circle stamped into crisp snow, as if it were made by a fairy, a snow sprite.

☆

A few weeks after I first heard of Andrea I've flown twenty-five hundred miles east to Guelph, Ontario, for a weekend seminar of Bagua and Xingyi with her. In the morning she instructs a dozen students in Xingyi, getting us moving through the basic stepping–striking combination, up and down the space in straight lines, like swimmers doing laps. There's even a turn at the wall, a reversal of direction, that reminds me of the competitive swimmer's flip. I recognize Xingyi's core moves from the afternoon I spent near Zheng Zhou, watching Madame Lü's students perform their blend of Xinyi and Xingyi on the hard-packed earth. It feels good, half a world away, to step inside those same actions, to try them on like a new set of clothes. Xingyi is all about sudden, straight-ahead, overwhelming, knock-you-on-your-ass power. The crucial concept is *beng,* the unstoppable force of an avalanche. There is no retreat. All blocks and strikes are carried out while stepping relentlessly forward. You're moving *through* the opponent, as if they're merely an obstacle to be knocked down and trod over to get where you really need to go.

I'm really here for the Bagua. After lunch it's time to learn circle walking, the basics of the art. The ideal circle is about twelve feet in diameter. You take a minute to let your back settle down into your hips, your dantien, consciously trying to lower your center of gravity. The arms come down comfortably, elbows slightly bent, each hand describing a C. Now turn your hands and torso slightly inward, so that as you walk you maintain that twelve-foot circle. Lift the foot with knee bent, keep it close to the ground, place it in front, kick it ever so slightly, set it down. Stay low. Grab the earth with the "palm" of your foot. This doesn't mean trying to clutch the earth as if the toes were fingers. The whole sole of the foot tries to hold the earth, through the bottom of the shoe. Each foot sticks to its own path. Two circles, one inside the other.

And that's basically it. Practice that an hour a day for three years and you will completely transform your body, you'll have unimpeded Chi, and you'll be ready to learn the martial applications of the art. Until your body has been transformed, there's not really any point learning the fighting skills that go with it, Andrea told us, although she did teach us a few, and had us run through them, just as a teaser. Early on she used me as a partner to show a technique, and I was amazed at her power when she knocked me in the chest with a forearm. It was just a demonstration, just a hint of her real strength, but it lifted me off the ground.

Mostly the two weekend afternoons were spent walking around and around in that twelve-foot circle. It sounds monotonous, but somehow it wasn't. What it was, was exhausting. In that backdropping posture, with bent knees, and hands turned inward, fifteen minutes at a time was all we could stand at first.

☆

At lunch the second day, while we lounged on the polished hardwood eating take-out sushi and miso soup, Andrea handed out photocopies of the lineage of Ma Gui Bagua. Ma Gui lived from 1854 to 1941. He learned Bagua from a certain Dong Haichuan (1798–1882). Dong chose to teach his complete system to Ma because Ma was a good student, who had trained with him since childhood, and more importantly, Ma was not a brawler. Dong's other top students liked to mix it up in street fights, sometimes to the death. It's not a wise investment to commit to passing on the full system to some impulsive character who could get himself killed tomorrow.

"Ma Gui was quite young when he learned the system," Andrea said, "so he was made to do really, really basic Bagua. It's down-to-earth, straightforward Bagua, which otherwise has kind of been lost. Most of it these days is pretty flashy."

I asked her if, besides the circle walking, there are forms to learn.

"No forms."

"So the basics can be learned quickly. We've already learned it in a day and a half."

"No no. It's the most difficult thing to learn to do right. Your body has to change before you can really do it right, but you can learn enough that you can practice on your own, and it will open up channels. You'll be making mistakes, but you will still be changing your body the way you need to, to do it right. You'll thicken the tendons, make them more elastic. The Chi will flow quite differently. It'll flow from the center of the body, down the center of the limbs. Even if you're doing it right, the circle walk is going to be really nasty, it's going to be really difficult. If it wasn't, it wouldn't change you. But if you get into it, it'll be the most amazing thing you've ever done."

Bagua appears to be keeping her young: she is fifty-one years old and doesn't have a grey hair on her head. Her love affair with martial arts dates to the 1970s, when a friend dragged her along to a Kung Fu class for moral support. "The teacher stuck me in a corner in a horse stance, and just left me there, happy as a clam, until he noticed me again two hours later," she remembers. "That was it. I just took to it."

In 1980 she set off for China to study Wushu at Beijing University, the first foreigner to major in Wushu since the art had been rehabilitated and reintroduced in 1977, in the thaw that followed the Cultural Revolution. "In '77–'78–'79 the faculty were incredible, they were all picked by ability, not marks; they'd been doing it ten years in secret, and were all traditionally trained," she says. Those were great days. Nowadays, a quarter of a century later, the Chinese penchant for bureaucratization has taken hold, and a spectacular unknown coming in from the cold would get the cold shoulder. But at that time it was, "Show us what you got." Andrea had some experience sparring, which the Chinese lacked, having been confined to practicing alone or in secret during those dark years of the Cultural Revolution. "I don't mind getting hit, but I don't particularly like hitting people, so I'm not a great sparrer," she says. "If I hit people too hard I always feel bad. I was usually the only woman, so I was used to sparring with men. You have to hit them a few times first, because most men will say, 'Oh, I don't hit girls.' *Doosh!*" She makes a sudden, fisted strike, stopping short of my head. "You have to bop them on the nose a few times first. Get them mad."

When she arrived in China they had no concept of Western style light sparring. "They were going heavy contact, full equipment, with throws," she remembers. "My teacher would grab my leg when I kicked him and throw me to the ground, because I was trained to hold the leg there, to show the point. He'd take it and throw me. I'd be sitting there waiting for my nose to stop bleeding, and he'd be shadow boxing around, going, 'Get up, get up.'"

Her Chinese teachers took her to watch competitions of other martial arts styles. "That's when I saw Bagua. I said, 'Whoa, what's that? I wanna do that!' It was this Bagua saber form, a girl about five feet tall with a sword about five feet tall too, describing beautiful circles, flowing up and down."

I was wondering about the vaunted Chi-generating powers attributed to Bagua. Andrea, a very practical and down-to-earth woman, downplays that part of it.

"You can feel Qi Gong, things a-tingling," she tells me, "and you can go with it, start shaking and bouncing off the wall if you want to. Personally, I just won't go there, that's not what it's about."

"What is it about, then, for you?"

"It's just about power in your body. The channels are open in your body, so you can be relaxed and still hit really hard. I know what blocked Chi feels like, and I know what unimpeded Chi feels like, and I'd rather feel unimpeded. When you're really moving from the center of your body, you move very fast and very powerfully. You're very stable, and yet mobile. You can do what you want."

☆

At lunch I pulled out some pictures I took in China, of Madame Lü's Xinyi school, and my Shaolin Kung Fu school. Among them was a photo of Jan in the school lobby, getting his head shaved while the Kung Fu kids crowded around him. I told Andrea all about his Iron Fist training, his brick breaking, his plunging of hands into boiling hot water, his swollen knuckles. She wasn't impressed. "Martial arts should be about your health first," she said. "I want a martial art I can be doing when I'm eighty. I don't want to be destroying myself."

That night I went off and drank herbal tea with Steve Higgins, who told me about the German lady in the laundromat, standing her ground against that punk. I already told you it made me think that I want a martial art I can do when I'm eighty. Now you know it was Andrea, that very day, who had lit the fuse.

23

☆

Seven Seconds of Sheer Terror

One Friday afternoon I went to watch Sifu Bob and Don the monk work out. I was psyched to see what the seventh level looked like, hoping it would be apparent even to a novice like me whether Don truly possessed superior powers. I'd mentioned Don to Wayne Unger, that cop who trains other cops in stress inoculation. I told him that Don pegged Sifu Bob as a three, Royce Gracie a five, and Don's self-assessment was seven. Therefore, with his arsenal of internal skills, Don should be able to beat Royce Gracie.

"He couldn't," Wayne said dismissively. "You can get so far out there, you forget what real fighting is: it's seven seconds of sheer terror, seven seconds of all-out violence. You can have all these fancy little moves, but quite frankly, I'm skeptical. There is nothing wrong with martial arts to develop character, but let's face it, it's still really about violence."

And that's the problem with going to watch Don give lessons in Kung Fu: there's no moment of all-out violence to take his measure. There are only respectful students, in this case, Bob and a friend of Bob's, a guy named Cathal, whose visit today is a one-off. He's more or less checking Don out too.

A barrel-chested Buzz Lightyear type of guy, Cathal is a former school principal, now living his dream running his own martial arts school. He has a specific goal today: "I was hoping what we could do is explore the mount," he says at the start. "I have yet to see anything that protects against the mount if the person on top is superior to you in strength. On our feet, if you are stronger than I am, there are so many equalizers. But when you're on top of me …"

Bob gets down on his back and Cathal mounts him, while Don—dressed in black jeans, an orange T-shirt, red fleece vest, and jade bead necklace—looks on. It's funny about Don. Remember earlier I mentioned Karen Armstrong's contention that it's tough to write a biography of the Buddha, because essentially, once he became enlightened, he had no personality? Don's a bit like that, so maybe he really is close to enlightenment. He's like the opposite of charismatic: he has no charisma whatsoever, he's a black hole you almost trip into, a vacuum you are sucked toward, which in a weird way makes him charismatic.

"The only thing I can see are pressure point techniques that would incapacitate that person," Bob says, lying on his back. He puts a thumb behind Cathal's ear to show one such point, but Cathal's not buying it.

"Jiu Jitsu guys teach hundreds of reversals, but it's all technical-based, not principle-based. I want a principle. I want to think about grappling not as a Jiu Jitsu guy, but as a Kung Fu guy; in other words, it's principle-based. I think the next evolution in the art will take on Jiu Jitsu, and not fight their fight. Take them on with something different. I feel like there's a void there."

Don says, "Eyes, throat, collarbone, and groin are the four vulnerables in our system. I don't think it's a coincidence that UFC doesn't allow eye gouging and fishhooking. I guess I don't understand why some of the simple things aren't done. Like a hit on the throat, a punch on the collarbone, a strike to the heart. A progressively percussive open-handed strike to the heart causes an intense electrical pain, and for a moment the person's heart stops. It's quite a jolt. I would see that as an effective method. Or a one-inch punch to the solar plexus."

"The most difficult person to control on the ground is the beginner," says Cathal. "Maybe that says something. We're missing some natural instinct."

But Don insists a percussive hit is the way to go. "One technique to develop the percussive power of that strike is, you take a coffee can and fill it with sand, tape it up with foam on the outside, and set it on a table or countertop. Now punch it with the back of the knuckles. You know you're doing it right when it doesn't slide or tip over—it actually slides back toward you."

"It's like concussive in the brain," says Cathal helpfully.

Don demonstrates lightly on Cathal's belly. "It's not doing this, it's *that*. Feel that? And that's doing it softly. It's a double hit, you can feel the wave. We call that 'jolting.'"

"Is that the basis of the famous one-inch punch?" asks Cathal.

"Yes, one-inch punch is just one example of it."

"Similar to the mechanism for chest compressions?"

"Yes. If you follow through, you can do damage to the lungs, and the person will spit up blood. It's very dangerous."

They move on. The best defense to being mounted, of course, is not to be taken down to begin with. Cathal's looking for the best way to stop a grappler lunging at you, wrapping your waist or torso in his arms, and taking you to the ground.

"Come at me," Don says. Cathal warily approaches, his hands up chest high. "If you do that I'll take your fingers," Don says. This time Cathal comes in lower, wrapping his big bear arms around Don's waist. "Attacking the head would be the way to go," Don says. He puts one hand on the back of Cathal's neck, and the other forearm up under the chin. "You've got a windpipe choke when you've got that," he says, gently cranking Cathal's neck and turning him aside. "I've watched my teacher do that on big wrestling dudes, and spin them off sideways so they fly through the air."

☆

Eventually they take a break, lounging on the mat, talking philosophy. At issue: When is a martial artist justified in using his skills? Virtually never, Don says. He tells a story of walking the streets downtown in the company of his Buddhist Master, many years ago. They passed the pub in the King's Hotel, then just called the King's, nowadays known as Steamers. Just then two drunks stepped out onto the sidewalk, and they started harassing the little Chinaman. His master asked Don to move across the street, fearing Don would interfere with violence. The two drunks did get violent, but Don's master allowed them to strike, dodging their blows. In the end he fell to the sidewalk, where from Don's vantage point, it looked like they were kicking him. Soon they tired of their sport and staggered down the street. Don hurried to his master's side. The old man jumped up and dusted himself off, not a mark on him. He had avoided every blow, at least according to Don.

Cathal argues that the two drunks should have been taught a lesson. They were allowed to wander away, having learned only that it's fun, and consequence-free, to kick an apparently defenseless little foreigner. They might lay a similar beating on the next innocent they stumble across. Cathal earnestly seeks to know: "At what point does a trained martial artist have a moral responsibility to step in and use his skills for good?"

"You cannot solve the world's problems," Don says. "When a timid person meets an aggressive person, the timid person will be beaten up. You cannot change that." He presents a scenario where good intentions make things worse. "A guy comes across a gang rape and interferes. He dies. Because the woman is a witness, now they have to kill her too. Is that the right outcome?"

"But as a martial artist, there is a moral duty to defend rights," Cathal insists.

"No. No. Because right–wrong is one of the worldly Dhamma roots."

"No, right–wrong is a universal. Molestation and murder of children, that's a wrong."

"I agree, that would be a wrong. But in Buddhist teaching that is part of a misunderstanding of the world. A baby who dies, a person who is mentally challenged, has a pure heart. However you imagine the afterlife, they will be further along than the greedy, lustful head of a company. The only thing a human being can do is recognize innocence and weakness, protect that. And the key is, you don't have to do that physically. You don't have to meet violence with violence. You don't have to stand up for rights with the attitude, *I have a right*. The Buddhist code is, Give no offense, and in your heart, take no offense."

☆

The next time I see Sifu Bob I ask him, "Remember how you told me Don is a seven, and Royce Gracie is a five?"

"Uh huh," he said.

"So I got it in my head Don could beat Royce Gracie—"

Bob started backpedaling. "On the ground, I'm sorry, I think Royce would take over. But on their *feet* …" He pauses a moment, and says, "Personally, I've never seen Don in a real fighting situation. He's a very knowledgeable fellow, but when it comes to technique and doing it at full speed, I don't know. Any Kung Fu move is very complicated and difficult to learn. Shaolin movements involve a lot of flowery deflections and pressure points, and then moving your way up to the core, so it's a hard one to answer."

I tell him what Wayne Unger told me—real fighting is seven seconds of sheer terror. There's no time for flowery. Bob more or less agrees. "I was in street confrontations when I was younger, and it feels like it takes five or ten seconds, although it really takes double that," he says. "Any technique I ever did to win was basic and simple. The complex techniques, I never had the ability to even think of trying."

24

☆

Writers and Fighters!

I f you want to know what fight tactics hold up through seven seconds of sheer terror, if you want to bear witness to what really works when two men try to hurt each other, then pretty much by default you end up back at the closest thing going to no-holds-barred combat: the Ultimate Fighting Championship. The UFC was sold long ago by Rorion Gracie and his partners; these days it's based in Las Vegas and owned by the Fertitta family, proprietors of a string of hugely profitable off-Strip casinos catering to the gambling urges of Vegas locals, as opposed to tourists. Less tacky glitz, better parking.

Royce Gracie won UFC 4 in 1993. By the time I got to Vegas they were up to number 57, which makes a bit of a mockery of the word "Ultimate": I mean, how often can you keep having an "Ultimate" Championship? But by now UFC is pretty much a brand name, known by its three initials. UFC 57 offered up an eight-bout card, the main event being a much anticipated rubber match between Randy Couture and Chuck Liddell, two top light heavyweights who served as competing team leaders on a reality television show about unknown fighters earning a shot at a UFC fight, making it the *American Idol* of no-holds-barred pugilism. The show was a big hit in the States on the Spike network. It had turned Liddell and Couture into television stars.

The fight sold out early, and the UFC turned down my request for press credentials, the bastards. I figured without a press pass I'd never get close to Liddell and Couture, the big drawing cards, so, looking for another fighter to focus on, I found a guy way down on the undercard by the name of Jeff "The Snowman" Monson, whose hometown is relatively close to me here on the West Coast. He's ninety minutes by ferry, then three hours' drive by car away, across the border in the USA. I googled Monson, and gleaned that he's a grappling specialist who has fought several times recently in Britain, and is most famous for a single incident: he once stripped off his shorts and paraded naked in the arena after losing a controversial decision at the Abu Dhabi World Grappling Championships. I liked the sound of that. Royce Gracie, while a perfect gentleman, was a little too cool and self-contained, or, to put it bluntly, he's wooden enough that he might have been carved from a tree trunk with a chainsaw. As an antidote, I was looking for someone extroverted and a little crazy.

☆

That's how I've ended up with a window table and a cup of coffee in a café called Plenty, in downtown Olympia, the capital of Washington State. The waiter is letting me use the phone on the bar to leave Plenty of messages for Jeff Monson to please come meet me here. I don't have a cell phone, and he's not answering his. There is nothing to do but leave messages. In the meantime I drink coffee and read a book called *Understanding Taoism* by Jennifer Oldstone-Moore, because even after climbing to the Golden Temple in Wudang and listening to Jarek for hours I still can't entirely say I do understand Taoism. Remember the *holy embryo*? I'm thinking at this moment Freud missed the mark when he attributed penis envy to women. It's men who have womb envy: women, without even trying, can miraculously produce an entirely new human being out of their abdomen. To match that, men in their jealousy have to invent all kinds of mystical nonsense about Holy Embryos and Immortality.

Logging trucks carrying loads of Douglas Fir—huge logs easily four feet in diameter—rumble right through this old downtown. Neo-hippie freak types keep walking past the window, reminding me that Olympia had its moment of fame in the 1990s as the birthplace of the Riot Grrrl movement, which coincided with Kurt Cobain and Courtney Love living here (the town was later immortalized by Courtney in the song "Rock Star": "Well I went to school in Olympia, Everyone's the same/They look the same/They talk the same/They even fuck the same"). Long after the media feeding frenzy had peaked (Young people doing something new and different!!), a mainstream magazine that apparently had only just heard about Olympia as the epicenter of "cool" phoned me, wanting me to go down and report on it. I told 'em it's far too late and I'm far too old: I'd feel like yesterday's man, like that sadly square *Time* magazine guy interviewing brash Bob Dylan circa 1965 in "Don't Look Back." Now here I am, a decade or so later, thinking, this town does have a nice funky hippie vibe, I'm glad to see it survived.

On the street outside, a soccer mom parallel parks an SUV with the bumper sticker, "Who Would Jesus Bomb?" Down the sidewalk in a wool cap and a jean jacket, here comes a stocky guy who could be Jeff. Looks like a young Ken Kesey, in town from the woods. Yep, must be him, he's coming in.

At five foot eight and two hundred forty pounds, he's built like a refrigerator. He takes off his hat to reveal a cue ball skull with serious looking scars on it, and a day-old unbandaged cut above an eyebrow. Then there are the ears: nasty-looking cauliflowers, a body alteration that takes years to achieve, worn exclusively and with pride by die-hard fighters. When we sit down and start talking, Jeff Monson turns out not to be a crazed extrovert at all, but shy, modest, and thoughtful, a guy whose background is mostly Olympic-style wrestling, beginning in high school, then at university in Portland. He coached wrestling at Minnesota while getting a master's degree in psychology. Then he came home to the Pacific Northwest to work as a social worker, but found he "still had the competitive bug." He started training in Judo, and then Pancrase—

"How would you describe Pancrase?"

"It's a lot of submission focus, working to finish the guy for sure. Kind of like kickboxing with submissions. Class C and B allows slaps to the face and punches to the body. You have to get to Class A before you can punch anywhere, but even in Class A you can't punch to the face on the ground, so in amateur ranks it's a bit safer. You wear knee pads and shin pads."

"And how did you turn pro?"

"It all started when I got an invitation to be part of a team going to go to Abu Dhabi for the World Championship of Grappling. Grappling as a sport is basically Jiu Jitsu with no *gi* on. It's wrestling and Jiu Jitsu combined, takedowns and submissions, with no striking. So the world championship was held in the United Arab Emirates, and I went as a nobody, an absolute nobody. I'd had two pro matches, pretty much underground matches. I came out of nowhere and won."

"You seem to be most famous for taking off your clothes."

He smiles. "What happened was, I won that tournament in 1999. In 2000 I took second, in 2001 I took second again, then I tore my biceps completely right after that, boxing. So I had to have reconstructive surgery coming back, and I basically just dedicated two years of my life to winning Abu Dhabi again, you know? So finally I'm ready to enter the tournament again, and that year it was being held in Brazil—it moves around from country to country, it's just called the Abu Dhabi World Championship because an Arab prince from Abu Dhabi with deep pockets finances it. So I'm in Brazil, fighting a fighter I beat to win the championship in 1999. He's a Brazilian, and this is in a big dome, with a huge crowd, and on national television.

"You know, I'm hard on myself, and if I don't think I won the match, I'm not going to complain about the decision. But this one *I absolutely dominated* the match, I mean, no question. I dominated, and they raised his hand! Inexplicably. Incredibly, really.

"And so I went and shook his corner's hand, shook his hand, not his fault, you know? And then basically flipped off the ref, and the judges' table, and then as I was in my corner getting my stuff, the crowd started chanting something in Portuguese, taunting me, mocking me, and I just lost it. I threw all my clothes in the crowd, and I was walking across the ring in my shorts, and as I left the ring I ended up throwing my shorts in the stands and being naked. They tried to arrest me, but my coach intervened and said, 'You know, you already screwed him in the ass, how do you expect him to have clothes on if you're screwing him in the ass?'" He laughs with a hint of embarrassment, remembering it. The smelly, sweat-soaked wrestling shorts he heaved into the crowd are now on display in Rio. "Memorabilia encased in glass in a sports bar. So that's okay."

Last year the Abu Dhabi World Championship of Grappling was held in California, and Jeff finally won his title back. "It had been six years, so it was really … yeah, it was … " He doesn't finish the sentence. Later he'll tell me the highs don't ever match the lows for him: "When you lose, it kills you inside, but when you win, the satisfaction doesn't correspond, or even out the crappiness you feel when you lose. When you win, it's like, 'Whew, I won, okay, next thing now.'"

☆

"What is it like to fight in England?"

"I like England, it's more laid-back than here for sure. I'd love to live in England. Boxing is king over there, and the grappling is poor, but they are really, really eager to learn, and to soak anything up. They're like, 'C'mon man, teach me—'"

His phone is ringing. It's his mother, they have a lunch date today and need to decide on a restaurant. "No, not that place," he insists. "They got Bread and Roses shut down. I won't go there." They settle on another place. He ends the call with, "I love you, Mom."

"What was that all about?" I ask. He explains that Bread and Roses was a local soup kitchen for street people. The owners of a nearby restaurant were instrumental in getting it shut down, claiming its proximity was bad for business. Classic NIMBY. Not In My Back Yard. So Jeff boycotts the restaurant.

"That shows a high moral standard on your part," I say.

"Do you know anything about me?" he asks.

"Not really."

"I'm probably more well known for my politics than the fighting."

"Oh yeah?"

"Yeah. There's a lot of people who don't support me at all."

"Within the fighting?"

"Within the fans, yeah."

"So what are your politics, that alienate people?"

"Just really far left, really outspoken against the war, outspoken against hierarchy and capitalism."

"Right on! That's like me!" We both laugh, and he looks at me warily to see if I'm serious.

"I belong to the IWW," he says. If you don't know your labor history, that's the famous Wobblies, the Industrial Workers of the World, a "one big union" movement that was founded in 1905, peaked in 1923 with about a hundred thousand members, mostly American, and has had zero political impact since about 1941, when everyone in America got behind the fight against fascism, and America came out the other end of that fight the undisputed capitalist heavyweight champion of the world. Lately a lot of people think the champ's become a bully, even in America. "That's why I like downtown Olympia," Jeff says. "Here and Eugene, Oregon, are the centers of political leftness I guess. Every month there'll be a blockade of the port—there's a Navy base here, where they ship out a lot of stuff to Iraq, so people get arrested protesting that every month."

Those kinds of politics don't sit too well with the average UFC fight fan, I suggest.

"Yeah. '*Beat 'im up! Hurt 'im!*'" He's mimicking the typical fan. "I spoke out against being in Iraq, and called the soldiers sheep, made some comments that should have been more directed towards the government, and people kind of ran with it. If you go to the online forums where fans discuss the fights, I'll have a ton of threats, hundreds of pages of 'Kill Jeff Monson, Jeff Monson's a commie.' It starts off that way but then it becomes a discussion of the war, politics, and religion, so in that way it was successful. I don't have any delusions of changing the world, but if I can just make people think, and not accept the status quo, then it's been successful, you know?"

"Will it affect how the crowd treats you in Vegas in a few weeks?"

"It'll be interesting to see," he says, then laughs nervously. "That's why I like fighting in England. They love anti-war sentiment. But here, the people who come to those fights aren't geared toward that direction." He pauses a moment. "Sometimes I just think I'm a big hippie, really."

"Where do you think that comes from?"

"I don't know. I grew up middle class, never lacked for anything, so it's not that I'm pissed off at the world, I just don't like the oppression I see, and I want to speak out about it. And not too many people get to do what they love. Like you, you obviously love what you do. Not many people get to do that, get to say I'm a writer, or a fighter. How many people get to say I do what I want to do? Instead of I can't wait till Friday, man."

This is something I love about Americans: they're the world leaders when it comes to follow-your-bliss pep talks. They're inspiring people, I find, far and away the most enthusiastic, go-for-it folks on the planet. Jeff has just inspired a little soliloquy in my mind:

Yeah, I may never be a fighter, but I'm a writer! Writers and fighters, are we that different? No! Throughout history, who changes the world, who battles injustice? Writers and Fighters! We gotta stick together!

☆

He may think of himself as a big hippie, but hippies don't generally dream of winning the heavyweight division of a blood sport like Ultimate Fighting. So where does that ambition come from? "It's a curse, I guess," Jeff says. "I grew up, wrestled in high school, never won the state title, wrestled in college, never won All American, never made the Olympics, I was just never fulfilled never fulfilled never fulfilled. I won Abu Dhabi, yeah, but there's something moving over me that just tells me I need to do it, to win the UFC, for my own well-being. Then I'd like to go to Japan and fight in Pride." Pride is a Japan-based Mixed Martial Art consortium, a competitor of the K–1 group Royce Gracie was fighting for when I met him in Vanderhoof. Japanese promoters pay the fighters better.

For his upcoming UFC bout, Jeff says, "I'm getting three thousand dollars, and three thousand more if I win. I'm hoping to make that much in endorsements too. I'm on a three-fight contract, and they can drop you at any time. They'll let me grapple, or maybe fight in England as long as it doesn't interfere with their fights. Big pay difference between that and going for the title. The main event, those guys are likely getting a quarter million each. We're trying to organize something like a union. There is a handful— maybe twenty, thirty guys—who can actually make a living out of this. Everyone else, if you don't have an income outside fighting, you're poor, living at the gym, or living with somebody. The UFC pay nothing. And there's no insurance: you can be in a fight and have twenty thousand dollars' worth of medical bills, and be out six months, they're not going to pay for any of that. How many other jobs can you get hurt on the job doing something dangerous, and they're not going to compensate you for the injury? So I'll fight for three and three, but you could break a leg and be out for six months. It's not lucrative like people think."

"But it looks slick when you watch it on Pay-Per-View; the production values suggest there's a huge amount of money involved," I say.

"There are huge amounts involved," Jeff agrees. "They are making millions and millions, and they don't pay us anything. Because everyone wants to be in the UFC, and if you don't want to fight they'll find someone who does. Supply and demand, right? There's always the Brazilian tough guy who'll fight for five hundred dollars, no doubt."

☆

In the evening we reconnect and I drive him out to a suburban Karate and kickboxing club where he's arranged to train. He's never been there before. His own club, a branch of a Florida-based club called American Top Team, is in the process of moving locations, and the new site hasn't been set up yet.

The first thing that strikes you about the gym is that in America, at least on the West Coast, they make full use of the luxury of space. You could park an airliner in here. There's a full-sized boxing ring in the far corner, where a couple of his regular grappling partners, Wesley and Joel, wait for him. As we approach, they're in mid-conversation. Wesley's saying, "I got round knees so it doesn't hurt as bad as some guys."

"I've been there," says Joel. "It's those skinny guys putting sharp little knees into your chest that really kill."

With very little warm-up Jeff is on the mat in the ring, wrapped like a pita around Wesley's falafels. He'll go five minutes straight with twenty-three-year-old Wesley, then three to five with Joel, who's in his thirties, then back to Wes, and back to Joel, so that in all, Jeff goes half an hour without a break. "In cardio terms that's like running a marathon," says Joel, whose day job is counselling teen drug addicts. "It involves all your body at the same time, it's like being underwater. Very unique sport, and not as testosterone-driven as people make it out to be."

To me grappling looks pretty much like two guys intent on buggering the other without being buggered in return. For a more knowledgeable take on what's going on, I get Joel to give me a play by play:

"Just real basic, passing guard, what he's trying to do is get around his legs, his legs are holding him in place right now, and the bottom man has a number of submission sweeps he can work, to try to get to a superior position, or finish the fight with an arm bar or choke. A smart fighter like Wesley is trying to keep his base nice and low, stay back on his heels, keep his head buried 'cause as soon as he lifts his butt he starts to get turned over. So this is almost a stalemate position. Wesley's doing a good job trying to defend, but really, it's just a matter of time.

"Now Jeff is sneaking that choke in," he continues. "There's a couple of ways you can choke: you can choke with the weight of the arm, or you can snake it all the way around and choke with the biceps and the blade. That's actually a wind choke as opposed to a blood choke, either way it takes so much out of you, it exhausts you even if you do fight out of it."

"The ring really swings a lot," I say. Under the terrifying pounding of two big men tossing each other around, it shudders and shakes severely. Someday soon it's going to come crashing down like the marriage bed in a Fatty Arbuckle two-reeler. Suddenly Wesley taps out and is up on his feet, face distorted in pain, hobbling and prancing around in quick little circles.

"Wesley's got a busted-up toe he got a few days ago, but it's not like a busted leg, you can fight through it," says Joel. "It just hurts a lot. Sprained ankles, broken toes, they're common from kicking someone in the leg. Any fighter at this level is fighting through injury."

"Do people get broken ribs?" I ask. Always curious about broken ribs.

"Quite a few. Especially a guy like Jeff can really squeeze you tight, and if you try to fight out of it, you can get caught the wrong way. But it's not enough to keep you from fighting. It's enough to slow you down, it hurts, but you don't stop. None of these fighters I know ever go into a fight completely healthy."

I don't say anything. I may not be an expert on submission wrestling, but I know first-hand what broken ribs feel like, and I can state with some authority: these guys are nuts. You gotta be a masochist to fight with broken ribs. Back in the ring, Wesley wants to give his broken toe a break.

"Oh, is Jeff gonna beat me up now?" says Joel, and he climbs in for his turn.

☆

Five minutes later, Wesley's back in there, and Joel, soaked in sweat that's half his, half Jeff's, tells me his martial arts history, starting as a teenager with Karate, then Kung Fu, then Jeet Kune Do, the art invented and popularized by Bruce Lee. Jeet Kune Do can be seen as a kind of precursor to Mixed Martial Arts, a "no style" style, taking the best elements of all styles, even Western boxing. You'll notice in some of his movies Lee doesn't stand like a traditional Kung Fu stylist: he's up on his toes, floating like a butterfly à la Muhammad Ali.

"Bruce Lee's whole concept was, this art is an evolving art. You get rid of what doesn't work. I think Bruce Lee would be a big supporter of this sport, and if Brazilian Jiu Jitsu had been more popular in his day, he would have been there. Because it works," Joel says.

"What happened to Jeet Kune Do after he died? Did it continue to evolve?"

"There's a bit of a debate. There's a split camp. A lot of people want to stay strictly with the old stuff, stay training the way Bruce said to. But others—the Burt Richardsons, Paul Vunaks—say Sifu Lee would have continued to evolve, and take from other arts. Jeet

Kune Do was a concept: learning to fight as skillfully as possible. Eliminate forms, just go with what works." He pauses as we watch Jeff and Wesley tangle on the ground. "This is fun," he says. "It's like human chess: you get to a certain position, and you know what he's trying to do, and you try to get there first. This sport has only been around ten years, so we're like pioneers, really. It's something I can tell my grandkids someday."

☆

On the way out the door we pass by a group of eight-year-olds on the mats, being tested on basic Karate moves. It always looks cute when little kids parrot what they've been taught. Compared with the intense focus I saw in kids the same age at my Shaolin school in China, these suburban American kids—uncertain, clumsy, and undisciplined in their flabby little bodies—are a joke. A minute later in the car, Jeff says, "Growing up as a kid, you think, 'This guy knows Karate, Oh my gosh he's got a black belt in Karate, don't mess with that guy.' But what does that really mean? He's followed some forms. Does that mean he actually knows how to fight? No. It teaches you techniques that you would never use in a fight. Like you would never keep your hands like those kids were doing. You'd keep them up, protecting your head, like with boxing."

I mention how the mother of that ten-year-old in Vanderhoof had said Brazilian Jiu Jitsu was more realistic because it mirrored the way kids fight in the schoolyard: they get each other in a headlock and twist each other to the ground.

"The reason people don't get knocked out fighting and end up rolling around on the ground is people don't know how to punch," Jeff says. "They use their arms, they don't use their body weight. Same thing with me, coming from a wrestling background, I didn't have any power in my punches, because I didn't use my hips. People not knowing how to punch makes Brazilian Jiu Jitsu more effective."

Jeff trains with a loosely affiliated pool of fighters based in Florida called American Top Team. That's where he's picked up the Jiu Jitsu to augment his college wrestling skills. "Most of the guys at American Top Team are Brazilian, right?" I ask.

"Yeah. Most of them came from Brazilian Top Team in Rio. It was a big thing when I joined, because a lot of them said, 'Don't let this guy on our team. He's an American, a gringo, he's going to take it and teach everyone here.' When I first started training there were guys who wouldn't train when I was in the room. Some of those guys are my best friends now. It's the culture, it took a while. Four years."

This is the last chance we'll have to talk until we meet up in Las Vegas in three weeks for his big fight at UFC. Tomorrow he's flying to North Carolina for a grappling tournament, then on to Florida to train with American Top Team. There are a million questions I want to ask, like, "So what is it about Leo Tolstoy's *The Kingdom of God Is Within You* that makes you say it's your favorite book, and the guiding template of your Christian anarchism?" But suddenly we're back downtown, and he directs me to pull up outside a tattoo parlor. "I've got an appointment."

"A Friday the 13th tattoo?" I ask. It's that special day, and some of the tattoo places in Olympia are offering thirteen-dollar deals, extremely cheap for a tattoo.

"No, a piercing," Jeff says. He seems a bit embarrassed about it, so I don't ask where. It's none of my business, really. But before he goes, there's one last thing I really want to do: touch those amazing cauliflower ears of his, those gnarled lumps on either side of his shaved head that look like blobs of chewing gum stuck on a balloon.

"You have cauliflower ears."

"Yeah, I got it in high school."

"How does it happen?"

"Any time you get a bruise in your body, your body sends fluid to repair the area, and it also sends calcium. In the ear the circulation is very poor, tiny capillaries, so when you get repeated blows, you get this calcium build-up, and if you don't take care of it, ice it, drain it, pack it, lay off it, then the blood flow decreases, and the problems get worse, the calcium builds up more. This is pure calcium now, it's like bone, there is nothing in it to hurt."

"Can I touch it?"

"Yeah, sure."

"Now that's amazing."

"It hurts like hell when you first start getting it but now it doesn't hurt at all. In Japan, it's like a status symbol over there."

25

★

The Babyfaced Assassin

The Mandalay Bay Resort and Casino is a fairly swank Las Vegas hotel, certainly better than the dump where I'm staying. I'm waiting in the lobby watching people check in, a lot of beefcake men, over-muscled gym junkies, here to watch the Ultimate Fighting Championship with their tanning salon girlfriends. There's an unofficial flying-out-to-Vegas uniform for these girls: tight black tank top, blue jeans shrink-wrapped around their asses, and three-inch black heels. And up top, sunglasses nestled like a tiara in tousled blonde hair.

I'm waiting for Jeff Monson to come meet me. Right now he's having his shorts inspected. The shorts he intends to wear in the ring when he fights tomorrow night need to be inspected and approved. When I phoned his room a minute ago, his wife, Jennifer, said he should be back soon. Jennifer sounds pretty excited to be here. Jeff had told me that when he first started fighting in Mixed Martial Arts, he kept the full truth of it secret from her; he told her he was going to wrestling tournaments, because he thought she wouldn't be able to deal with the brutality of these no-holds-barred events. But when he started coming home all cut and bruised by flying fists and savage kicks, he had to come clean. She was upset at first, but in the course of time she settled down and accepted it—in fact, now she's more into it than Jeff in some ways, tracking the careers of all the fighters, and keeping up with the gossip of the game.

Guess what? Mandalay Bay has two hotels, with two separate lobbies, and I'm sitting in the wrong one. I'm in the little boutique hotel off in the corner, where the muscleheads bring their mistresses, seems like. Jeff's in the regular hotel where the check-in counter's a hundred yards long and the line-up is fat-assed middle Americans, mixed with Chinese people who aren't fat exactly, but by Chinese standards look plump with affluence and lack of exercise. Anyhow, two lobbies means Jeff and I miss each other completely, which means the next time I see him is three hours later at the official weigh-in, at the eight-thousand-seat Event Center where the fight will play out tomorrow night. Jeff's down on the floor where the sixteen fighters, their handlers, and their corner men are all mixing and mingling, making me jealous that I'm missing some great dialogue, but I take solace in the fact that those bastards who got press credentials are only marginally closer than I am; we're all stuck in the stands, only they're a bit closer and I'm in with the plebes, three thousand beer-drinking hardcore fans, a lot of them wearing T-shirts that say things like *Fighting Solves Everything,* or *When in doubt, Knock 'em out,* or *Brazilian Jiu Jitsu: The Pitbull of Martial Arts.* My favorite T-shirt slogan of the day is practically a short story: there's a silhouette of a rifle, and underneath, the beginning of the Marine Corps Rifleman's Creed: *This is my rifle, there are many like it, but this one is mine. My rifle is my best friend. It is my life. I must master it like I master my life.* The women favor tank tops to show off their shoulder tattoos. I like the one with the

Greek masks of Comedy and Tragedy well-rendered, and an aphorism underneath: *Laugh now, Cry later.*

The reason the crowd is so huge is that the weigh-in comes right
after a Meet-the-Fighters autograph session, featuring headliners
Randy Couture and Chuck Liddell. It was quite the mob scene.
Huge hotel security types—flatheads in cop-like uniforms—had
their hands full dealing with overeager fans like the teary-eyed
woman who thought she had a right to jump the three-hundred-
yard queue because "I drove thirty hours to get here!"

I'm doing my journalistic duty, conducting an informal survey
to see if anyone knows about Jeff Monson and his leftist politics.
Apparently not. He may be the World Grappling Champion but
he's still an unknown with this bunch. Most of these fans know
nothing of Mixed Martial Arts outside what they've been spoon-
fed on Spike TV's UFC shows. The weigh-in's emcee, Joe Rogan,
host of the popular reality stunt show *Fear Factor* and a commen-
tator on UFC's Pay-Per-View telecasts, introduces Jeff by calling
him a "true American," but no one seems to catch the reference.
When Jeff strips to his shorts and steps on the scales, the guy sitting
beside me proclaims, "That's a monster!" He's two hundred thirty-
nine pounds; his opponent, one Brandon Lee Hinkle, is two
twenty-seven, but looks almost lean by comparison. He's five
inches taller at six foot two, and he's known to be a devastating
puncher with weak grappling skills. The two of them shake hands
cordially enough—there's none of the ego-driven posturing some
of the other fighters display. I do notice one thing, though: at the
end, when he descends the six-step staircase at the side of the stage,
Jeff is definitely favoring a leg.

I make my way down to the railing near the fighters and call out
to get Jeff's attention. We agree to meet in the lobby—the *other*
lobby—at five, and he'll take me to a nearby gym, where I can

watch as he runs through his last work-out before the fight. "My trainer and corner men are meeting me in the lobby too, you won't be able to miss us," he says.

☆

In the lobby at five o'clock sharp there's a big, handsome blonde guy standing around waiting. "For Jeff?" "Yeah." Only much later will I figure out this is Josh "The Babyfaced Assassin" Barnett, at one time the youngest title holder in UFC history, and now a professional wrestler fighting mostly in Japan. But at this point, to me he's just a guy helping Jeff out. And he doesn't seem too happy. The first thing he says when the other two corner men show up is, "What's that muscle that runs down the thigh like a sheath, the fascia? Idiot ripped it last week in a five-hundred-dollar grappling tournament."

"You gotta admire it though," says Dan Lambert, one of the others, a Florida businessman who bankrolls American Top Team. "Jeff loves to fight. It's better than a fucking Brazilian who won't get out of bed." He's teasing a smallish, athletic-looking Brazilian, another Top Team fighter, who's tagging along with the group, who never says anything and whose name I never catch.

"I don't know why he wants to work out now anyway," says Josh. "I'm not gonna let him do *anything*."

"Aw, he just wants to break a sweat," says the second corner man, a paunchy ex-wrestler named Wade.

Soon Jeff arrives and the six of us wait around for a limo. "How'd that grappling tournament in North Carolina go?" I ask him.

"All right. I had one two weeks ago, and one last week. I won, but I tweaked my leg a little. I'm kinda limping around. Hopefully it'll be better tomorrow," Jeff says. "Hey, I got shirts for you guys," he tells his team.

"Yeah, they say *Kill Bush,*" Josh says sarcastically. "I was there when he wore that."

He's talking about a tournament in Portland, Oregon; what the T-shirt in question actually said was *Assassinate Bush,* and Jeff was seen wearing it on the Jumbotron in a pre-fight video introduction. The crowd booed. Jeff won his bout, and in the post-fight interview in the ring his efforts to explain the T-shirt morphed into a rant against American foreign policy. The organizers cut the mike, according to Josh.

"No they didn't," Jeff says.

"Yes they did."

Later Jennifer will tell me the public display of that T-shirt prompted the Secret Service to drop by their house for a little visit, just to make sure Jeff didn't mean it literally.

☆

The limo takes us to the Ricardo Pires Brazilian Jiu Jitsu Combat Club, in a strip mall ten minutes from the hotel. Two huge sweat-soaked men are flaked out on the floor after grappling, and a little four-year-old girl runs between them, trailing an empty Cheesies bag behind her like a windsock. Jeff lies back on the mat, pulls a cell phone and a single credit card out of his pocket, and tosses them ten feet to where the mat meets the concrete wall. His toenails are painted bright pink.

Around him a half-dozen local grapplers are pairing off, casually slapping palms before the start of each tussle. There's a beautiful camaraderie here. I can see the attraction. You go hard for a bit, break a good sweat, then feel you've earned the right to laze on the mat shooting the shit. After stretching out, Jeff gets up and comes back with boxing gloves.

"I guess you want to hit now," says Josh.

"Yeah."

"Okay, but you can't hit hard, because you don't have wraps on."

Josh puts on padded mitts to take the punches. Wade has changed into sweats and is grappling some of the locals, but in between he watches the boxing, calling out things like, "Jeff, keep the hands up!" Even to me, it's apparent Jeff has a bad habit of dropping his hands from where they should be, up protecting his face.

He looks a bit like a fish out of water in a boxing ring. Josh is much more nimble, juking and jiving and giving flat-footed Jeff playful taps around the head with the mitts. There's a trace of sand on the canvas—we're in the desert after all—and in the harsh light it glitters underfoot like stardust fallen to earth. Jeff complains about it, he's slipping too much in his bare feet. It almost sounds like pouting. "Don't think about it," says Josh. "Don't worry about the little things, just concentrate on what you need to do. Just bring 'em home. I don't care how hard the punch is, just bring 'em home." He means bring the hands back to protect the head after throwing punches.

When the boxing's done they get back on the mat, with Wade acting as Jeff's practice dummy. All three advisors—Wade, Dan, and Josh—subject him to a barrage of comments:

"Once you get top position, keep it and work the shit out of it, okay?"

"Circle the head. When in danger, circle the head. Make him carry two hundred forty pounds."

"Don't you think he grabs the throat, tries to come around, and spins him like a wrestler?"

Jeff is lying across Wade, hesitating with his options. Pummel his face with his fist, or lock his arm down so he can smash his face with his forearm? "Lock the head, push the chin in, you know that one?" says Wade.

"He does now," says Josh.

"Remember, it's not fancy, but it works every fucking time," says Wade excitedly. "I use the blade here." He means the sharp bone of the forearm that leads toward the thumb, pressed against the opponent's neck to choke him out.

"And push the nose up, or rip the cheek! If you're behind him, don't be one of those guys dicking around back there," says Josh. "Be a killer, rip that face off, hit the soft spots, finish him off! Brandon's a gamer. He's not that skilled but he gives it everything he's got. You gotta neutralize that. You're the great neutralizer, Jeff, but instead of just stalling or riding him out, punish him. Being on bottom should be hell for this person."

They brainstorm another move, a face lock. Wade says, "I haven't seen that one in a long time," prompting them to trace the move's history back to its possible originator: "Wasn't he called the Malawian Bone Crusher or something?"

Now it turns from strategy to nostalgia, from training to a bullshit session while lying on the mat. The name of one fighter brings up another, and another, who "sucked as a fighter."

"Naaah. When he first took his *gi* off, he wasn't comfortable, but he never sucked."

"He was all about the triangular arm bar."

Meanwhile Jeff says almost nothing. After ten minutes he finally mutters something so soft I can't hear him. Josh says, "Don't worry about it, Jeff. For every punch he puts on you, land three on him."

"He's not a threat to submit you," Wade says.

"Someone asked me how this fight's gonna go," Josh says. "I said, second round, you'll end it with a choke."

☆

While the other guys are changing back into their street clothes, I corner Josh and tell him it seemed to me like they'd overloaded Jeff with advice.

"I just wanted to reinforce things he already knows," he says. "All this stuff he knows and uses. You gotta keep his mind fresh. If he sticks to the game plan, he'll be fine."

"And the game plan?"

"I want him to keep his pace up high; I want him to beat the guy with conditioning; I want Jeff to make it a grappling match, because I know Jeff will win. I want him to win every little battle they have, be it a hand, or getting a head free, anything like that. Winning all those little battles is going to take the will to fight out of the guy."

"Is it tough for someone from a wrestling background like Jeff to pick up the boxing skills?"

"You gotta go in thinking, 'This is a fight, this is not about winning by points,'" says Josh. That reduces everything to a brutal simplicity: "Are you in there to win a fight, or are you in there to get beat up?"

☆

In the limo back to the hotel the Brazilian finally says something. "That kid is good, man." He's talking about a teenage boy at the club who was game enough to take them all on, repeatedly.

"He is," agrees Wade. "I submitted him seven times. My bitch. Caught him with the reverse armbar, got him with the guillotine."

The five of them talk of foot locks and guillotines, double wrist locks and chicken wings.

"That's not a real move, that's bullshit," says Dan.

"What do you mean it's bullshit, you tapped!" Josh answers. "You talking about where I put the knee on your shin bone and pull a toe hold, or are you talking about the one where you try to put me in half guard, and I knee bar you with my legs, my hip?"

"Wade did that knee on my ankle, pull on my toe, and I said, Bitch, I am not fucking tapping to that, you can break it off. I'm not tapping to that fucking thing, it's not a legitimate submission hold!" Dan says.

"Thank you!" says Jeff.

"I didn't tap, but I didn't walk for three days."

Josh says, "I don't care if you tap or not; if you tap it makes my job easier. It's your fucking leg, buddy. If you get it just right though, you can break a shin bone."

"Oh man, it hurt like a bitch," says Dan.

"What other bullshit holds are you talking about, Jeff?" says Josh.

Jeff doesn't answer. Wade says, "Did you get him in a Boston crab?"

"No, I never got Jeff in a Boston. He's kinda hard to bend over like that," says Josh.

"I don't think he bends that way," says Dan.

"Yeah, exactly. He puts his legs together and skids around; you can't bow his back like that. No, I went after his legs trying to get something, and my legs were wrapped up into his armpits, so I ended up pulling his knees one way and stretching his body the other."

"That's crap. Elbows and shins, breaking toes off, and other crap," says Dan.

"Two words of advice: if you don't like it, don't tap," Wade declares.

Josh agrees. "Hey man, it's been good to me as a professional wrestler," he says proudly.

☆

The three cornermen came from different times and places in Jeff's life, and didn't know each other well. They shared a common love of grappling and wrestling, but the talk eventually meandered from that subject into political philosophy, and they agreed a ten percent flat tax would be more fair than the current graduated tax rates, and then Wade said to me, "Wait a minute, you know who you remind me of? You look just like Steve Forbes. Say Flat Tax. C'mon. Flat tax."

Now I don't know if you know who Steve Forbes is, or what he looks like. Google him, find a photo, and you will see that it is no compliment to be told you look like him. Dude is worth four hundred million bucks, and blew a shitload of cash running in the presidential primaries on a flat tax platform, and was widely mocked and derided for his trouble, in part because looks-wise he's a goofy, jowly, nerdy doofus. To drive images of Steve Forbes from my head, I asked the guys why the UFC pays its fighters such crap wages, and that started a short discussion that led to Wade demanding of Josh, "You were guilty, right?"

It turns out that once upon a time, (2002 to be exact) this self-same Josh Barnett, AKA The Babyfaced Assassin, was the UFC's reigning heavyweight champion. Then he was accused of taking performance enhancing drugs, and stripped of his title. Barnett appealed the Nevada State Athletic Commission ruling. "They never had any solid proof I took anything," he says. He arranged an independent retest, and it seemed to vindicate him, but whatever the case, justly or not, he was tainted by the charges, and the powers that be at the UFC were in no mood to reinstate him, because even before he had been accused of drug use, he'd been demanding they renegotiate his contract. To put it in Biblical terms, he was cast out of the UFC tents into the desert. If you want to sustain the metaphor, Josh wandered to the encampment of another tribe, settled among them, and prospered. Josh Barnett went to Japan.

"I've won one of the most distinguished titles in the world, King of Pancrase, worked fights in K–1 and Pride, and been on the covers of magazines over there that don't even have anything to do with martial arts," he boasts. "I've had a comic book autobiography, and I'm in four video games, I've been on television—there is so much more cross-over over there. I've brought them a character and a persona they can have fun with, and I knew if I stayed in UFC none of that would have been available to me."

Josh started fighting professionally at the tender age of eighteen. "I had high school wrestling, some Judo and Muay Thai and kickboxing. I really learned almost all my technique and trade from Matt Hume at Pankration, his club in Seattle. I learned submission wrestling, and many more stand-up skills, and catch wrestling." Catch wrestling, or Catch as Catch Can, originated in a legendary gym in Wigan, England, called the Snake Pit. The two great masters of the art, Bill Robinson and Karl Gotch, both trained there under a guy named Billy Riley. The Snake Pit no longer exists. "Funny enough, Catch as Catch Can isn't prominent in England anymore," Josh says. "But it used to be world renowned back in the early 1900s. It's what wrestling was, back in the 1800s, when pro wrestlers really plied their trade. It wasn't an entertainment spectacle like the WWE: it was legitimate wrestling with submissions."

☆

The true heyday of wrestling was the three decades leading up to the First World War. In the 1920s scandals over fixed fights plagued the sport, as they did boxing at the time. While boxing tried to clean up its act, wrestling promoters went the other way and turned the art into a circus act of fixed fights, where "unless you're missing some chromosomes you couldn't possibly think it's real," as wrestling historian Jake Shannon puts it. Shannon is executive director of Scientific Wrestling, who put up a fascinating website at scientificwrestling.com. He says the bridge between that golden era of legitimate wrestling and our present age is a Belgian named Karl Gotch, who is still alive, eighty-one years old. Gotch spent three years in the Second World War in a German labor camp, and afterward worked as a legitimate amateur wrestler, and also as a professional wrestler to make a living. He travelled the world accumulating fighting skills, including a stint at the infamous Snake Pit. By the early 1960s Gotch had moved to Japan. According to Shannon, "Gotch had quite a repertoire, and an immense amount of knowledge. He's a tough guy. Anyone he ever wrestled will tell you he's the toughest they ever met. So he went to Japan, kicked everyone's butt over there, and they started calling him Kamasima, the God of Wrestling. He started training all the big fighters over there. He actually was corner man for Antonio Inoki, when he fought Muhammad Ali in 1976." Inoki reclined on his back on the mat and kicked Ali in the shins and knees all night, bruising him severely. Some say Ali's footwork was never the same after that. "Basically, any submission wrestling out of Japan has Karl Gotch's stamp on it," Shannon says. "He really kept the lineage alive."

Josh Barnett told me Japanese wrestlers train in what's called Gotch style wrestling. "All the training in the gym is for real, even though they might go out in the ring and work a match, meaning the outcome might be predetermined," he said.

Later I asked Jake Shannon, "So in Japan, the worked matches and the legitimate matches are all mixed up, and someone like Josh Barnett is doing both?"

"Yeah. When they train they really do learn how to do submission wrestling, but then sometimes they'll do the worked matches. There are promotions up and down the gamut, there's pure worked, semi-worked, full shoots, semi-shoots."

"Full shoots means … ?"

"Not worked at all."

"Okay, so do people know what they're watching when they go watch it, or are they sometimes confused about it?"

"Sometimes you can't tell if it's worked, sometimes you can, because you'll see them do some stupid move, where you think, 'That is ridiculous, there is no way he could pull it off.'"

"Do you think it's fair to say the rise of Mixed Martial Arts events like UFC has caused a revival in these almost forgotten techniques?"

"Most certainly. The funny thing is, the first promotion to do this kind of thing was Pancrase."

"But doesn't Pancrase present itself as the ancient wrestling art of Greece, as practiced in the ancient Olympics?" I asked. I'd done a little homework.

"Right. That was Karl Gotch's idea. Pankration was the first to do a real shoot match. That's where Ken Shamrock came from, and that's why they brought him over to fight Royce Gracie in the very first UFC. My opinion is, Ken was at a real disadvantage for that, because in his training, they never use the bathrobe thing the Brazilians wear, so he got choked out by Royce, who used his jacket. Now they've standardized the rules, and unless it's special rules, you can't go in wearing the bathrobe."

"The *gi*," I say, helpfully. Obviously he knows that, he's just making a point.

"The *gi*. Thank you."

☆

"For a catch wrestler, one of the great precepts of the art is, *Why be on bottom when you can be on top?* In the old times you could lose by being pinned, so people would not roll to their back. They'd use their legs, or what the Brazilians refer to as the guard," Josh told me. "But in catch there's emphasis on the ability to neutralize and immobilize a joint from any position, especially using neck cranks, ankle locks, as well as arm locks. Jiu Jitsu for instance doesn't prescribe neck locks nearly so much, or leg locks as much, whereas the catch wrestler certainly is interested in attacking and controlling the neck, because the neck is the fulcrum of the entire body. Wherever the neck and the head go, the body will follow, so if you are controlling the neck you are controlling his body.

"There were some famous American wrestlers known for their catch skills, like Frank Gotch out of Iowa, he was known for his toe holds, which is a submission hold. Then there was Martin Farmer Burns, who could hang himself with a noose around his neck, just hang there, because his neck was so strong. Then there was a guy, Ad Santel, who in the 1920s went to Japan, and beat the World Judo champ, and declared himself the champ, which raised the ire of the Japanese, but he kept beating them all, until they gave up on him. Catch was really one of the earliest martial arts."

If you're fighting in a modern Mixed Martial Arts event under rules similar to the UFC, where almost anything goes except eye gouging, fishhooking, and elbows to the face, then the long lost art of the toe hold suddenly rates a second look, along with neck cranks, ankle locks, and many other antique wrestling moves that have nearly faded from the collective memory, except as parodies of themselves in the scripted cartoon theatre of World Wrestling Entertainment and its ilk. Jake Shannon says, "There are three bread and butter holds that catch wrestling is known for. One, neck cranks, which are dangerous, and they can actually break someone's neck quite easily. Two, the double wrist lock, which is like a chicken wing or whatever, where the arm is bent downward at a ninety degree angle, and three, toe holds. It's called a toe hold not because you're actually trying to target the toe, you grab the person's toe and crank the ankle, so it's an ankle submission really. Toe holds are *very* legitimate."

☆

Hopefully now you have a better appreciation of what Jeff and his corner men were arguing about in the limo in Las Vegas ("I'm not tapping to that fucking thing, it's not a legitimate submission hold!"). I might have learned more then and there, except when Wade asked Josh if he was guilty, it pretty much killed the conversation. Soon we were back at their hotel, the Mandalay, which by Vegas standards is upper middle class, and I went back to my hotel, Circus Circus, which by Vegas standards is lower middle class. I ordered some takeout Mexican food from the Yellow Pages, and stumbled into the bathroom with a gut full of refried beans and cheese, looked in the mirror, and for the first time in my life thought, Steve Forbes. I used to think of myself as a handsome devil but I've gotten jowly in the five years since I married. So I sank into a mild depression. Las Vegas always does that to me anyway. "What Happens in Vegas Stays in Vegas" is the semi-official motto of the place, they even use it in television commercials; but the slogan deserves a coda: what happens stays, yeah sure, uh huh, except for sexually transmitted diseases and credit card bills. Those go home with you. At the heart of the slogan is a wink wink nudge nudge, encouraging you to pull something crazy and sexually profligate, then slink back to your loving wife and family with a *secret*. The place is crawling with male conventioneers who've bought into that fantasy, and there are strip clubs and hookers galore ready to turn any craving into a commercial transaction. The main drag, The Strip, is confettied with brightly colored wallet-sized advertisements for blonde goddess whores, handed out by sunburnt five-foot-nothing illegal Mexicans. Most guys who take a card from them give it only a glance before letting it flutter to the pavement. While tourist families rubberneck the mammoth casinos, the man-made lakes and faux Eiffel Towers, their little kiddies are fixated on what's at their feet, trampling the million tits and asses of the most tawdry litter in the world. No wonder I get depressed. In this vulnerable mental state I started worrying about this book, that it lacks a big catharsis. I was supposed to earn a black belt and discover something deep about myself by overcoming my fears. Everyone expects major catharsis from their "narrative non-fiction" these days. "His life changed forever, yours will too when you read about it!!" That's what the blurb should say. But this book seems on course to fade out with a whimper, not a bang. What to do? Oh what the hell, be Taoist about it. Go down, not up. Stay hidden. Just accept it.

26

☆

Punish This

It's fight day at Mandalay Bay, and the sports book is thrumming with business. There are maybe two dozen giant television screens on the forty-foot-high wall above the betting counter, and every one of them is tuned to a different sporting event. On a Saturday afternoon in February, that means horse racing, hockey, and mostly college basketball. The chairs for spectators have an arm that flattens out like a beaver tail for taking notes, and the guys slumped in the chairs have the heavy-lidded blasé look of hardcore gamblers, except for a woman who shrieks and leaps out of her seat every time a kid drains a three-pointer in a game between Utah and New Mexico. Tucked in one corner of the wall are the odds for tonight's UFC fights, but only the top five of the eight bouts are listed, and Jeff's is not among them. Damn. I was going to put some money on my man.

Four clean-cut American model citizen types stand in a small crowd milling around the UFC odds board, trying to figure out how to read it. They've flown in for the weekend from Orlando, Florida, where lately they've made it a ritual to watch UFC fights on Pay-Per-View while drinking Budweiser and tearing the meat from flaming hot chicken limbs at an establishment called The Wing House. They're neophyte Vegas gamblers. For people like them the casino provides a guy in a blue blazer, circulating through the crowd like the host at a cocktail party. When he comes over to help out, it's finally understood: Liddell's the favorite, you gotta bet fifteen fifty to make ten dollars. For Couture, bet ten and you can make thirteen fifty. The Mandalay Bay employee, one Jay Rood by name, says, "Eight to nine thousand" when I ask how many fans the Event Center holds, "but for this kind of fight they don't pack them in there like they could, because of the volatility of the crowd." He's amazed at yesterday's mass hysteria at the weigh-in. A weigh-in for a fight between the best boxers in the world might draw a hundred and fifty people. "We were leery about the UFC at first, whether it was legit or not, or if it was like the WWE," he says. "The Fertittas really stuck with it through some lean times." We agree that getting that Ultimate Fighter reality TV show going on a cable network is what turned the tide. It gave Liddell and Couture personalities.

One of the Orlando gang claims demand for fight tickets has driven the price of seven-hundred-dollar floor tickets up to three thousand dollars on eBay. I came down to Vegas worried I'd have to haggle with a scalper, but managed to score a ticket at face price by checking back at the box office three times this morning for last-minute returns. I'm in the cheapest seats, but it still set me back a hundred bucks.

☆

Two hours to kill before the fight. Think I'll wander downstairs to the counter where reporters who rate can pick up their press credentials. Hey, there's Joe Rogan. You know what? The guy can't cover five feet of Mandalay Bay broadloom without being accosted by folks who recognize his celebrity. I hesitate to call these people fans—they're not necessarily fans of his, they'd do the same for any famous person. "Hey, Joe, can I—" No one asks for an autograph anymore, everyone has a cell phone that takes pictures, and it's not enough to have a picture of Joe Rogan to prove you actually met him, it's gotta be a picture of *Joe and you,* with arms around each other like bosom pals. If you're with someone, you get them to take the picture, then return the favor by taking one for them; if you're solo, you hold Joe close and take the picture yourself, an intimate double portrait snapped at arm's length. Joe's a pro at smiling without looking insincere. Posing on autopilot. A bride and three bridesmaids ducking out of a wedding reception squeal at the sight of him and come barreling over for a group shot, causing Joe's smile to actually show signs of wear and tear. Maybe it's because a shrieking bride attracts an even bigger crowd of rubberneckers, all going, "What the fu— hey, it's that *Fear Factor* dude! Let's get a photo with our phones!" But just then Joe's pocket starts ringing, he pulls out his own phone and answers it, and everyone backs off, granting him temporary privacy. There's a lesson here for mid-range and higher celebrities: if you want to cross a crowded room quickly, pull out your cell phone and talk into it.

☆

At last the doors open and I can settle my ass into Section 203, Row H, Seat 9. What can I tell you? The crowd is younger and more beautiful than I'd expected. The men have spiky gelled hair and any woman with a respectable cleavage has gone out of her way to display it in the most flattering light possible. I feel like a *Girls Gone Wild* video's gonna break out any minute. Getting to my seat involves squeezing past a fine-looking Latina in a black tank top with PUNISH THIS in big pink letters across her tits. I think it's safe to say the men are into BJJ, Brazilian Jiu Jitsu, and the women into BBW, Brazilian Bikini Waxing. I think I've said enough about where my mind's wandering. I'm a happily married man, I shouldn't be subjected to scenes like this. I'll say one more thing: almost half the crowd are women, and they shout louder and more fervently than the men. One sitting directly behind me tells her friends, "This is like my Super Bowl." When the first fight starts, she's on her feet, yelling, "Let's go, KING!! You sucker! Fuck yeah! Knock 'im out, bitch!!"

☆

Jeff's is the second fight of the night. On the long walk from under the stands to the ring he ignores the cheering crowd, and looks vaguely peeved, like he just got a credit card bill much higher than expected. His opponent, Brandon Lee Hinkle, bounces in next, playful and a bit oafish, reminding me of Kevin Kline in *A Fish Called Wanda*. Because they are fighting in an octagon-shaped ring surrounded by a chain link fence, there is, strictly speaking, no corner for the corner men. From where I sit, Wade appears to be doing most of the talking, before he, Josh, and Dan are ordered out of the octagon. The fence is bolted shut behind them. Jeff and Brandon are alone with a referee. A bell sounds, and he gestures for them to come together and do whatever they need to do to make the other guy surrender or lose consciousness.

☆

Here are my notes, covering the full four minutes and thirty-five seconds of Jeff's fight, from start to submission:

J has him down.
Elbow, elbow!
C'mon keep yourself

I can't bear to look away, and I pretty much hold my breath the entire fight. It's not so much that I want Jeff to win—I just don't want him to lose. He's already told me how devastated he gets when he loses. In part I'm being selfish: we're supposed to all go out for dinner afterward, so if he loses instead of wins, dinner will be funereal instead of fun. But there's much more to it than that, I surprise myself that I care so much. My body scrunches up into pre-wince mode, getting ready to fully wince if Brandon Lee Hinkle should start landing his reputedly heavy fists on Jeff's eyes, ears, throat, or nose, and blood starts to flow. But the fight doesn't play out like that. There's almost no punching: it goes straight to the ground and becomes two guys rolling around. Later, Josh will be kind enough to give me a post mortem play by play:

The minute Brandon started to engage, Jeff shot for a take-down, which Brandon defended very well, but that was fine for us, because Jeff is very good at reversing from the bottom onto the top. So even though he didn't get the takedown, he did eventually put Brandon on his back. Brandon actually was able to roll Jeff over and get into a side control position, and I wasn't really worried, but I felt if there was any opportunity for Brandon to win the fight, it could be from there, from some sort of cut.

But Jeff once again got right up underneath him and put him on his back, and at that point I knew it wasn't going to go much longer. My basic instruction was just continue to move, don't stop moving, don't stop working; as tired as Jeff may get by pressing the action, I know Hinkle will be three times more tired. Eventually it was just a matter of getting something he was comfortable with, and that's when he got the choke.

☆

That sounds all cool and collected because it's hindsight, but when you are in the moment it's another matter. It's heart-stopping, especially that moment when it looks like Jeff has him, and Hinkle pretty much gets up off the ground with Jeff on his back, and throws him off. Josh is right, in all likelihood that Herculean effort made Hinkle three times more exhausted, and when Jeff almost immediately gets back on top of him, he doesn't have it in him to be Herculean twice in two minutes. I'm thrilled giddy for Jeff when he gets the choke and Hinkle's body goes limp. The referee knocks Jeff off him, Jeff stands up and raises his arms in a kind of subdued, businesslike celebration, like it was all part of an evening's work, and I have tears in my eyes. For a while the vanquished Hinkle becomes the center of attention in the ring because it takes a few tense minutes to revive him, and when at last they do, he thinks the fight is still on, and struggles to get up and re-engage the battle. It's tragic and comical at the same time. Poor fallen warrior is only adding to his humiliation. The cruel crowd is laughing at him.

Joe Rogan comes into the ring as he always does, to interview the winner, and talks with Jeff for a while but the PA is so lousy you can't hear a word until the very end, when Joe says, "Looking forward to seeing more of you."

"Thank you," says Jeff, and then he brings both fists up by his head, and shouts, "Jiu Jitsu!" There's no "assassinate Bush," or "U.S. out of Iraq." The UFC folks have asked him not to say anything political.

☆

Whew! My man won! Feels good. I feel drained. Now there's a bunch of other fights to sit through. Last night in the casino I met this Australian guy named Elvis Sinosic, who's come halfway around the world to fight another guy who's come a quarter of the way around the world, the Italian Alessio Sakara. Sporting a rather dubious record of six wins, eight losses, and two draws, Elvis is a nice guy, sweet, unassuming, soft-spoken, who runs a martial arts club back home in Concord, New South Wales, specializing, according to his blood-red business card, in Brazilian Jiu Jitsu, Thai Kickboxing, Mixed Martial Arts, Self-Defense, Wrestling, Yoga, and Kids. I liked that: that a martial artist capable of fighting at this level would be back home next week teaching kiddies in after-school classes. It reminded me of Sifu Bob, a man with lethal talents, who also hires himself out to host martial arts–themed children's birthday parties at the Academy, cake included.

I'm supporting the outrageously red-headed Elvis one hundred percent as he enters the octagon, but from the get-go his chances take a grim turn. Sakara, who is eleven years younger and sports a thirteen-and-three record, lunges at my man, wraps him up in a bear hug, and throws him down hard on his back. Obviously Elvis could use a lesson from Don the monk in neck cranks and percussive punches. He's got no defense. Sakara, on the other hand, is primarily a boxer, and clearly lacks the wrestling or grappling skills to secure a submission. His fight plan appears to be "Beat on Elvis's face until the ref in his mercy orders an end to the bludgeoning." But the ref, inexplicably to me, is not moved to interfere. Remember Andy Pi in Beijing telling me how awestruck he had been, watching Royce Gracie's exquisite, revelatory technique in the first UFCs, "winning fights without having to beat people up, without hurting them"? Well, this fight is nothing like that. This fight is all about administering a beating. The ref has to keep reminding young Sakara that it's all right to sit on Elvis's chest and destroy his face with forearms and fists, but not all right to nail him in the eye socket with an elbow bent sharp as a pick-axe. Of course, he only points this out *after* the elbow finds its target, and then again after it strikes a second time.

Elvis's face is awash in blood as red as his hair—in fact, it's hard to tell where the hair ends and the blood begins. Blood is dribbling and splotching the mat all around his skull, but Elvis is a gamer: he keeps trying to cover up, and even lands a few of his own from his back. But he's taking a severe beating, and after a while it's not funny, it's unpleasant to watch. The crowd goes eerily quiet, and for a moment I think it might be because they're having a collective breakthrough in conscience, that the nauseating battering of poor sweet Elvis has caused them to question their perverted interest in watching people pummel each other senseless. Then a lone voice among the eight thousand yells out, "Booorrring," and there's a great twitter of laughter, then wide applause. They're not re-examining their core values after all, they're just plain bored. The fight is too one-sided.

The seat beside me has been empty until this fight. The guy who now claims it has hardly touched his ass down before he's asking me out of the side of his mouth, "They sanction this crap? I'm amazed they allow it. It's like a street fight."

Turns out he's in town from New Jersey and someone's given him the ticket, otherwise he would have never come near this joint. He's in his fifties, sharp-minded, disdainful. "Look at the demographics," he says. "It's a young, white crowd. Muscle-heads, a lot of 'em on steroids. They drug test these fighters?"

I tell him the Nevada State Athletic Commission does. The same regulatory body that tests boxers.

"How much do these guys make?"

I tell him about Jeff getting three grand, plus another three for winning.

"Three grand? I'll lose more than that at the tables tonight. How can they live on that?"

Jeff had told me of guys living in the back rooms of gyms, unable to afford rent. When I pass that along, Mr. New Jersey says,

"Meanwhile, the guys who own it are making millions, I bet. They need a union."

Later I dig up the financial numbers: a live gate of three million three hundred thousand dollars, and an estimated four hundred ten thousand Pay-Per-View buys at $39.95 apiece. That's another sixteen million dollars. Total earnings, nineteen million bucks. And the fighters see three grand? It is outrageous.

Down in the octagon, Elvis's fight is done. Bathing in his own blood but still conscious, frisky even, he's up on his feet, awaiting the inevitable unanimous decision, and in the crowded post-fight cage, he's trying to catch up with his torturer to give him extra hugs, but the Italian's body language says, "I just beat the crap outta you—quit dripping blood on me and get lost." Joe Rogan interviews the victorious Sakara in the ring, but the PA muddles it all to mush. The cynic beside me mutters, "No loss. Not exactly a Mensa meeting going on down there."

☆

I've got fight fatigue. There are plenty of fights to go, but I'm only half watching. I'm more interested in the crowd. Seated on my right are two twenty-something couples from Colorado who epitomize all I was saying earlier about BJJ and BBW, hair gel for men and push-up bras for the ladies. One of the gals disappears down to the souvenir stand, and comes back a bit later wearing a newly purchased white T-shirt. For some reason she has covered up the top half of the slinky black "Party in Vegas" dress she arrived in. She's angry about something; she flings a plastic bag at her boyfriend, screeches, "Here's your stupid T-shirt!" and skitters in her high heels down the stairway and out the exit. We never see her again. Twenty minutes later she phones her girlfriend's cell and tells her to tell the boyfriend she's taken her luggage and is headed for the bus station, to catch the first bus back to Colorado right now. Her boyfriend says, "What? Tell her she's—" then cuts himself short, slumps back in his chair, and makes an unhappy, impotent face, like, "Don't tell her anything, just let her go." Eavesdropping on their little drama, I'm feeling slightly voyeuristic, and thinking, Thank God I'm not twenty-something anymore, pulling or putting up with infantile tantrums.

I should tell you one more thing: in the feature event, Chuck knocked out Randy, and in the crowd around me a lot of women cried.

27

☆

Resist Not Evil

Now that he's a winner, Jeff is instantly a hot commodity. In the afternoon before the fight, he had wandered through the casino pretty much unrecognized. Now, an hour after the last bout, he comes up an escalator from the basement and is dumped off in the middle of hundreds of waiting fight fans, and they all know who he is. All the men want to slap his back and tell him, Great fight. Beautiful girls with cleavage want to cuddle close for a photo. A guy in a wheelchair wants to tell him about his website, www.farfrumwalkn.com, celebrating Mixed Martial Arts fights between guys in wheelchairs, and another guy, on crutches because of a degenerative disc disorder, wants to know what kind of weight training he should do. "I want every opinion in the world, except my doctor's," he says. "Damn doctor says stop lifting weights altogether—No way!" Jeff takes time for one and all; he even gives the crutch user his email address, telling him he'll consult his chiropractor and send him a training regimen geared to his condition.

An uncredentialled documentary crew sticks their camera in his face and starts firing questions. "It's the hardest sport in the world," Jeff tells them. "You gotta know kickboxing, boxing, grappling, Jiu

Jitsu, and wrestling, and if you're bad at any one of them, people will find out quick, because there are so many tapes of the fights around."

"And does your mother watch the fights? Have you called your mother yet?"

"She doesn't watch," Jeff says. "She's scared. She doesn't want to see me hurt anybody, and she doesn't want me to be hurt."

☆

After what seems like hours, we make it to the elevators that will take us up to his room, where his wife, Jennifer, waits with Darren, his chiropractor, and Darren's buddy Deiter. Darren and Deiter are from Florida, and they're wearing puka shell necklaces.

Jeff dumps his duffel bag on the floor and wanders off to the kitchenette, where he drinks a huge amount of water. "You missed how Jeff drinks his protein drink," says Darren. He points to a plastic picnic cooler, the size that can easily hold a dozen cans of beer. "He pours the powder in the cooler, adds water, picks up the whole thing and chugs it down."

"Is your check in here?" Jennifer asks Jeff, poking around in the duffel bag. She's plump with a punk look, in a short leather skirt and black stockings I'd call fishnet except the holes are circular and of various random sizes. Jeff comes back from the kitchenette and pulls a bunch of crinkled and dog-eared papers out of the bag's side pocket, dumping them on the floor, where they contribute to the general clutter of the place. Clothes and papers are strewn haphazardly around. It's hard to find a place to sit down. Jeff, sifting through the papers, finally finds the check and hands it to her.

The amount is less than she expected. Jeff tells her they deducted the state licensing fee out of it.

"You had to pay for the license yourself?" she asks, incredulous.

"A hundred and twenty-five bucks."

"They're a racket," she snarls.

☆

She and Jeff absent themselves to the kitchenette for a bit. There are double hinged doors they can close for privacy. I start explaining to Darren and Deiter what the hell I'm doing here, and then I show off my recently acquired knowledge of Bagua by demonstrating the circle walk, slightly scaled down from the ideal circumference because the room is mostly taken up with two double beds pointed toward that standard-issue great honking piece of furniture hotels hide the television in. "The key is settling your back down into your hips before you even start," I tell them.

"Sounds like you're working the multifidus," Darren says.

"What's that?"

"The multifidus is the deepest muscle in the back. It basically goes from vertebra to vertebra; it's part of the core muscle group, one of the major muscles. It's very deep, very small, but it's an *intrinsic* muscle. You have large muscles, big ones that have lots of big power moves. But what people miss in training are the core muscles, to get the balance, the coordination, the speed, the agility—a lot of that comes from the core. For big power shots people train the slow twitch fibers, but they fail to train the fast twitch fibers, or the core muscle groups. That's what makes the difference between an athlete and just a meathead, a guy that picks up a lot of weights but doesn't know how to use that muscle mass. You get someone who knows how to train the fast twitch fibers and the core muscle groups, and then make it powerful, where you can use the speed, the agility, the balance, the coordination, all coming from the core, you've got someone dangerous. Then you give him technique, and you have a fighter."

"How does that relate to Jeff?"

"A lot of training they do is balance. In and out of guard. Have you seen what they do in Jiu Jitsu, in training, where they are in guard, and they go to half guard, they do a little pick-up of the foot, and kick off the hip, and they switch? They work the obliques, the abdominal muscles, thigh muscles, all these different muscles. With balance comes neuro-muscular re-education—you can educate the joint to recognize where it is at all times. They learn to take hits, get hits, and find center. It's all about finding center.

"It gets really deep into neurology, muscle re-education. That stuff you showed us, that martial art—"

"Bagua."

"Yeah, Bagua. It makes perfect sense. You can't do anything without a strong foundation. I've been fine tuning Jeff's structure for some time, so there is no neurological interference and he gets maximum performance from the brain. My fighters I treat a lot like my ballerinas. I work with a lot of ballerinas. And the ballerinas and the fighters have lots in common, because if a ballerina loses center it's obvious, they can't do a thing. Same with a fighter: if for just a second they lose center, Boom! The fight is over."

Jeff comes out of the kitchen, turns his back to us, and casually strips down to change into jeans and a T-shirt. No underwear. He really is quite the specimen, two hundred thirty-nine pounds, all muscle, much of it covered with tattoos. He's got a big hammer and sickle on his leg, for example; that's a rare one these days. I'll tell you about the arms a bit later. Right now he wants Darren to work on him a bit—his back is killing him. So Darren gets him to lie on his side on the bed, and then gets over top of him and prepares to heal.

"C-5, C-6 is subluxated. We're going to contact that exact segment and set it back into proper position." As an aside to me, he says, "I know his X-rays, I wouldn't just do this to anyone. That's it, right there." He jumps around on Jeff like a midget trying to kick-start a motorcycle. But the bed is proving too soft and springy to get the good pressure. "You should get on your knees on the floor, a pillow under each knee, and lie forward onto the bed," he suggests. Then he feels around some more. "He has a lumbar disc in the L5 position that's got to come up a bit. That's twisted. Feel it?"

"Yeah," says Jeff.

Darren attempts a "gross manipulation."

"I feel good now," Jeff says.

"Oh yeah, there it is," says Darren. "And then we're actually going to leave, right? It's midnight. We are all so proud of you, Jeff. I was screaming so loud I lost my frigging voice. Okay, where are we going?"

"He wants to eat," Jennifer says. "House of Blues have food."

"We just missed half the show," Jeff says. Joe Rogan has invited Jeff to come watch his stand-up comedy act at the House of Blues, the live rock club in the casino. Jeff was supposed to call someone to set it up.

"Did you call him?" Jennifer asks.

Jeff doesn't say anything.

☆

Ten minutes later we're all loitering outside the House of Blues, because the guy at the ticket wicket don't know nothin' about no comps, plus the show's sold out and already underway. Jeff is such a mild-mannered guy he just takes it, and wanders away to sit glumly at a row of slot machines barking their tinkly siren song like a kiddie carnival merry-go-round on steroids. He tinkers with his cell phone, trying to get through to the guy he was supposed to call. Meanwhile Jennifer is pleading with a beefy bouncer type and getting the cold shoulder.

This is the moment where I actually prove useful, for once. In this entire book, I can't think of a time I've proven myself useful yet, so I'm overdue. The closest was when Jarek was hungry coming down Wudang Mountain in the dark, and I pulled Fancy Smell biscuits from my knapsack. Oh yeah—and I drove Jeff to grappling practice in Olympia. It's good to be useful once in a while. Otherwise you're just the guy tagging along writing everything down.

Here's the deal: we're being denied access by a bunch of over-muscled bouncer type guys projecting a Don't Fuck With Me attitude. Testosterone rules, but there is hope. Among the lugheads in black T-shirts I spot a splash of lipstick, our red lifebuoy in a dark sea of manly indifference. Hooray, a woman works here. I catch her eye and go talk to her.

"See that guy over there? That's Jeff Monson."

"I know. I saw the fight. He was awesome."

Five minutes later, we're in the Etta room, named in honor of blues legend Etta James. It's a VIP box with two big comfy couches, looking down on Joe Rogan in mid-performance from just above stage left, the closest, most intimate seats in the house. Jennifer stretches out on one couch, Darren, Deiter, and I share the other, and Jeff lies on the floor, on account of his back. "Dude, your back is *torqued*," says Darren. "We'll get it tomorrow."

"We need something hard, not that bed," says Jeff.

"All we need is a bench."

We watch Joe Rogan deliver a series of comic riffs, standard nightclub material about women who don't like to give blow jobs, or the self-loathing he always feels immediately after masturbating. People in the crowd keep buying shots for the waitresses to plunk on the stage at his feet, and he keeps draining them down his throat and tossing the empty shot glasses over his shoulder. He's getting wasted. The more he drinks, the faster they come. There's a long rambling monologue poking fun at gullible Christians who accept Noah's Ark as Gospel truth. Not exactly cutting-edge comedy. When the show's over and the curtain closes, we're behind the curtain with Joe, and suddenly it's hushed and private. We yell down to him from our box, and he yells back up, "Jeff Monson? Come on down!"

When we get there, it's clear Joe's loaded. "I'm high as giraffe pussy," he burbles happily. Deiter, who's the easygoing opposite of chatty Darren, has said nothing all night, but he loves that line. "I'm gonna have to use that," he says.

Turns out Joe Rogan is a huge Jeff Monson fan. He has even entered the fray to defend Jeff in an online forum for fight fans, the one where Jeff laid out his anti-war, anti-Bush, anti-capitalist message, and watched the death threats roll in. "I've saved a lot of your posts on my computer," Joe says. "Everyone wants to believe we live in a perfect world of white light protected by Jesus, and all the Communists and Nicaraguans are evil! It's bullshit! We're stuck with alpha-male chimpanzee bullshit patterns, and you're telling about, we should be looking after people who can't defend themselves. That's a heroic position for a pro athlete." He goes into a long soliloquy about how brave Jeff is to speak his mind publicly in an age of conformity ("You're a true American hero—fuck Jefferson and Washington, they were just going with the flow!"), even managing to work into it Jeff's infamous Abu Dhabi nude scene: "You definitely should have won, and you're walking around naked! No one wanted to get in your way!"

The conversation's a bunch of disjointed assertions that collide like bumper cars. Jeff, sober and extremely earnest, will say, "The Soviet revolution was a good thing, until the Bolsheviks took it over, and turned it from a social revolution into a political revolution." And Joe will answer back, "Who wrote history? White male rich fucks!" He's drunk and shouting, but it's genuine, and he's funnier now than he was onstage. He notices Jeff's tattooed arms and wants a closer look. Jeff, the Tolstoyan Christian Anarchist, gets a bit shy and says, "You won't like them." One arm is "Jacob wrestling the angel," and the other is "Angry Jesus."

"I'm going to get a full-sleeve tattoo, I've already had it designed," says Joe. "It's Buddha in a Kung Fu pose, with a dimethyl triptamine molecule in his hand." None of us are exactly sure what that is, so he tells us that in REM sleep, the brain floods with this chemical, and there's a book by a Dr. Rick Strassman (*DMT: The Spirit Molecule*) about the benefits of taking it as a psychoactive drug. "It puts you in another dimension, it's mushrooms times a million, plus aliens," he says. "Fifteen seconds in, you're communicating with entities who reveal life is just a process to trick you into reproducing." This amazing drug, Joe says, teaches you that Life is about Love. But Jeff already knows that, because his favorite book is *The Kingdom of God Is Within You: Christianity Not as a Mystic Religion but as a New Theory of Life,* by Leo Tolstoy. The last long letter Tolstoy ever wrote was a response to a letter from Gandhi, who had written to tell him of the tremendous impact the book had made on him. In the book Tolstoy argues that Christ's central message, delivered in the Sermon on the Mount, is "Resist not Evil." Non-resistance to Evil, in other words turning the other cheek, means never fighting evil with violence, because you are then committing evil yourself. This is why the two sides in any war always end up portraying the other side as evil.

They're right, the other side is evil. What they fail to admit is that they are evil too. The only way to fight evil without becoming evil yourself is to fight evil with love.

☆

At the mention of Love, Joe Rogan introduces a friend of his, a tanned Dutchman who has stood at his side and said almost nothing so far. "This is Rob Kaman, the greatest kickboxer of all time," Joe says. "He figured it out! He took a deep breath!"

Many people do consider Rob Kaman the greatest kickboxer ever. He's pushing fifty now. Prodded by Joe, he tells us a tale of how he was meditating recently, the good old-fashioned drug-free way, sitting in the mountains, not moving for three hours, until he became overwhelmed, and frightened, by how much love he felt for his family, his friends, the entire world. "Then I realized I didn't have to be frightened of this love. I just had to give it away."

Joe grabs his buddy Rob's shoulder, slaps him heartily on the back, and pronounces with tremendous feeling, "This guy is a bad motherfucker! He is not thinking of himself, he is not selfish. He is saying, here is reality!"

"No one can be a good fighter if they're bullshitting themselves," Jeff says.

"Competition made me vicious, made me a fucking animal," says Kaman. "As long as you have the urge to fight, you will never love. Fighting comes from inner turbulence."

"Mine's from never being accepted by my step-dad," says Jeff.

"Exactly!" Joe howls. "My mom was twenty-nine, my step-dad was twenty-four. I don't blame him, he was too young, he wasn't ready. He didn't know what to do with a kid."

"I'd love to have a philosophical chat with you sometime," Jeff tells him. They try to enter each other's number into their cell phones, a process that proceeds in comical fits and starts on account of Joe's inebriation and clumsy thumbs. At last Joe says, "I'm calling you now," and Hallelujah, Jeff's phone rings.

28

☆

Going in Circles

I've been faithfully doing my Bagua. On any given morning, from about ten to ten thirty, you'll find me out in the back yard, bent-kneed, back sunk, ground-gripping my Frankenstein frog walk in a twelve-foot circle. Eventually I'm going to wear a perfect, hard-packed, bare-earth zero in the grass, which will be fine. I'll feel like I've accomplished something. I'll show it off. When people drop by I'll say, "Wanna see my Bagua circle?"

I like it. It's exhausting, and it makes me sore, but it's easier to stick to than the Kung Fu kicks, punches, blocks, and forms, for me anyway. I think it's because it's circular, there's no beginning or end, you don't have to say to yourself, what should I do now? It's a bit like driving a car—when the mind wanders, you come back to find you're on autopilot, doing what you're supposed to be doing. My circle walking is having a positive effect. I don't know about unimpeded Chi, but it's definitely lowering my center of gravity. I'm not as flighty, tippy, and up on my toes anymore. I'm getting grounded.

☆

My friend Merwan came by recently to see the baby, and told me he'd started to do some "silk reeling" exercises with a Chen style Taiji teacher here in town named Gordon Muir. Merwan thought he was pretty good. Then, freaky coincidence, I was listening to a tape of a talk I had with Andrea Falk, weeks after I'd recorded it, and I'd completely forgotten about this, but I'd asked her if she knew any competent teachers here in Victoria. The only name she gave me: Gordon Muir.

So I phoned up this Gordon Muir, and within a few minutes he had asserted that Chen style Taiji is the most devastating martial art there is, and we had arranged to meet at the food court of a mall equidistant between us, so that I could suss him out a bit, see if we fit. He's on the tall side, relaxed, fifty-six years old, and I took to him immediately. "I'm on the Eternal Spring path," he told me. "Eternal Spring is this Chinese idea that you age, it's not possible to stop aging, but you remain strong, and robust, and keep all your faculties, until one day you topple over." The best way to go.

Gordon started in martial arts way back in 1962, in Judo, then moved on to Karate. By the mid-1970s he was a third-degree black belt and a professional kickboxer. "I had a five-year career, had some pretty good fights, fought some well-known people," he told me. "But I was dissatisfied with the training, because I felt there was no further to go. You could only get so fast, and so strong. So I kept looking around for something more, and I encountered a book by a guy named T.T. Liang.

"His book really annoyed me because I wanted photos to show me how to do it right, but his book was all theory and ideas, and translations of the classics, things like that. Then I finally got into it. I must have read it three or four times. So then I wanted to find Master Liang, and no one could tell me where he was. 'He's retired, not taking students.' So I back-burnered it. A couple of years went by, and I saw an article by him in a Kung Fu magazine. There's a beautiful photo of him with double swords looking really cool and everything, and it said he lives in St. Cloud, Minnesota. And I was in Winnipeg, three hundred and fifty miles north, so, coincidence.

"I thought about calling him, but since he was supposed to be retired, not taking students, I figured if I phone him he'll just say no," Gord continued. "So I got two weeks off from my boss, drove down there, I had a heck of a time finding him, but I did. He was semi-retired, still teaching out of his basement. His students were telling him, 'Master Liang, he came from Canada, different country altogether, he's here to see you.' And Liang says, 'Better come back next week.' 'No no, T.T., he's from another country, he drove all this distance to see you.' 'Better come back next week.' So I came back the next week. Four and a half days later, I had learned the whole long form."

"What was he like as a Master?"

"I really liked him. A strange man, but he was very intelligent."

"Strange how?"

"He was a tail-puller."

"What's that?"

"He would figure out how to push your buttons, then push them frequently, just to get a rise out of you. He would say, 'In Taiji, if I push you, you have to yield, and even if I push you with my mouth you have to yield.' Another saying was, 'If I say something to you and you get mad, I win; if I say something to you and you laugh at me, you win.' He was doing verbal Taiji with you. He had a lot of sayings, very big into sayings, because he wanted things to stick in your head. One of his teachers, Cheng Man-Ch'ing, he was a very famous Taiji Master, and a true Chinese gentleman, which means a master of the five excellences. In China, these are medicine, painting, calligraphy, poetry, and

Taiji. So he was a very cultured person. T.T. would say, 'Cheng Man-Ch'ing, five excellences,' then he would point to himself and say, 'T.T. Liang, drunkard, spendthrift, gambler, womanizer'—and the last one I can't remember. In his youth he'd lived the dissolute life of a wealthy guy in Shanghai, he had every venereal disease, he was a drunk and drug addict. Doctors told him he was going to die, and that's when he sobered up and went out and found a Taiji Master. But he was a rascal right up to the end."

"And what was his style like?"

"He was a Yang stylist, very, very soft. Their saying is, 'Always yield, four ounces overcomes a thousand pounds.' T.T. was the softest Yang stylist I ever met—you couldn't touch him, but he would knock you down every time. He was yielding and soft, but at the same time very strong. He did things to me I wish I could go back and have him do again, because I was a hard stylist then, so I didn't know what he was doing. Even now I have no explanation for what he did to me, and this is thirty years later."

"So you never got to a level where he could teach you that stuff?"

"He would always teach you at your level, and a lot of stuff he did at high levels, none of the students could replicate. I don't know why, whether we weren't capable, or we were Caucasian and he was Chinese, and he didn't want to pass on the full knowledge to us."

☆

The book by Master Liang that so impressed Gordon is still in print. *T'ai Chi Ch'uan for Health and Self-Defense: Philosophy and Practice* includes translations of ancient classics, including one attributed to Wudang Mountain's own Zhang San Feng, the semi-mythological inventor of Taiji, and plenty of T.T. Liang sayings too. My favorite: "If I believe entirely in books, better not read books. If I rely entirely on teachers, better not have teachers."

Gordon continued to study with Master Liang until the teacher's death. Afterward, he began to doubt the usefulness of Yang style. "If it's just some drunk in a pub, no problem, but I couldn't imagine, if it's a serious fight, what am I going to do with Yang style Taiji? So I eventually shifted to Chen style, and when I hit Chen style I thought, 'Wow, this is fantastic, this really fills in a lot of theoretical and physical holes that Yang style had, that I couldn't figure out.' My current teacher, Chen Zhonghua, is exactly what I've been looking for since I started doing internal martial arts. His Chen style is complete; I would say that he's got the art. T.T. is a bit of a question mark in that regard, because I don't really know what it was he did."

"You told me on the phone you consider this Chen style Taiji the most devastating martial art going," I said.

"Anywhere. Anywhere. It's the most devastating, there is no doubt. They just tear your body apart, it's not kid stuff at all. They're breaking bones, they're smashing limbs, it's really, really fierce. Not that you *have* to do that. You take it to a certain degree, and it's only health."

I told him about my experiences at the Taiji fest at Wudang, and how Jarek had insisted, like Andrea with Bagua, that Taiji involves completely retraining the body. "It's a complete rewiring," he agreed. "A lot of people have the idea that Taiji is slowed down, relaxed external movement. They think, all I have to do is learn how to relax. I have to say to them, it's really not that relaxed. It's not tense, but it's a balance. If you are too loose, you collapse. You have to have strength, but we pull out strength from somewhere else, it's completely different from what a hard stylist does.

"Internal guys, their strength always comes from the ground, up into the body, and out through the hands. You are always trying to make the connection of various parts of the body down into the ground, so if you come to me and start grappling, what you find is you are grappling the ground. All I'm doing is giving you pathways into the ground, and you're thinking, 'How can I get hold of this guy? I can't do a thing to him, it all leads to the ground.' So it's very frustrating when you fight an internal artist."

I ask him why, at Mixed Martial Arts events like the UFC, there's plenty of talk of kickboxing, grappling, Jiu Jitsu, and wrestling, but nobody ever mentions internal arts like Taiji. Gordon says it's because Taiji has a stigma of being for old people, of being a discipline for ex-fighters looking for health and longevity. He says if a good Taiji Master could get hold of a diligent, athletic teenager, then in five or ten years, if that kid were to enter UFC, "he would go in there and destroy everybody in the ring. We need to find some young person to turn into a champion. The problem is, you train a hard style guy for six months, and he'll be able to pull some of that out in a fight, maybe. But a Taiji guy, the lights are out for three years. We have to train you to *give up* your muscle and *give up* your power. Most people don't trust enough to give up that attachment to power."

☆

In China, silk is a textile so ancient and central that it's embedded in the culture through commonplace metaphors. It's common knowledge that if you try to pull the delicate thread from the cocoon of a silk worm, it's very easy to tug too hard and break it. So you need a soft continuous circular motion to extract the silk, which also describes the movements of a series of Taiji exercises called silk reeling. These exercises are designed to pull energy up from the earth into your legs, your hips, your shoulders, and eventually out through the hands. I got a bit of a shock when Gordon told me the silk reeling movements he teaches were developed by a Beijing-based Taiji Master, Feng Zhiqiang. Oddly enough, when I was in Beijing, I had paid a visit to Master Feng, and beneath giant black and white portraits of his mentors Chen Fake and Hu Yaozhen (nicknamed "One Finger Shakes Heaven and Earth"), I watched him demonstrate his art, which he calls Chen Style Xinyi Hunyuan Taijiquan. I didn't know enough about Taiji then to ask skillful questions, I just wanted to be in his presence.

At one point he bade me hold out my palm, and he swished his hands above and below it in small circles like a sorcerer casting a spell, telling me I should soon feel a tingling sensation. "I could make it very painful for you, without touching you," he claimed. "But at my age, it's too exhausting for me." I concentrated on my hand, waiting to feel the tingling. Did I? Maybe a little. Or maybe I just said I did to be polite. Hard to say now. My translator, Geoff's secretary Ling, said she definitely felt it.

So now months later, I find myself back in my hometown, learning Master Feng's basics. What I like most about Gordon's teaching style is he makes sure to demonstrate the martial applications of the exercises, and to that end, in one class he struck a kind of half horse stance beside me, asked me to place both my hands on his shoulder, and bade me push him over. It was like his lower legs were bolted to the floor, and his upper torso attached to them by a frictionless ball socket at the hips. With the slightest shrug, he deflected all my pushing force down into his legs, like lightning seeking the ground. It was impressive because he was not "resisting" me at all, just shrugging me off.

☆

The Chinese say that once someone has been your master, they stay your master for life, regardless of whether you move on to another. Sifu Bob taught me a lot about comportment, and dignity, and how to carry oneself in the world. Although I'm no longer training at his school I still look up to him. When I went out to tell him face to face I wouldn't be back, he was out in the sunshine behind the club, sorting balloons for a children's party later in the day. He gave me his sincere blessing, and I went on my way. As I was leaving, there was a little boy in the reception area, in a crisp new Academy uniform, waiting to be called through by Bob for a lesson. No more than eight or nine years old, he was running around bouncing off the walls, singing some goofy pop song, acting like any kid that age, but as soon as Bob's voice called his name, his comportment completely changed. He was suddenly all business, stiff and solemn, trying desperately to act the part of a little macho man. I could almost hear Bob teaching him what he taught me, first and foremost. Rule number one: Relax.

☆

When we were at Wudang together Jarek gave me a short verbal primer you might call The Four Conditions Needed to Master Taiji, borrowed from the four conditions needed to master Taoist meditation: *fa, cai, lü,* and *di.*

Fa means method. "To practice something you need a method, and so you need to find a teacher who will transmit to you the true method," he had said. "They always talk about fate and destiny, which means you were destined to meet your teacher."

Cai means time and money. "You need to practice free of any concerns that your family might starve."

Lü means friends and partners, "people who will help you in your practice. In the Taoism of old, if someone was spending years meditating in a cave, then the others had to bring him what he needed to live there. But in martial arts it's mainly friends who help with ideas and practice. Like pushing hands. When you push hands with your master you land on the wall. When you push hands with your friends, you can experiment, and gradually improve."

Di is place, the fourth factor. "In Taoism it's a place where someone was meditating and achieved immortality. This is a good place. It has a certain atmosphere, some kind of energy. It sounds superstitious but there are places that give you a good feeling, and others that give no feeling at all."

☆

I'm feeling good. I figure I've got three of the four essentials in place, the only question mark being the time aspect of *cai,* what with baby Gigi eating up every free moment. The kid will grow eventually, and I'm not in a hurry. It's not in the spirit of Taiji to be in a hurry. In the meantime she loves to imitate daddy doing Taiji, gleefully flailing her arms and legs about, showing off that she's still chock full of original Chi. In Gord I've found the best possible master for me—a sincere artist and a gentleman, with a reputable lineage in an art that's appropriate for my age and ambition. I've got a notebook full of stick-figure renditions of the moves, like the book Jan the smiley German teenager kept at Shaolin, and after each class I try to add one or two exercises to my notebook repertoire of movements. I try to practice what I know every day. My body is being re-educated. I'm letting the body do what needs to be done, and leaving the mind to follow.

Acknowledgments

First and foremost one is due to Toby Mundy at Atlantic Books, it was all his idea. Later he wouldn't let me call this book what I wanted to—*The Humble Scribe Dreams of Kung Fu Revenge*—which is probably just as well. Thanks goes to Helen Reeves at Penguin Canada for seeing merit in the proposal. Sarah Castleton, Laurel Sparrow, Shima Aoki, and Martha Magor all pitched in too. I'm grateful to the indomitable Anne McDermid, the hardest working agent in showbiz.

In the martial arts world, first up is a heartfelt thank you to the ever cool and classy Bob Holland. The China part of this book could never have happened without the Polish juggernaut, Jarek Szymanski. Jeff Monson was gracious under great stress. Thanks to Andrea Falk for teaching me to go in circles. Gordon Muir is still teaching me things, and putting up with a very spotty attendance record. If I've left anyone out I'll catch you in person. And lastly a great big hug full of love vibrations goes to my Shundorbo, for putting up with me, and for being an endless source of loving support.

BRIAN PRESTON lives on Vancouver Island with his wife, kids, and in-laws. He has been writing for a living for sixteen years, mostly for Canadian and American magazines. *The New Yorker* called his first book, *Pot Planet*, gimlet-eyed and often hilarious. For a long time he thought by gimlet they meant the alcoholic beverage, but then he discovered a gimlet is also a very sharp woodworking tool resembling a corkscrew.